Saudi Arabia in the 1980s

William B. Quandt

Saudi Arabia in the 1980s

Foreign Policy, Security, and Oil

WITHDRAWN

THE BROOKINGS INSTITUTION
Washington, D.C.

Library of Congress Cataloging in Publication data:

Quandt, William B.
  Saudi Arabia in the 1980s.

  Bibliography: p.
  Includes index.
    1. Saudi Arabia—Foreign relations.
  2. Saudi Arabia—Politics and government.
  I. Title.
  DS227.Q36   327.538   81-18086
  ISBN 0-8157-7286-6   AACR2
  ISBN 0-8157-7285-8 (pbk.)

            1 2 3 4 5 6 7 8 9

THE BROOKINGS INSTITUTION is an independent organization devoted to nonpartisan research, education, and publication in economics, government, foreign policy, and the social sciences generally. Its principal purposes are to aid in the development of sound public policies and to promote public understanding of issues of national importance.

The Institution was founded on December 8, 1927, to merge the activities of the Institute for Government Research, founded in 1916, the Institute of Economics, founded in 1922, and the Robert Brookings Graduate School of Economics and Government, founded in 1924.

The Board of Trustees is responsible for the general administration of the Institution, while the immediate direction of the policies, program, and staff is vested in the President, assisted by an advisory committee of the officers and staff. The by-laws of the Institution state: "It is the function of the Trustees to make possible the conduct of scientific research, and publication, under the most favorable conditions, and to safeguard the independence of the research staff in the pursuit of their studies and in the publication of the results of such studies. It is not a part of their function to determine, control, or influence the conduct of particular investigations or the conclusions reached."

The President bears final responsibility for the decision to publish a manuscript as a Brookings book. In reaching his judgment on the competence, accuracy, and objectivity of each study, the President is advised by the director of the appropriate research program and weighs the views of a panel of expert outside readers who report to him in confidence on the quality of the work. Publication of a work signifies that it is deemed a competent treatment worthy of public consideration but does not imply endorsement of conclusions or recommendations.

The Institution maintains its position of neutrality on issues of public policy in order to safeguard the intellectual freedom of the staff. Hence interpretations or conclusions in Brookings publications should be understood to be solely those of the authors and should not be attributed to the Institution, to its trustees, officers, or other staff members, or to the organizations that support its research.

Foreword

IN THE BRIEF PERIOD of the 1970s the Kingdom of Saudi Arabia was drawn into a bewildering array of international issues: rivalry between the superpowers, escalating oil prices, Arab-Israeli wars and negotiations, inter-Arab squabbles, global financial instability, the consequences of the Iranian revolution, and aid to dozens of countries in the third world. Heads of state and prime ministers descended on Riyadh in record numbers, as did bankers and businessmen.

Oil, of course, was the basic reason for Saudi Arabia's unprecedented international involvement. Sitting atop the largest proven reserves of petroleum in the world, and capable of producing oil at very little cost, Saudi Arabia earned $225 billion from oil during the 1970s—over $60,000 per capita. In 1980 alone oil income amounted to another $95 billion.

One result of this boom was a massive spending program that in many ways brought about a socioeconomic revolution in Saudi Arabia. Though the Saud family still rules and the political continuity of the kingdom remains unbroken, King Khalid's reign has been influenced by internal and external events that have stretched the capacity of the Saudi political system.

In this study of Saudi foreign policy, William B. Quandt analyzes the threats confronting the kingdom, the Saudis' capacity to deal with them, and the role of the United States in Saudi Arabia's future. He discusses the points of stress in the "special relationship" between the kingdom and the United States, offering some guidelines for the conduct of future U.S.-Saudi relations.

Quandt, a senior fellow in the Brookings Foreign Policy Studies program, has written three other books on the Middle East and has twice served on the National Security Council staff, where he dealt with some of the issues in U.S.-Saudi relations covered in this book. He acknowledges the assistance of many Saudis—officials, academics, journalists, businessmen, and students—during the four trips he made to Saudi Arabia in the course of his research. Believing that they prefer anonymity, Quandt has not named them but remains grateful for their hospitality and candor.

The author also thanks Robert C. Ames, Ambassador Hermann F. Eilts, David E. Long, Roger B. Merrick, Theodore H. Moran, Harold H. Saunders, Ambassador Christopher Van Hollen, and Marvin Zonis for stimulating and useful suggestions after they reviewed the manuscript. Among his Brookings colleagues, John D. Steinbruner, director of the Foreign Policy Studies program, was supportive throughout the project, and Christine M. Helms was particularly helpful in keeping the historical record straight—her own study of Saudi Arabia was a valued resource. James F. Hitselberger provided research assistance, Ruth E. Conrad typed endless drafts, and Clifford A. Wright checked the manuscript for accuracy. Tadd Fisher edited the book, and Diana Regenthal prepared the index. For all these efforts, the author is sincerely grateful.

In a study of this sort the question of accurately transliterating Arabic words and names always arises. For some very common names, standard Western usage is maintained. Otherwise, a simplified transliteration from Arabic is employed, without any diacritical marks. Specialists will be able to tell the original spelling; nonspecialists will be spared meaningless symbols. Consistency has been valued more than making distinctions among all the letters of the Arabic alphabet.

Most of the research in this study was made possible by grants from the Ford Foundation and the Rockefeller Foundation, whose assistance is deeply appreciated. The Department of Energy also provided support for research in the area of energy and national security. Some of the work on Saudi oil policy was begun under the auspices of the department and will be carried further in a subsequent more detailed study on the subject.

The opinions in this book are those of the author and should not be ascribed to the Ford Foundation, to the Rockefeller Foundation, to the Department of Energy, or to the trustees, officers, or other staff members of the Brookings Institution.

BRUCE K. MACLAURY
President

October 1981
Washington, D.C.

Contents

Map of Saudi Arabia and the Middle East

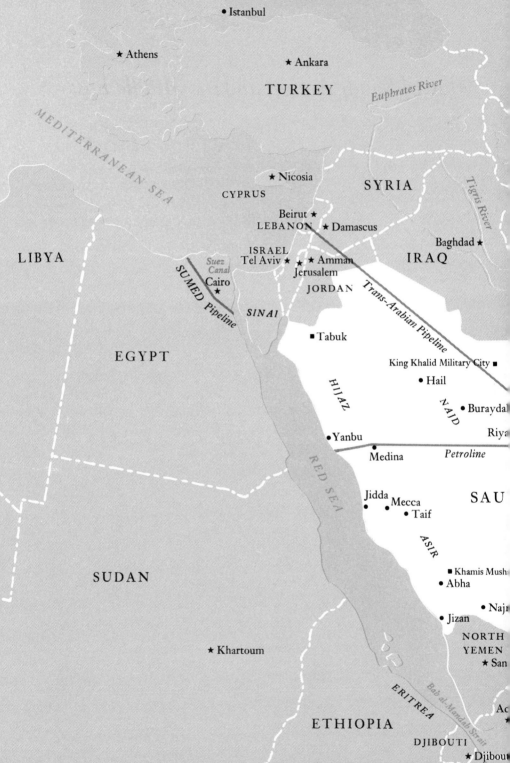

Chapter One

Saudi Security in the 1980s

TRY TO IMAGINE the international repercussions of any one of the following developments during the 1980s:

—The Saudi regime is overthrown by radical military officers. In the ensuing turmoil, oil production drops to almost zero as personnel of the Arabian American Oil Company leave the country.

—Iranian aircraft attack and destroy a significant portion of Saudi Arabia's oil-producing facilities.

—Saudi Arabia announces that for "technical reasons" oil production will be reduced immediately from 9 million to 5 million barrels a day.

—Saudi Arabia decides to upgrade its diplomatic dialogue with the Soviet Union. The Saudi foreign minister travels to Moscow and expresses an interest in purchasing Soviet weapons.

—Israel launches a preemptive strike against Saudi Arabia's F-15 and airborne warning and control system (AWACS) aircraft, destroying virtually all of them.

—North and South Yemen declare unity and announce their common determination to recover lost territory in the Asir and Jizan regions now held by Saudi Arabia. Yemeni troops cross the border into Saudi territory, supported by Cuban-piloted MIG-21s.

With luck, Saudi Arabia may get through this decade without any of these events taking place. Any one of them, however, would send shock waves throughout the world and would have immediate, perhaps dramatic, effects on the international economy, the regional balance of power, and the rivalry between the superpowers.

Because Saudi Arabia sits atop the largest and most easily exploited reserves of petroleum in the world, it inevitably is being drawn into the center of international politics. What the rulers of the Saudi Kingdom do or fail to do can have major consequences. What happens in this

I

little known country is therefore of concern to statesmen, bankers, businessmen, and strategists throughout the world.

For Americans, the stakes involved in the U.S.-Saudi relationship are particularly great. No country has benefited more from relations with Saudi Arabia than the United States. American oil companies have made enormous profits. American business has had a disproportionate share of the Saudi market. The American military has played a major role in the development of the Saudi Armed Forces. American diplomats have easy access to Saudi rulers.

Despite the apparent intimacy of the U.S.-Saudi relationship, however, strains are felt everywhere. On questions of oil prices, the Palestinians, and the appropriate response to the Soviet challenge, Americans and Saudis are often far apart. Little remains of the confidence and goodwill that characterized the relationship in some earlier periods. Motives are constantly being questioned on both sides. Irritation is more commonly expressed than appreciation. Little understanding exists in Washington of the realities of Saudi Arabia. The same is true in reverse. For two countries fated to deal with one another on an extraordinarily complex range of topics, this is hardly a firm foundation on which to build.

Americans need to transcend their stereotype of Saudi Arabia as a feudal desert kingdom awash in oil. Both the limits and the possibilities of Saudi foreign policy must be appreciated. Some effort to see the world from the standpoint of Riyadh is required in Washington, and not because the Saudis have any monopoly on wisdom or statesmanship. They do not. They are often parochial and shortsighted in their views, as are their American counterparts. But the Saudis do function in a geostrategic setting that must be understood. Their resources for conducting foreign policy are limited, despite great wealth. The threats to Saudi Arabia are substantial and cannot be wished away, as both Saudis and Americans often try to do.

Perhaps more than most regimes the Saudi leadership sees its long-term prospects as intimately influenced by events beyond the kingdom's borders. Inter-Arab politics, the Arab-Israeli conflict, the superpower rivalry, the price of oil, the rate of inflation in the West—all of these can have immediate and possibly destabilizing effects in Saudi Arabia. For a regime whose legitimacy cannot be taken for granted and therefore must be anchored in meeting the expectations of its population, the misconduct of foreign policy could be fatal. A loss of control over oil reserves, the inability to defend the territory of the kingdom, or the mishandling of foreign exchange assets could be devastating for the House of Saud.

The United States occupies a crucial place in Saudi foreign policy, and thus in determining the future of the kingdom itself. This study seeks to improve the basis for American policy toward Saudi Arabia by analyzing the threats to the kingdom and the capabilities of the Saudi regime to deal with those threats.

External Concerns

Oil is the key to Saudi Arabia's future, its wealth, and its status in the international community as well as the source of many of its dilemmas and concerns. Just as oil can be translated into prosperity and power, it can also serve as a magnet to draw an energy-conscious world toward the Persian Gulf. Great wealth is thus accompanied by great danger.

If geography has blessed Saudi Arabia with oil, history has been less kind. For just as Saudi Arabia has come into its own as an economic power to be reckoned with in the world, its surrounding environment has been thrown into unprecedented turmoil. Iran is in the throes of revolution. The Arab world is divided. The Soviet Union has invaded nearby Afghanistan. And the United States often appears to be an uncertain ally. This is a far cry from the Saudi vision, perhaps need, of a stable Middle East, free of radicalism and generally inclined to cooperate with the industrialized powers of the West that can translate oil into development and can provide the security umbrella under which conservative regimes in the region can hope to prosper.

As a traditional monarchy deriving part of its legitimacy from adherence to fundamental Islamic tenets, Saudi Arabia during much of its brief history as an independent state lived in comparative isolation from the rest of the world. While most Arab states were being swept by various ideological currents—nationalism, socialism, and communism—Saudi Arabia remained attached to its own strict interpretation of Islam. European colonialism, which left such a strong imprint on much of the rest of the Middle East, largely bypassed the Arabian Peninsula, and thus Western influence was late in making itself felt.

Physical isolation reduced the danger of foreign intervention in internal Saudi affairs, allowing the Saud family to consolidate its power and to dominate its weak neighbors where possible. Serious external threats were deflected to some extent by the Western presence in the region. Up until the mid-1950s this arrangement worked fairly well. The British played a security role in the Persian Gulf, Iraq, Jordan, and Egypt. The Americans were visibly present in Turkey, Ethiopia, Pakistan, and Iran. The Soviets were nowhere in sight. And Saudi Arabia, having been knit together by a remarkable combination of force and persuasion, of conquest and inducements, was on the verge of financial well-being as substantial oil revenues began to flow.

Both wealth and security were by-products of Saudi ties to the West. Saudi Arabia was in many ways a passive partner, reaping benefits while exerting little effort. This passivity, however, could not last indefinitely in the face of dramatic changes all around Saudi Arabia.

The demise of the Western-dominated security system surrounding Saudi Arabia began in 1955-56 with the virtually simultaneous appearance of the Soviet Union in Egypt, the intensification of the Arab-Israeli conflict, and the emergence of Arab nationalism as a powerful force under the leadership of Egypt's President Gamal Abdel Nasser. Shortly thereafter, in 1958, Syria and Egypt joined together in a self-styled revolutionary United Arab Republic, civil war erupted in Lebanon, and the British positions in Jordan and Iraq collapsed.

The Saudis were alarmed as revolution appeared to be sweeping the Arab world. Monarchies seemed destined for the dustbin of history. What had gone wrong? From the Saudi viewpoint, the twin evils were Zionism and communism. Because of their conflict with Israel, Arab states such as Egypt and Syria were obliged to turn to the Soviet Union for arms. As Soviet influence grew, so did radical, even secular, ideologies such as Nasserism and the pan-Arab nationalism of the Baath parties in Syria and Iraq. Were it not for Israel, concluded many Saudi leaders, the Soviets never would have gained a foothold in Egypt; and without the Soviets in Egypt, the Middle East would be a far safer place for conservative regimes such as Saudi Arabia.

Compared with the relatively tranquil situation in which Saudi Arabia found itself in 1953 at the time of the death of King Abd al-Aziz ibn Abd al-Rahman Al Saud (often known in the West as Ibn Saud), his sons confronted a radically different set of challenges in the early 1980s. Not only had British power in the area significantly receded, but also the United States had had a difficult time playing a stabilizing role in the region. Iran, intensely anti-American, sought to export its "Islamic revolution" to surrounding countries. Ethiopia was under Marxist rule.

Turkey was nearly bankrupt and Pakistan was unstable. So much for the traditional pillars of the American position in the area.

Nor was the Arab setting more reassuring as the 1980s began. Egypt had made a separate peace with Israel, resulting in a break between Egypt and most Arab countries, including Saudi Arabia. The Palestinians were frustrated, organized, and armed, and they openly demanded that Arab oil producers use their resources to advance the cause of Palestinian rights. Lebanon seemed to be disintegrating as communal conflicts intensified, and Syria was locked into a dangerous conflict with Israel that was being fought out at Lebanon's expense. Iraq was flexing its muscles while seeking to assume the mantle of Arab leadership. But Iraq was also at odds with Iran, and the risk of protracted conflict between these two neighbors posed difficult dilemmas for the Saudis. North Yemen was shaky and South Yemen was allied with the Soviet Union. Meanwhile Israel continued to occupy Arab lands, including East Jerusalem, an issue of particular concern to the Saudis.

As for U.S. policy in the region, after the Camp David accords the Saudis came to believe that Egypt and Israel had been chosen to play the leading parts in American Middle East strategy. The Saudis could not be certain whether U.S. interests extended much beyond their oil. The failure of the United States to back the shah of Iran in 1978–79 did not go unnoticed in Riyadh. In an attempt to reassure the Saudis, President Ronald Reagan stated on October 1, 1981, that the United States would not permit Saudi Arabia "to be an Iran." This sweeping commitment, however, raised as many questions as it answered.

Finally, as the Saudis surveyed their immediate environment they noted that the Soviets had developed political and military positions of considerable strength. The Soviet invasion of Afghanistan in December 1979 was seen by Saudis as one more step in the Soviet strategy of encircling the oil-rich Persian Gulf. Soviet troops and advisers were in Ethiopia, South Yemen, Afghanistan, Libya, and Syria. Iran was a tempting target for Soviet subversion. Kuwait had purchased some arms from Moscow and a large Soviet embassy operated there. Iraq, while more independent of the Soviet Union than in the past, was still a source of radical, secular ideology. And the assassination of Egypt's President Anwar Sadat on October 6, 1981, opened a new period of uncertainty in the largest and most pro-American Arab country.

Faced with these sources of threat and causes for anxiety, the Saudis, limited in human and material resources but having vast amounts of oil and money, tried to shape a foreign policy suited to their modest capabilities, an effort designed to provide a sense of security and to help shield their own population from disruptive and destabilizing influences from abroad. They still believed that stability in the Middle East would be enhanced if only the Palestinian question could be resolved. But they were also aware that more was required to defend Saudi interests. Isolation was no answer, nor was exclusive dependency on the United States. Arab consensus, as much as the Saudis might seek it, usually proved to be fragile at best. And Islamic solidarity failed to provide a strong alternative, as fashionable as it might have become in recent years.

The Saudis confronted a very uncertain future, shackled with the weight of tradition and a history that provided few clues as to how to cope best with the new array of challenges to their security and well-being. External events would have a great influence over Saudi Arabia in the years ahead. And if the Saudis failed to shape those events, at least to some degree, they might find themselves overwhelmed. Faced with such bleak prospects, the Saudis felt a deep ambivalence toward the United States, which was a source of both anxiety and security for them.

Internal Concerns

For the current generation of Saudi leaders, foreign policy has been intimately related to domestic stability. The prospects for Saudi economic well-being and development have been and continue to be heavily dependent on the outside world. Saudi oil has been discovered, extracted, and marketed by foreigners. Economic development has required massive purchases of goods and technology. Social change has involved the import of teachers and doctors and the export of Saudi students to be trained abroad. Manual labor and construction is almost entirely done by foreign workers who outnumber the entire Saudi labor force. Military modernization has required arms, advisers, and training from the United States and Europe, and perhaps Pakistan in the future.

With time, the Saudis hope to reduce this dependency on foreigners, but the indefinite future entails continued Saudi connections with the industrialized West—the source of technology, goods, security, and markets for oil—and with the Arab and third world countries that provide much-needed skilled and unskilled manpower. Any serious, sudden disruption in these relations would have immediate domestic consequences.

Just as Saudi Arabia must look beyond its borders to develop relations that promote development and security, it is from abroad that the most dangerous threats to Saudi Arabia emanate. But it is not the classical concern of military conquest by powerful neighbors that worries the Saudis, nor is it the fear of Soviet invasion. Rather, it is the danger that instability, conflict, and radical ideologies in the Middle East will adversely affect internal Saudi developments. The Saudi leadership enters the 1980s with as great a preoccupation with subversion, ideological warfare, terrorism, blackmail, and propaganda as with outright military threats.

The early 1960s were a particularly important period in shaping the foreign policy views of the current generation of Saudi leaders. Beginning in 1958 Saudi Arabia found itself in sharp conflict with the revolutionary forces in the Arab world that were responsive to Egypt's President Nasser. This coincided with a period of uncertain leadership in Saudi Arabia, as King Saud ibn Abd al-Aziz's mismanagement of the kingdom's domestic and foreign policies led other members of the royal family to curtail his powers. Under these circumstances Saudi Arabia was particularly vulnerable to attempts at subversion and destabilization. The outbreak of civil war in Yemen in late 1962 brought Egypt and Saudi Arabia to the verge of direct conflict, further raising the fear of Egyptian intervention in Saudi internal affairs. Plots were uncovered in the armed forces. Several air force pilots defected. A small group of "Free Princes" established itself in Cairo and openly criticized the regime.[1] Embryonic leftist and nationalist parties were organized. The Saudi leadership felt very much on the defensive. Finally, Saud was pushed aside and Crown Prince Faisal ibn Abd al-Aziz succeeded him as king in 1964.

Egypt's subsequent defeat in the 1967 Arab-Israeli war resulted in the deflation of Nasser's prestige. His troops were withdrawn from Yemen and a truce was struck between Riyadh and Cairo. In return for a sub-

1. One of the Free Princes, Talal ibn Abd al-Aziz, currently involved with the UN International Children's Emergency Fund, gave a revealing interview on Saudi foreign policy to *Al-Nahar al-Arabi wa al-Duwali*, April 7–13, 1981, pp. 18–19 (see Joint Publications Research Service, *Near East/North Africa Report*, 2122, JPRS 75777 [May 28, 1980], pp. 262–67). Talal provides some background on his role in urging King Saud to end the Dhahran basing agreement in 1961.

stantial subsidy to Egypt, Saudi Arabia was spared further propaganda attacks and attempts at subversion. In the next years Saudi Arabia remained on reasonable terms with most Arab countries and King Faisal embarked on a cautious but determined program of modernization and development. The decade from 1967 to 1977 was an unusually stable and prosperous one for the Saudis.

Because of their belief that domestic developments can be seriously affected by events in the Middle East, the Saudis are extremely attentive to the shifts of power and opinion around them. If they believe they can shape those events by drawing on their own resources, they will go to considerable lengths to do so. When the source of danger is beyond their reach—for example, Israel or the Soviet Union—they will urge the United States to act. When all else fails, they will try to remain uninvolved in regional turmoil, adapting as needed to the ebb and flow of events.

The Middle East after Sadat

Anwar Sadat's death came as a shock to the Saudis. They had not supported his policy of peace toward Israel, but they had recognized in him a potential force for stability and moderation in the region. His demise raises questions about how far any Arab leader will be prepared to go in cooperating with Washington or negotiating with Israel.

In the post-Sadat Middle East, Americans will look more toward Riyadh than ever before as a central element in the Middle East equation. Pressures will mount on the Saudis to show leadership in rebuilding an Arab consensus that includes Egypt and on the question of the Palestinians.

Whether the Saudis can meet such expectations will be one of the many challenges confronting them in the 1980s. To understand the dilemmas facing the Saudi leaders, one must look more closely at the source of threats to the kingdom, the topic dealt with in part I; the Saudi capabilities for dealing with them, covered in part II; and the prospects for the U.S.-Saudi relationship, which constitutes part III.

Part One

The Setting of Saudi Foreign Policy: Threats to Stability

Saudis often speak of their country as being encircled by hostile, pro-Soviet forces. But reality is considerably more complex. The Saudis find themselves almost uniquely at the intersection of a number of strong crosscurrents. This creates for them a web of involvement with the world that precludes a return to comfortable isolation.

First and foremost, the Saudis are caught up in the complexities of inter-Arab politics. Virtually every movement, party, or faction in the Arab world has at one time or another sought to placate, overthrow, or enlist the support of the Saudi regime. An endless parade of Arab leaders and officials passes through Riyadh seeking aid, responding to summonses, uttering veiled threats, or simply paying obeisance to the richest country in the Arab world. Only Egypt's President Anwar Sadat in recent years openly treated the Saudis with contempt and scorn, dismissing them as ignorant bedouins. But even Sadat kept a back door relationship with the Saudis, and his successors are likely to try to ease the strains between the two countries.

Inevitably Saudi Arabia's prominent role in Arab politics leads to involvement in the Palestinian question and the Arab-Israeli conflict. On this issue the Saudis have tried to play it safe, conforming to an anti-Israeli line in public, while refraining in practice from becoming too deeply involved in the diplomacy of the Arab-Israeli conflict. The Saudis have typically been concerned bystanders, supporting with varying degrees of emphasis Arab rights, the Palestine Liberation Organization, the idea of a negotiated peace, and the hard-line stance of some "rejectionists," all the while hoping that the conflict will eventually be resolved on terms that will reduce the dilemmas they confront. For in their view, as long as Arabs seek Israel's withdrawal from the territories occupied in the 1967 war, Saudi oil and Soviet arms will remain essential

9

weapons to bring pressure on the United States to extract concessions from Israel. As the military option loses credibility, more thought is given to using Arab economic power as the primary adjunct to diplomacy.

It is only a short step from the Saudis' preoccupation with the Arab-Israeli conflict to their concern for maintaining their reputation as a champion of Islam. If Saudi Arabia loses its prestige as a defender of Arab rights, as protector of the holy places of Mecca and Medina, and as a bastion of pure Islamic values, the regime will also have lost much of its credibility and legitimacy. Thus it is particularly important for Saudi Arabia to identify with Islamic causes—such as opposition to Israel's claim to sovereignty over all of Jerusalem and to the Soviet invasion of Afghanistan. Saudi aid goes primarily to Muslim countries in the third world, and at times the Saudis seem to try to export their conservative religious views along with their aid, as in the case of Pakistan. In supporting the quixotic and repressive regime of Idi Amin in Uganda, the Saudis were aiding a Muslim leader who had broken ties with Israel. That was enough to ensure him a degree of Saudi backing and eventual refuge after his ignominious demise.

The Islamic dimension of Saudi foreign policy has been reinforced by the challenge of the Islamic revolution in neighboring Iran. The Ayatollah Ruhollah Khomeini's regime not only is outspokenly in favor of exporting revolutionary Shiite Islamic ideas—which have some appeal to the Shiite minority in eastern Saudi Arabia—but also has argued forcefully that Islam and monarchy are incompatible. This theme, and the model of an Islamic republic, have attracted the interest of many conservative Muslims, including some in Saudi Arabia. As different as the shah may have been from the current Saudi leadership, the Saudi royal family is not anxious to hear a potentially powerful neighbor push the comparison too far.

The Iranian revolution highlighted the tension in the Middle East between radicalism and conservatism and between modernity and tradition. Saudi Arabia sharply opposes forces calling for violent change in the status quo, whether from the Marxist left, the Islamic right, or any of the variations and combinations of those ideological currents now found in the Middle East. In the past the greater fear had been of the left, but following Nasser's death the center of gravity in the Arab world moved toward the center and Saudi Arabia felt less vulnerable to attacks from the left. Only South Yemen seemed beyond the pale, and the Saudis were even prepared to make some conciliatory gestures toward Aden.

If the Arab left seemed weakened by the late 1960s, Marxist regimes in Africa, such as Ethiopia, and the Soviet presence in Afghanistan were distinct sources of concern for Riyadh. The Saudis also seemed uneasy with militantly Islamic regimes, such as Muammar Qadhafi's Libya. The attack on the mosque in Mecca in November 1979 by religious fanatics reminded the Saudis that extremism could come from the right as well as the left, a lesson that had been learned from the case of Iran.

The ideological contest in the Middle East parallels but is not always identical with the superpower rivalry. For nearly a generation the Saudis have been firmly on the side of the United States in its global rivalry with the Soviet Union. No ongoing diplomatic or economic relations exist between the Saudis and the Soviets, although some trade with communist countries takes place. During World War II the Saudis allowed the United States to build an airfield at Dhahran. Beginning in 1946 the United States made use of Dhahran as part of its global strategy aimed at the Soviet Union. This caused the Saudis to be somewhat uneasy, but nonetheless King Saud agreed in 1957 to renew the lease for five years in return for economic and military aid of about $180 million.[1] Despite the termination in 1961 of the Dhahran arrangement, the United States has clearly remained a strong supporter of Saudi security, as massive arms sales in the late 1970s demonstrated. An important symbol of American involvement in the defense of Saudi Arabia has been the U.S. Military Training Mission, which has operated in the kingdom for three decades.

Saudi Arabia has not given up on the "special relationship" that ties it to the United States, but strains are evident. The Saudis speak publicly of keeping both superpowers out of the Middle East and are reluctant to allow the United States to establish any permanent military facilities on Saudi soil. For both political and economic reasons, the Saudis are turning to Europe and Japan for goods and services, including military equipment. Disagreements over the Arab-Israeli conflict are sharp and persistent. And on the crucial issue of oil production, the Saudis have tried to straddle the line between the use of oil to advance Arab political interests and their desire to cooperate with the United States.

The Saudi dilemma concerning oil policy highlights one other dimen-

1. See Malcolm C. Peck, "Saudi Arabia in United States Foreign Policy to 1958," pp. 166–67, 226–32.

sion of Saudi foreign policy. Saudi wealth and consequent political influence are derived from two sources: the revenue generated by oil production and the industrialized West's ability to translate that income into development, goods, services, and secure investments. To maximize their political and economic gains, the Saudis need to be attentive to the positions taken by other members of the Organization of Petroleum Exporting Countries. In theory Saudi Arabia is one country that could break the power of OPEC to set prices far above the costs of production. But to do so would be self-defeating. At the same time, the Saudis have no interest in crippling the economies of Western Europe, Japan, and the United States, nor of weakening the value of the dollar, some $80 billion of which they hold as investments. Thus the Saudis feel tied to both oil producers and to consumers, to price moderates and price hawks.

As the Saudis shape their security and foreign policies for the 1980s they will be acutely conscious of the network of interests and conflicts in which they are now entrapped. Pushed and pulled in various directions, they will try to find a safe middle ground, a consensus position that will minimize pressures and threats. Whether the Saudis can maintain such a posture in such a volatile region and with so much at stake is a question only the future can answer. For the moment, an appreciation of their dilemma requires a closer look at the web of involvement in which the present Saudi leadership finds itself.

Chapter Two

The Arab World
and the Palestinians

SAUDI ARABIA within its present borders and under the rule of the Saud family is a recent phenomenon. Today's ruling generation can still remember when some of the peripheral areas of the present-day kingdom were under the control of rival Arab leaders. It was King Abd al-Aziz's most impressive triumph that in the 1920s and early 1930s he was able to subdue or persuade most of the tribal groups and settled areas of the peninsula to accept his leadership. Force, persuasion, and religion went hand in hand as the Saud family extended its sway to the Eastern Province, then to the north, west, and south. In this process the British set limits on the geographical expansion of Saudi power into their own spheres of influence in Jordan, Iraq, the Persian Gulf coast, and Oman.[1]

It was through confrontation with other Arab leaders and tribes that the Saudis tested and asserted their power, and on virtually every border there were disputed claims that left a legacy of ill will. Many of these have yet to be resolved. This has meant that Saudi Arabia has always been involved in inter-Arab disputes. The Hashemites in Iraq and Transjordan, for example, were seen as bitter enemies and competitors for political leadership in the Arabian Peninsula, even though Britain generally managed to keep the conflict contained.

Saudi preoccupation with the Arab world is not simply a function of geography and history. It also reflects the religious, linguistic, and cultural character of the population. Several thousand Saudis may take pride in belonging to the ruling Saud family, but the other 4 million to 5 million citizens of the kingdom identify themselves by tribe, family, and region, with the Arabic language and Islamic religion as their common denominator.

1. See Christine Moss Helms, *The Cohesion of Saudi Arabia.*

If Saudis take their "Arabness" seriously, it is not primarily as proponents of abstractions such as Arab unity or Arab nationalism. These concepts, as appealing as they may sound, have often been used as weapons against Saudi Arabia by various radical movements. If there has been a pattern in Saudi dealings with the Arab world, it has been to seek hegemony in the Arabian Peninsula, while elsewhere trying to ensure an equilibrium of power to prevent challenges from Egypt, the Hashemites, or any other major Arab power.

Unable to dominate the Arab world by itself, Saudi Arabia has opposed claims of Arab leadership by others while encouraging a flexible network of inter-Arab alliances to maintain some balance in the region. When the Hashemites in Jordan and Iraq seemed to be on the ascendance in the early 1950s, the Saudis sided with Egypt. A few years later, when Nasser had brought Syria into the United Arab Republic and the Hashemites in Baghdad had been murdered, the Saudis threw their weight behind moderate forces in the Arab world in order to limit Nasser's power. Alliances have been formed, then broken, with the Saudis seeking as much freedom of maneuver as possible, hoping to exercise a moderating influence to achieve their ends while avoiding isolation or entrapment in the crosscurrents of inter-Arab rivalries.

Although Saudi Arabia will doubtless be a key player in the game of Arab politics, it is unlikely to exercise consistently strong leadership. This is partly a matter of limited resources and partly a matter of style. The Saudis shun controversy and conflict with the major Arab powers, trying to stay on speaking terms with radicals and conservatives, Baathists and monarchs. In this way Saudi leaders believe they can help shape a moderate Arab consensus. Discretion, not boldness, is the watchword in Saudi dealings with Arab issues.

Egypt

Of the neighboring Arab countries, none has so preoccupied the Saudis as Egypt. The Saud family has little reason to harbor fond feelings toward Egypt. In the early nineteenth century Egyptian troops intervened in the Arabian Peninsula to check the power and ambitions of the Saud family. More recently, Egypt under President Nasser waged an intense propaganda and subversive war against Saudi Arabia in the late 1950s, culminating in the proxy war fought in North Yemen from 1962 to 1967. During that inconclusive struggle Egyptian planes bombed Saudi territory on several occasions.

After President Nasser's death in September 1970 relations between Cairo and Riyadh improved rapidly, and from 1972 to 1977 there was even talk of an Egyptian-Saudi axis in the Arab world. Some Saudis hoped that a stable, moderate Arab consensus could be built with Egyptian muscle and Saudi money. Combined with a "special relationship" with Washington, this would be the best guarantee of Saudi security.

But this vision was short-lived, and after President Sadat's unilateral move toward peace with Israel, diplomatic relations were broken and Saudi aid to Egypt was suspended. Sadat's response was to speak disparagingly of the Saudi leadership, although just before his death he was urging the United States to help its Saudi friends.

Whatever the ups and downs of Saudi-Egyptian relations at a given moment, Saudi Arabia cannot ignore Egypt. As the most populous Arab country, Egypt is an immense source of skilled and semiskilled manpower, something that Saudi Arabia desperately needs. Egyptian teachers and doctors are found everywhere in Saudi Arabia, and the break in economic relations in 1979 did not affect the status of Egyptian workers.

Egypt is also the largest military power in the Arab world, and it is clearly in Saudi Arabia's interest that Egyptian forces not be used against the Saudis or their allies. Egypt, for example, has indicated a willingness to provide military assistance to Somalia, Sudan, Morocco, and indirectly, even Iraq. In each case this parallels Saudi policy of providing economic and political support for these regimes. While less anxious to see Egyptian troops anywhere in the Arabian Peninsula, the Saudis realize that in some circumstances the presence of Egyptian forces might be essential. When Kuwait was threatened by Iraq in 1961, the willingness of Egypt to send a peacekeeping force under Arab League mandate helped to defuse the crisis. But the memory of the Yemen war has not faded, and the Saudis worry that Egyptian forces in the peninsula could be a disruptive element rather than a source of stability. As is often the case, this leaves the Saudi leadership with a deep concern with Egypt's military might and ambivalence toward how it might affect Saudi interests.

Saudi Arabia's economic future is also affected by developments in Egypt. For years Saudis have been aware that virtually all their wealth is derived from oil moving through the Strait of Hormuz. Some of that oil reaches Western markets through the Suez Canal, as do many of the products that Saudi Arabia imports in return.

During the brief period of good relations with Egypt in the mid-1970s, the Saudis sought to develop an alternative route for some of their oil that would require Egypt's cooperation. A partially Saudi-owned (15 percent) pipeline, SUMED (Suez to the Mediterranean), was constructed to carry oil from the Red Sea to a port west of Alexandria. By 1980 it was carrying over 1.5 million barrels of oil a day to market.

The Saudis also completed two parallel pipelines (Petroline) across the peninsula in 1981 so that some Saudi oil and natural gas liquids could bypass the Strait of Hormuz and be delivered directly to the Red Sea port of Yanbu. There the gas is to be processed into petrochemicals and the oil sent on to European markets, partly through the SUMED Pipeline and partly through the Suez Canal. When fully operational, the two pipelines will initially handle 1.85 million barrels per day of Saudi oil and nearly 300,000 bpd of natural gas liquids.[2] This will create a significant degree of dependency on Egypt as a cooperative partner in this enterprise.

With these common security and economic interests, why have Egypt and Saudi Arabia found themselves in opposite camps in the aftermath of President Sadat's peace initiative toward Israel? Many observers professed surprise that Saudi Arabia broke with the moderate, pro-Western regime of President Sadat in 1979 to align itself with such improbable companions as the Soviet-supported regimes in Iraq and Syria, as well as the Palestine Liberation Organization (PLO).

From the Saudi perspective, what did Egypt's separate peace with Israel mean? And why did the Saudis see it as a threat to their own interests? Without Egypt, it is commonly believed, the Arabs can neither make war nor peace with Israel. If this is true, Egypt's defection means that other Arabs are faced with Israel's overwhelming military superiority, which precludes war as a credible Arab option. Even with

2. The capacity of the SUMED Pipeline may be increased to as much as 2.4 million bpd. Petroline could carry 2.35 million bpd if additional pumping stations were built, and some analysts have speculated that capacity could be expanded ultimately to as much as 4 million bpd. The gas pipeline could also be made to carry crude oil, but pumping stations would have to be added. See Roger Vielvoye, "Saudi Oil Development Thrusts West," *Oil and Gas Journal* (July 7, 1980), pp. 74–78; and Bakr A. Khoja, "The Pipeline Contribution to the Middle East Oil Trades," *OAPEC Review*, vol. 5 (February 1979), pp. 26–29.

the weight of Egypt on their side, the Arabs were unable to defeat Israel militarily, including in 1973. If force is effectively eliminated because of Sadat's policies, this leaves diplomacy backed by economic power as the only alternative to prolonged stalemate. But the diplomatic deck, they believe, is stacked against them.

The Saudi assessment of the conflict with Israel is that the Arabs have few bargaining cards now that Egypt has made peace. The Syrians alone cannot challenge Israel without turning their own country into a Soviet base. The PLO can pursue armed struggle, but the major monuments to their military efforts thus far have been "Black September" 1970, when they were crushed by Jordanian forces, and the war in Lebanon in 1975–76.

In their frustration the Syrians, Palestinians, and Jordanians inevitably look to Saudi Arabia as the only element on the Arab side that can help obtain some semblance of balance in the conflict with Israel. This means that Saudi oil would have to be put at the disposal of the Arab cause, violating the long-held belief of King Faisal that short of extreme circumstances, oil and politics should not be mixed.

Of course, it has always been a myth that oil was unrelated to the Arab-Israeli conflict, but it has nonetheless been in the Saudis' interest for some ambiguity to cloud the issue and for crucial decisions on production and pricing to be made by them rather than by angry Arab radicals. Egypt's isolation heightens the pressure on Saudi Arabia to use the "oil weapon" in the struggle with Israel and removes Egypt as a source of support against those pressures.

As long as the Palestinian issue festers, the Saudis fear, the surrounding Arab world will be threatened by instability, the Soviets will be a source of arms and diplomatic support for some Arab regimes, and Saudi Arabia will be asked to use its oil to force the Americans to extract concessions from the Israelis. Meanwhile the Saudis see the United States embracing Egypt as its preferred partner in the Arab world, and this calls into question the durability of the U.S.-Saudi special relationship. It is bad enough when Israel uses its political clout in Washington to cast doubt on Saudi Arabia, but it was even worse when President Sadat inveighed against the Saudis. In the search for advanced U.S. weaponry Egypt and Saudi Arabia have to some extent become competitors, and it is galling to the Saudis to see impoverished Egypt gaining access to the American arsenal at the U.S. taxpayer's expense, while Saudi Arabia is only grudgingly granted permission to buy extra fuel tanks and missiles for F-15 jet aircraft that are being purchased at what seem to be inflated prices. This sense of irritation may have been somewhat tempered by Sadat's support, just before his death, of the sale of AWACS aircraft to Saudi Arabia. In time, some rapprochement between Riyadh and Cairo seems possible.

The "Radical" Arabs

While the Saudis have had their share of quarrels with all their Arab neighbors regardless of the nature of their political systems or their ostensible ideological leanings, since the early 1950s they have been particularly concerned with signs of Arab radicalism, especially on the left. Arab radicalism not only has been anticolonial and anti-Western but also, more dangerously, has often been populist, activist, antimonarchical, progressive, secularist, and frequently pro–Soviet Union. For the Saudi leadership, which has been wedded to the concepts of monarchy, Islam, and tradition and which has valued stability and order, at least since the 1940s, the prospect of revolutionary change in whatever guise has been a threatening one. Equally dangerous has been the willingness of the radicals to invite the Soviets into the Middle East.

Beginning with the Egyptian revolution in 1952, the Saudis witnessed a series of violent upheavals in the Arab world in the name of the people, nationalism, and social justice. Traditional monarchies were on the defensive everywhere. The attack was led under many names: Arab nationalism, Nasser's slogan after 1956; Arab unity, a favorite of the Baath party and Nasser after 1958; social justice and equality, Nasser's theme after 1962 and that of an assortment of Marxists and communists throughout the 1960s and 1970s.

The results of Arab radical challenges to the status quo were impressive. The Egyptian monarchy was swept away in 1952. The Iraqi royal family was murdered in 1958 and replaced by a regime that included nationalists, Baathists, and communists. Syrian political life slipped to the left in the mid-1950s, then went through a brief period of unity with Egypt from 1958 to 1961, before settling down to Baathist rule of one variety or another from 1963 on. The conservative Imamate of North Yemen was overthrown by Egyptian-backed republican forces in 1962. Algeria gained its independence that same year with the fiery socialist leader Ahmad Ben Bella as its first president. The British flag over Aden came down in 1967 and power was turned over to militant nationalists with strong Marxist leanings. Two years later the tottering regime of King Idris I of Libya was ousted by a young nationalist, Muammar Qadhafi, whose rhetoric was borrowed from Nasser and Islam.

In each of these cases conservative, Western-oriented regimes, mostly monarchies, succumbed to some form of Arab radicalism. In each instance, when the dust settled the influence of the Soviet Union seemed to have advanced a bit further into the Arab world. The Saudis were worried and on the defensive. If an internal challenge to Saudi Arabia were to be mounted, it was widely assumed, it would be in the name of the people and social justice, against the privileges of the House of Saud and the corruption spawned by oil wealth. Such a challenge could count on support from abroad from one or more radical Arab regimes.

To deal with the threat from Arab radicalism, the Saudis have resorted to a wide range of tactics. Least effective were clumsy attempts to buy influence and politicians, including an abortive attempt by King Saud to finance an assassination attempt against Nasser.

If covert action was not the Saudi strong suit, economic aid proved to be a more persuasive instrument. Nasser's anti-Saudi crusade was blunted at the Khartoum conference in August 1967 by generous offers of aid from Arab oil-producing countries, including Saudi Arabia, to the militarily and economically prostrate Egypt. Syria, Jordan, and eventually the PLO were also recipients of Saudi largesse. For King Faisal, who took the lead at Khartoum in organizing economic support for the confrontation states, aid to these rival regimes was a prudent form of insurance, even if it provided little real leverage.

By keeping channels open to the radical Arabs and by providing some aid, the Saudis hoped to be in a position to exert moderating influence and to exploit internal changes that might bring new leaders to the fore. This gamble seemed to pay off in 1970, a critical year in inter-Arab politics. In September Nasser died and was succeeded by Anwar Sadat, someone the Saudis preferred to Nasser, even though Faisal held Sadat personally responsible for the Yemen conflict. A few months later the leftist regime in Damascus of Salah Jadid was ousted by the more pragmatic Hafiz al-Assad. In each case the Saudis sensed an opportunity to encourage a trend away from dependence on the Soviet Union and toward greater inter-Arab cooperation.

Fortunately for the Saudis, just as they began the game of wooing Egypt and Syria toward centrist positions, Saudi oil revenues were rapidly increasing. This made Saudi Arabia a much sought after friend in the Arab world. When Sadat finally ousted the Soviet advisers from Egypt in July 1972, the Saudis were delighted and were more than willing to help Egypt economically.

In courting Egypt and Syria, however, Saudi Arabia risked being drawn into the Arab-Israeli conflict. Egypt and Syria, along with most other Arab states, were unprepared to accept the post-1967 situation. Diplomacy seemed to offer few openings. War, coupled with the use of oil as a political weapon, became the choice of Sadat and Assad. But war was risky for the Saudis. If the Arabs lost, a new wave of Arab radicalism might follow. Pro-Western regimes would come under great pressure. Soviet influence might grow even stronger, as it did after 1967. But if Saudi Arabia remained aloof while Egypt and Syria fought, or if it openly opposed the recourse to hostilities, it would also be vulnerable to charges of colluding with imperialism and Zionism.

Not surprisingly, King Faisal tried to warn the West in spring 1973 that war was coming, in the hope it would be avoided by effective diplomacy. But his warnings were not heeded; Egypt and Syria went to war on October 6, and two weeks later King Faisal unsheathed the oil weapon against the United States. In 1967 some Saudis may have taken silent satisfaction in the demonstrated incompetence of the Egyptian and Syrian armies, but 1973 was another matter. Most Arabs saw the war as a victory of sorts, and the Saudis took credit for having played an essential part. Henceforth they would not be allowed to remain on the sidelines and plead that the oil weapon was a two-edged sword that should never be wielded.

If the 1973 war marked the high point of Saudi cooperation with the leading Arab arms clients of the Soviet Union, Egypt, and Syria, that common front did not last for long. Two years later Egypt and Syria were at odds, leaving the Saudis in an awkward position. Late in 1976 Saudi Arabia tried to bring Sadat and Assad together, but the rapprochement was short-lived. Sadat was soon moving on his own toward peace with Israel, leaving Syria with the so-called rejection front.

As Saudi relations with Egypt deteriorated, and to a lesser extent with Syria, the Iranian revolution of 1978–79 accelerated Iraq's move away from its previous isolation. With Iran in chaos, Egypt expelled from the Arab League, and Syria in turmoil, Iraq saw the opportunity to make a bid for leadership in the Arab world. The Saudis, anxious not to find themselves at odds with their newly assertive and potentially powerful neighbor, began to work to improve Saudi-Iraqi relations.

On ideological grounds this seemed a strange match. The Baathists in Baghdad were secular socialists. They had long been identified in the West with extreme positions, had a reputation for violence, and had concluded a Treaty of Friendship and Cooperation with the Soviet Union. But by 1980 Iraq had somewhat tempered its position on the Arab-Israeli dispute, had edged away from Moscow's embrace by opposing Soviet actions in Afghanistan and in Ethiopia, and had broken its close ties to the Marxist regime in South Yemen.

The Saudis, perhaps self-servingly, took some credit for these developments, but whatever the reason the stage was set for an unprecedented degree of cooperation between Baghdad and Riyadh. Both regimes were worried about the Islamic revolution in Iran; both expressed concern about the superpower rivalry in the Persian Gulf; both opposed the Camp David accords; and both had an immense stake in OPEC pricing decisions.

While the new relationship with Baghdad was hedged with qualifications and was probably not destined to last indefinitely, it did demonstrate that Saudi Arabia was prepared to cooperate with so-called radical Arab regimes if that might reduce pressures in inter-Arab debates. For example, early in 1981 the Saudis allowed Iraq to take delivery of 100 East European tanks at Saudi Red Sea ports. This soon became a regular practice, with East European and Soviet ships calling at the small port of Qadima north of Jidda to unload shipments of arms for Iraq. By fall 1981 more arms were reaching Baghdad via Saudi Arabia than by any other route. At a time when Iraq was actively at war with Iran, Saudi support was particularly important.

Saudi leaders hoped that Baghdad would continue its policy of nonalignment and that the Iraqis might curtail their disruptive actions in countries of special interest to Saudi Arabia, such as North Yemen and Oman. While harboring few illusions about the ultimate compatibility of Iraqi and Saudi interests, the kingdom's leadership was prepared for pragmatic accommodations with Baghdad.[3] For example, within OPEC a joint stand by Saudi Arabia and Iraq on prices would be very hard to resist since together they account for well over one-third of OPEC's total productive capacity. Thus Riyadh has a strong incentive to discuss oil policy with the Iraqis. One concrete example of cooperation on oil

3. On Saudi-Iraqi relations, see Adeed Dawisha, *Saudi Arabia's Search for Security*, pp. 21–23.

might be a pipeline from Basra in southern Iraq across Saudi Arabia to the Red Sea, a project that was seriously discussed in mid-1981.

If Saudi Arabia has gone to some lengths to keep channels open to Syria and Iraq because of their influential roles in inter-Arab politics, relations with the regimes in Libya and South Yemen have been more episodic. Libya's Qadhafi has been something of an enigma to the Saudis. He is outspokenly pro-Palestinian and uses the language of Islamic revival. In his early period he seemed to be anticommunist as well. But Qadhafi is also a revolutionary with ambitions of leadership in the Islamic and Arab arenas. In addition he has become heavily dependent on the Soviet Union. Finally, when Qadhafi publicly challenged the right of the Saudis to control the holy places of Mecca and Medina in late 1980, the Saudis broke diplomatic relations with Tripoli.

South Yemen, while more of a direct danger to Saudi interests than Libya, maintains diplomatic links with Riyadh. Relations, however, are uneasy as the Saudis waver between policies designed to unseat the communist regime in Aden and those that might temper the radicalism of the South Yemen rulers. Aid is offered, then withdrawn. Tribal dissidents are kept on a Saudi retainer, to be unleashed if Aden's policies become too troublesome. While the Saudis have learned to live with Marxists in Aden, it is no secret that they see South Yemen as an enemy and are developing their modest military capabilities to deal with threats from that quarter.

The "Conservative" Arabs and Client States

If foreign policy were simply a reflection of national interests, one might expect Saudi Arabia's natural allies in the Arab world to be other conservative, Western-oriented regimes. A Saudi-led "moderate" bloc would have strong incentives to contain radical, destabilizing trends, to limit Soviet influence, to cooperate on regional security, and in the cases of the few remaining monarchies, to resist republican notions.

As much as the Saudis value regional stability and fear Soviet-sponsored radicalism and subversion, they have not found it easy to forge close ties with other Arab conservatives. While Egypt's unwillingness to follow the Saudi lead is easily understandable, the persistent problems for Saudi Arabia in dealing with other Arab conservatives require a historical perspective.

The Inner Circle

As the Saud family expanded its power in the Arabian Peninsula in the first three decades of this century, clashes occurred with all the political entities surrounding what came to be the Kingdom of Saudi Arabia. Armed conflict, tribal warfare, and attempted subversion were part of the Saudi experience with the Hashemite rulers in Transjordan and Iraq, with the sheikdoms along the Persian Gulf, with the Sultanate of Oman, and with Yemen. Disputes over borders, religious differences, and dynastic rivalries ensured less than cordial relations between Saudi Arabia and most of its immediate neighbors. Although some of these sources of tension have subsided in importance, they are never very far beneath the surface.

Saudi relations with the inner circle of conservative regimes—Jordan, Kuwait, Bahrain, Qatar, the United Arab Emirates (UAE), Oman, and North Yemen—have wavered from outright hostility to cautious cooperation and to periodic attempts to develop patron-client ties. This has left the rulers of these states wary of Saudi intentions and often contemptuous of Saudi pretensions and high-handedness. The Saudis may be rich, but few of their immediate neighbors hold them in high regard.

This is particularly true in the case of Jordan, where objective national interests and lingering historical rivalries set the two countries at cross-purposes. Jordan is relatively poor but occupies a crucial geographic position that helps shield Saudi Arabia from Syria and Israel to the north. Jordan is a central player in the Arab-Israeli dispute and in inter-Arab politics and is one of the few remaining monarchies in the Arab world. It also has a comparatively able military force and a demonstrated ability and willingness to work on behalf of stability in the gulf region, Oman, and North Yemen. Thus one might expect a substantial amount of Saudi aid for Jordan to help ensure its buffer role, to enhance its modest "peacemaking" capabilities, and to contain radical trends in the Arab world. But King Hussein is also a Hashemite, great-grandson of Sharif Hussein, one-time ruler of the Hijaz region, who was driven out of the Arabian Peninsula by the father of today's Saudi rulers. It was only one generation ago that the Hashemites and Saudis were still trying to unseat one another. Little wonder, then, that a mutual antipathy lingers on. The Saudis profess not to take Jordan very seriously. The Jordanians lament Saudi arrogance and inefficiency and fear that revolutionary upheaval cannot be far off.

Despite these expressions of distaste for one another, Jordanian and Saudi leaders are in frequent contact. No Arab head of state is received in Riyadh more frequently than King Hussein. In recent years high-level Saudi-Jordanian talks have occurred on the average of once every two months, often involving King Hussein and King Khalid ibn Abd al-Aziz directly. This has resulted in substantial Saudi aid to Jordan, a modest degree of military cooperation on regional issues, and a common stance on the Arab-Israeli conflict. But an undercurrent of distrust remains, and the Saudi-Jordanian connection is far from being a firm alliance founded on mutual interests.

If King Hussein is treated as a fellow monarch, albeit from a rival clan, the rulers of the Persian Gulf sheikdoms are generally viewed by the Saudis as lesser tribal leaders who for one reason or another—usually British protection—managed to remain outside the Saudi embrace. At best, these ministates should behave as dutiful clients, following the Saudi lead in inter-Arab politics.

Kuwait has been most reluctant to fit the mold of an obedient client. As a significant oil producer with a population of more than 1 million, Kuwait has developed a distinctive political identity and an independent foreign policy. Kuwait consistently supports the Palestinian cause— about one-fourth of its population is made up of displaced Palestinians— and its intellectual life is dominated by Arab nationalist concerns. Virtually every political current in the Arab world finds expression in Kuwait. Pressures for political participation are sometimes accommodated. Parliamentary elections took place in early 1981. Conspirators, some hostile to Saudi Arabia, have occasionally been able to operate out of Kuwait. Unique among the gulf sheikdoms, Kuwait has formal diplomatic relations with Moscow, has allowed a large Soviet embassy to function since the mid-1960s, and has recently begun to purchase some Soviet military equipment. If Jordan is seen from Saudi Arabia as a useful buffer against Soviet influence, Kuwait is viewed as a potentially dangerous opening wedge in Moscow's search for acceptance on the Arab side of the gulf. Saudi-Kuwaiti contacts are frequent, involving questions of oil as well as regional politics, but Saudi influence in Kuwait is limited.

The smaller emirates of Bahrain, Qatar, and the UAE are more inclined to follow the Saudi lead. Bahrain's greatest attraction for some Saudis is as a nearby oasis for entertainments denied them at home. On a more strategic level, however, the Saudis are apprehensive over Iranian designs on Bahrain and the possibility that Shiite militancy in Bahrain could provide a bad example for their own Shiite minority. In the hope of strengthening Saudi-Bahraini ties, the Saudis plan to build a causeway from the mainland to the island.

Qatar, as the only other political entity that shares Saudi Arabia's adherence to the strict Wahhabi interpretation of Islam, is somewhat more securely anchored to the Saudi sphere of influence than other gulf states and therefore is taken more for granted. Periodic visits take place, but Qatar is not a major actor in any of the arenas that interest the Saudis.

The UAE is another matter. First, it has enough oil to make it a significant member of OPEC. Second, Saudi Arabia has long made claims to parts of the territory of the UAE. Third, the Saudis were concerned about instability after the British withdrawal from the gulf in 1971 and therefore threw their support behind the creation of the UAE as the best means to prevent disruptions in this sensitive region. These concerns have led to a surprisingly active diplomacy between Saudi Arabia and the UAE. In July 1974 agreement was reached on most of the disputed border between the two countries.[4] Subsequently the UAE generally followed the Saudi lead in OPEC meetings on price decisions. Given the potential for conflict over territorial issues, the Saudi-UAE relationship has evolved comparatively smoothly.

Saudi-Omani relations are particularly complex, for once again common interests are offset by historical and religious antipathies. From a religious standpoint the Ibadi sect in Oman is looked down upon by the Wahhabis of Saudi Arabia. More concretely, the Saudis clashed with Oman in the early 1950s over the Buraymi Oasis and into the 1960s conducted a campaign among the tribes of Oman, and even in support of the Ibadi Imam, aimed at weakening the authority of the sultanate.[5]

In 1970 the British assisted Qabus bin Said in ousting his father and in establishing a more "modern" style of rule. One of Sultan Qabus's first acts was to visit Saudi Arabia and to seek financial aid for his impoverished realm. The Saudis were alarmed at the outbreak of guerrilla war in

4. It is still difficult to find an authoritative map of the UAE-Saudi border. The Saudis have dropped their claim to the Buraymi Oasis. In return they have received a corridor of land to the sea just south of Qatar. A major undeveloped oil field lies astride the UAE-Saudi border and discussions have been held on sharing the output once the field is exploited. See the map and discussion in J. B. Kelly, *Arabia, the Gulf and the West*, p. 211.

5. See ibid., pp. 113–30, 158–59, for a colorful account of the unhappy history of Saudi-Omani relations.

the Omani province of Dhofar, seeing the Marxist regime in South
Yemen as the instigator of the troubles. As a result, the Saudis offered
several hundred million dollars in aid to Qabus. But the Saudis remained
on the sidelines, leaving Britain, Iran, and Jordan with the task of defend-
ing the sultanate. By the time the war was essentially over in 1975, Oman
could count on a modest income from oil and was less in need of Saudi
help.

Saudi-Omani relations soon became lukewarm, with only intermittent
contact. The Saudis disagreed with Qabus on the Egyptian-Israeli peace
treaty, and they initially expressed concern at Oman's willingness to accept an American military presence in the country. By early 1980, however, Crown Prince Fahd ibn Abd al-Aziz had conveyed to President
Jimmy Carter his willingness to see the Omani island of Masirah developed as a forward staging area for the U.S. Rapid Deployment Force.

In view of Oman's involvement with American force planning for the
region, one can anticipate that the Saudis will pay increasing attention
to developments in Oman, but the prospects for very close cooperation
seem modest. Oman is unwilling to accept client status, and the Saudis
have generally seen Oman as somewhat remote and firmly tied to the
British and Americans.

Despite the many issues that divide Saudi Arabia and the Arab princi-
palities of the gulf, they have in common a desire to prevent Iranian or
Iraqi hegemony and they are all trying to preserve conservative social
and political structures in the face of serious internal and external
threats. With these points of common interest, Saudi Arabia, Kuwait,
Bahrain, Qatar, the UAE, and Oman established in early 1981 an Arab
Gulf Cooperation Council, with a permanent secretariat in Riyadh. The
Saudis were pleased with their part in bringing the group together but
were anxious not to define its goals as regional defense. While privately
gratified that Iraq was not a member, Saudis did not want to convey the
impression that the council was designed to oppose Iraqi ambitions in
the area. It remained to be seen whether the council would find a real
role for itself in the complex politics of the gulf region.

If Saudi Arabia has been somewhat successful in gaining a dominant
voice in the affairs of its Arab gulf neighbors, North Yemen has been a
less pliable client. Saudi diplomacy has been severely tested over the
years by Yemen, and a legacy of mistrust and paternalism lives on.
Within the lifetimes of Saudi Arabia's current rulers, two armed con-

flicts have occurred between Saudi and Yemeni forces. In the early 1930s Saud and Faisal, the brothers of today's Saudi leaders, led military campaigns that established Saudi predominance over the disputed Asir and Jizan provinces. Following a generation of relatively peaceful relations after the Treaty of Taif was signed in 1934, Saudi-Yemeni relations deteriorated sharply when Republican forces backed by Egypt overthrew the conservative imam in 1962. For five years thereafter, the Saudis fought a proxy war with Egypt in North Yemen. Much of the country remained under the control of tribal forces backed by the Saudis.

Egypt's withdrawal from Yemen after the 1967 Arab-Israeli war opened the way for a new phase in Saudi-Yemeni relations. The Saudis retained their ties to some tribal groups, but they also began to deal with the republican government in Sanaa in the hope of keeping it from coming under excessive Soviet influence. By the late 1970s the Saudis were deeply engaged in Yemeni affairs, with aid programs paralleling less obvious forms of political manipulation. So great was Saudi influence that it was widely believed in Sanaa that President Ibrahim al-Hamdi was assassinated by the Saudis in October 1977 to make way for a more sympathetic regime under President Ahmad Hussein al-Ghashmi. Whatever the truth, there was little doubt that Saudi Arabia was very concerned with Yemeni affairs.

The specific reasons for Saudi involvement in Yemen are not difficult to discern. Apart from disputes over territory, the Saudis worry that Yemen could easily come under leftist influence, which would result in a substantial Soviet presence in the country. This would provide another platform for attempts to pressure and subvert the Saudi regime. Border disputes would doubtless erupt, forcing the Saudis to choose between fighting a Soviet-backed regime or acquiescing and seeking political accommodations. In addition Yemen currently supplies a large proportion of Saudi Arabia's unskilled work force. Estimates run around 500,000 or more. If Yemen were to be ruled by a regime hostile to the Saudis, this large Yemeni population in Saudi Arabia might be used as a destabilizing element.

In any event, the Saudis seek to keep the most populous country in the Arabian Peninsula within their own sphere of influence, rather than see it follow in the path of South Yemen. It is not surprising that Yemen receives very high priority in Saudi foreign policy, although the Saudis seem to display a patronizing and sometimes contemptuous attitude that

has done little to win the hearts and minds of Yemenis. Yemeni irredentist claims to the Najran and Jizan regions, as well as to parts of the
southern Asir, add to mistrust on both sides of the border.

The Outer Circle

If the Saudis' relations with their immediate conservative neighbors
have often been intense and complex, the more remote traditional and
moderate Arab regimes have usually been on good, if sometimes formal,
terms with Riyadh. Morocco and Sudan, for example, have both been
recipients of substantial quantities of Saudi aid. As a fellow Arab monarch, King Hassan II of Morocco has been particularly successful in
gaining backing for his military adventure in the western Sahara. In return, Morocco tends to support the Saudis in inter-Arab circles, despite
King Hassan's well-known disdain for the eastern Arab world.

In recent years a number of Saudi rulers have tightened their personal
ties to Morocco, buying property, vacationing there, and even marrying
Moroccan women. This has not been a guarantee of cordial official relations—Saudi aid was suspended in the late 1970s over concern with how
it was being spent—but it has helped provide a solid underpinning for
Saudi-Moroccan ties.

Sudan has been of concern to the Saudis because of its involvement in
the Horn of Africa dispute between Ethiopia and Somalia since the late
1970s, as well as its close ties to Egypt. In addition Sudan has at various
times been threatened with leftist pressures, and the Saudis have no
desire to see a pro-Soviet regime in Khartoum. Thus they have provided aid to Sudan, in return for which President Gaafar Muhammad
al-Numeiry muted his enthusiasm for the Camp David peace process as
it unfolded after 1978. Numeiry is a frequent visitor to Riyadh, but the
Saudis have tended to keep Sudan on a tight leash. For example, in 1980
the Saudis were reluctant to finance the purchase by Sudan of American
military equipment as long as Sudan maintained diplomatic relations with
Egypt.

Lebanon occupies a special place in Saudi foreign policy concerns,
not because of any intrinsic interest in Lebanon, but out of concern for
the consequences of developments in the often beleaguered country for
the broader region. The risk of a general Arab-Israeli war being ignited
in Lebanon obliges the Saudis to pay close attention to developments
there. During the worst of the Lebanese crisis in the mid-1970s, the

Saudis had a highly regarded and effective ambassador in Lebanon. He returned to Beirut in 1981 to help devise an acceptable "Arab solution" to the crisis surrounding the city of Zahle and the installation of Syrian surface-to-air missiles near that besieged Christian town.

By helping to defuse the crisis the Saudis hoped to win credit in Washington, to reduce the need for Syria to depend exclusively on the Soviets, and to remove a possible flashpoint for a Syrian-Israeli war. It was clearly these objectives that motivated Saudi diplomacy more than any concern for the Lebanese dimension of the crisis per se.

The Saudis find themselves in the awkward position of wanting to support "moderate" forces in Lebanon but being reluctant to back openly the pro-Western Christian militias because of their close ties to Israel. This leaves the Saudis with a policy of support for the PLO, which periodically challenges the authority of the government of Lebanon, and Syria, which is viewed by many Lebanese as an occupying army. When the Saudis do try to influence events in Lebanon, it is by talking and offering aid to the PLO and Syria, and even the Christian militias, as much as by supporting the legitimate government.[6]

The Palestinians and the Conflict with Israel

When the Saudis talk about the Arab world, they evoke ideals of unity, solidarity, and cooperation that have become part of standard Arab political rhetoric. Their own experiences, however, have taught them that inter-Arab politics is a rough-and-tumble arena, where competition, maneuver, and concern for reputation are everyday facts of life. Despite their awareness of these harsh realities, they seem to believe that the Arab world would be considerably less turbulent and threatening were it not for Zionism and the existence of the Arab-Israeli conflict.

The Saudi image of a manageable Arab world, in which their security and domestic development could be best protected, approximates the balance-of-power model of international relations. As a relatively weak power, the Saudis seek to prevent domination by any single Arab coun-

6. For a brief period the Saudis contributed a contingent to the Arab League–mandated Arab Deterrent Force in Lebanon. Eventually the Saudis along with the Sudanese withdrew their troops, leaving Syria as the only member of the ADF. In early 1981 the Saudis reportedly suspended financial support for Syrian forces in Lebanon. The restoration of this subsidy was one element in the mid-1981 diplomacy of trying to defuse the explosiveness of the Lebanon issue.

try. For example, quite apart from the ideology he propounded, Nasser was a threat because he sought Arab unity under Egypt's tutelage.[7]

The key to survival in the balance of power game is flexibility of alignments. To prevent one state from gaining too much power, others must band together. Ideology should not be a primary consideration in calculating moves and countermoves. Neither friendships nor enmities can be taken for granted. The well-executed maneuver is as much admired as high-minded principle. The game is played with a certain relish, accompanied by large doses of cynicism.

Saudi ability to compete in this environment required that Egypt not become too strong, that no outside power intervene to upset the balance, and that ideology remain muted. In these circumstances Saudi Arabia could use its key resource, money, to win the support of others and to establish a buffer of weak, semidependent clients along its borders. Military power was not a crucial ingredient in this contest as long as actual conflict could be prevented by shifting alliances and by counting on some deterrence from the shadow presence of the major powers who had a stake in Saudi survival. Tribal feuding provided a good education for the Saudis who had to play the game of inter-Arab politics.

During the 1950s this model broke down and was replaced by one much more threatening to Saudi interests. First, the flexibility of inter-Arab alignments was reduced by the presence of a common adversary, Israel. Second, the Soviet Union was invited into the area as a major supplier of arms to selected countries, thus enhancing the war-making capabilities of Egypt and Syria in particular. Third, Arab politics became intensely ideological, with the nature of the regimes in various Arab countries becoming matters of concern for all Arabs. Nasser could appeal to the Arab masses over the heads of their leaders and thereby threaten to bring down governments.

From the Saudi perspective, Israel was largely responsible for the collapse of the old order and the entry of the Soviet Union into the region. To many Saudis, it was Israel's ability in 1947–48 to defeat the conservative governments of Egypt, Syria, Iraq, and Jordan that set off a wave of military coups in the Arab world. Displaced Palestinians became a radicalizing force in Arab politics as they sought support for their usurped rights. Those regimes friendly to the West found themselves

7. A useful interpretation of Saudi foreign policy from the balance-of-power perspective can be found in Robert R. Sullivan, "Saudi Arabia in International Politics," pp. 436–60.

on the defensive when Britain, France, and the United States seemed to side with Israel. By contrast, the Soviets could present themselves as champions of the Arab cause, especially after their offer of arms to Egypt and Syria in the mid-1950s.

Apart from these reasons for concluding that Israel's challenge to the Arabs was a destabilizing force, the Saudis also felt some antipathy for Israel on religious and cultural grounds. Most Arab countries had some experience of hosting Jewish communities. Relations with these communities were rarely idyllic, but the idea of Jews living alongside Muslims and Christians was not unknown. For the Saudis, however, Jews were almost totally foreign. No significant Jewish community existed in the Arabian Peninsula outside of Yemen in modern times. Few communications between the Saud family and Zionist leaders ever took place.[8] Many Saudis failed to see much distinction between Judaism as a religion and Zionism as a religious political movement. Until quite recently the anti-Jewish forgery *The Protocols of the Elders of Zion* could easily be found on public display in Saudi Arabia. Few Jews were allowed into Saudi Arabia for any reason. And King Faisal's tirades against Israel often seemed to be tinged with more than a trace of hostility toward Jews.[9]

If religious and cultural hostility reinforced Saudi antipathy to Israel on political and strategic grounds, the issue of Jerusalem further complicated the picture. As the guardians of the holy places in Mecca and Medina, the Saudis could not be indifferent to the third most sacred place in Islam, the al-Aqsa mosque in Jerusalem. Faisal did in fact pray at al-Aqsa on one occasion when the Saudis contributed to the restoration of the Dome of the Rock mosque.[10] After 1967 these Islamic shrines came under Israeli control as East Jerusalem was annexed. Faisal was particularly adamant in his insistence that Arab Jerusalem must be free of Israeli domination, and he spoke of his desire to pray again at al-Aqsa before his death, something he was unable to do. His successors continue

8. See H. StJ. B. Philby, *Arabian Jubilee*, pp. 206–09, for an account of his contacts with Chaim Weizmann in 1939. On one occasion Philby hosted a lunch for the Saudi representative to the Palestine Conference, Fuad Bey Hamza, and David Ben-Gurion.

9. See the account of King Faisal's first meeting with Secretary of State Henry Kissinger in November 1973 in Edward R. F. Sheehan, *The Arabs, Israelis, and Kissinger*, pp. 70–73. In 1981 President Ronald Reagan's reaction to the first substantive letter he received from King Khalid was to note that the Saudis appeared to be "anti-Semitic."

10. King Faisal visited Jerusalem in February 1966.

to focus attention on Jerusalem, although some of them seem less concerned with the idea of a Zionist-communist conspiracy.

The Saudis' opposition to Zionism was not enough to ensure their wholehearted support for the Palestinians. Before 1967, in fact, the Saudis had not been deeply involved with the Palestinian movement. In part this was because the Palestinian activists of the day were typically either leftists or followers of Egypt's Nasser.

In the aftermath of the 1967 war, however, Nasser was no longer much of a threat to Saudi Arabia. The new dynamic force in the Arab world seemed to be the Palestinian resistance, a collection of guerrilla fighters, old-guard nationalists, and young idealists. By 1968 all the major Arab countries were competing for influence within the PLO. The Syrians controlled one group, the Iraqis another. Libya, Algeria, and Kuwait all had their favorites. But the center of the PLO, the Fatah organization led by Yasir Arafat, tried to remain comparatively free of control by any single Arab regime.[11] To maximize his ability to maneuver, Arafat sought support from several sources, the most important being Egypt and Saudi Arabia.

Support for Fatah served several purposes for the Saudis. First, it was a relatively inexpensive insurance policy. No leader in the Arab world, especially in the late 1960s and early 1970s, wanted to be branded as anti-Palestinian. Since Saudi Arabia hosted nearly 200,000 expatriate Palestinians, there was an added reason to want to be on good terms with the most widely accepted spokesman of the Palestinian people. Second, the Saudis felt that Arafat was a comparatively moderate leader, with nationalist goals, who would not foment revolution in the Arab world. Thus it was worth strengthening his tendency in his rivalries with the other more leftist, pro-Soviet factions such as the Popular Front for the Liberation of Palestine. Third, Arafat and most of his immediate colleagues were Muslim, unlike the leaders of the PFLP and the Popular Democratic Front for the Liberation of Palestine, and in some cases had been associated with the Muslim Brotherhood movement in Egypt. This helped convince the Saudis that they did not represent a dangerous radical trend.

Saudi support for the PLO has had its ups and downs over the years, but the Saudi commitment to the Palestinian cause has been surprisingly strong and predictable. Yasir Arafat is one of the most frequent visitors

11. See William B. Quandt, Fuad Jabber, and Ann Mosely Lesch, *The Politics of Palestinian Nationalism.*

to the kingdom, and Crown Prince Fahd is particularly close to Arafat. Within Fatah's inner circle, Khalid al-Hassan is also on very good terms with the Saudi leadership.

The Saudis have supported the idea that the PLO is the sole legitimate spokesman for the Palestinians and have publicly and privately called for the establishment of an independent Palestinian state. In the Saudi view a Palestinian state would go far to satisfy the demands of most Palestinians. They would thereby cease to be a radical, destabilizing force in the area. Saudi Arabia could hope to gain some influence over such a state by providing aid.[12] The Saudis simply do not share the Israeli fear that a mini-Palestine would inevitably be irredentist, therefore radical and pro-Soviet, resulting in a Soviet base in the Middle East.

Rightly or wrongly the Saudis profess to believe that a political settlement of the Arab-Israeli conflict, including the creation of a Palestinian state, would reduce the dangers they now see in the Middle East. Not only would the inter-Arab environment become more manageable, they think, but the risk of war would also be reduced. Thus to the surprise of some the Saudis continue to insist that a solution to the Palestinian issue is a matter of urgent concern and top priority to them.

Conclusion

History, culture, geography, and national interest combine to make the Arab world the primary arena for Saudi foreign policy. On occasion, issues outside the Arab context will capture the attention of the kingdom's leadership, but Arab concerns consistently rank near the top of the Saudi agenda.

Developments in Syria, Iraq, Egypt, Lebanon, and Jordan are watched carefully for the impact they may have in the Arabian Peninsula. The neighboring emirates along the gulf, Oman and the two Yemens, are also a constant preoccupation for the security-conscious Saudis.

12. The limits on Saudi influence over the PLO were reflected in the PLO's decision not to attend the Arab summit meeting in Amman in late November 1980. The Saudis had pressed the PLO to attend. The Syrians had argued against the PLO's participation. Under these conflicting pressures the PLO went along with the Syrians, who have direct military control over them, and not with the Saudis, who hold the purse strings only.

It is not primarily sentiment or ideology that draws Saudi Arabia into inter-Arab politics. Rather, it is the sense that Saudi Arabia's own well-being is directly affected by what happens in the Arab world. When the Arab world is deeply divided along radical versus conservative lines, the Saudis feel uneasy. When Soviet influence seems on the rise in any major Arab country, the Saudis feel threatened. When the Palestinian issue flares up, the Saudis are immediately on the spot, for they control the oil that many Arabs believe could be used as an effective weapon against Israel and her supporters.

For a country as deeply involved in Arab politics as the Saudi Kingdom, it is perhaps surprising that the Saudis are rarely found in a position of strong leadership. In part this reflects the reality that Saudi Arabia, for all its wealth, is not a powerful country. Militarily and demographically it is not in the same league as Egypt, Iraq, Syria, or Algeria. In terms of skilled manpower, even Jordan has more to offer than Saudi Arabia. Lebanese and Palestinians, not Saudis, influence Arab intellectual, political, and cultural debates.

Instead of trying to lead the Arab world the Saudis have sought to play the role of moderator of inter-Arab conflicts, as the brokers of an often elusive Arab consensus. To this end—which serves Saudi interests well by keeping external pressures at a minimum—the Saudis have sought to remain on speaking terms with nearly all Arab regimes.

Since the death of Egypt's President Nasser, the Saudis have deliberately tried to open normal relations with Cairo, Damascus, and Baghdad. These ties have had their ups and downs, but Riyadh has always wanted to be on good terms with at least one of these capitals, as well as with the Palestinian movement. In this way threats from Arab radicals can be defused, propaganda attacks against the kingdom can be contained, and the sharp polarization of Arab politics that characterized the early 1960s can be avoided.

As a medium-sized player in the inter-Arab political game, but one with resources that many others may covet, the Saudis have a strong interest in preventing the hegemony of any single Arab state in the region. A balance of power, with shifting alliances to maintain equilibrium, is strongly preferred to a unified Arab world under someone else's leadership. Only in the peninsula itself have the Saudis shown a propensity to act as a hegemonic power, but even this has been beyond their reach.

If these patterns continue, one can expect the Saudis to maintain a wide network of Arab relations, to work quietly behind the scenes to contain inter-Arab conflicts, and to use their financial clout to win some degree of influence in major Arab capitals. With a strong pragmatic sense, Saudi Arabia will keep open the possibility of eventually welcoming Egypt back into the Arab fold—in part to counterbalance the growing influence of Iraq.

Finally, the Saudis will remain committed to the Palestinian cause, for no other issue in the Arab world is potentially as divisive as this one. After a generation of nationalist agitation on behalf of Palestinian rights, no Arab regime is prepared to abandon the struggle entirely, whatever the sentiments of the ruling elites may be toward Palestinians. To do so would be a sign of weakness, of abdication in the face of Israeli intransigence, of capitulation to American pressure.

Unwilling to abandon the Palestinians, yet unable to take the lead in negotiating a settlement of the Palestinian issue with Israel, the Saudis are left with the unenviable task of trying to limit the negative consequences of the stalemate, while pleading with the United States to do something to ease the strain, to solve the problem for them. Much of the Arab world looks to the Saudis as holding the key to the Palestinian issue, a misconception perhaps, but one that adds to the kingdom's sense that it cannot remain aloof from inter-Arab politics, from the Palestinians, or from Israel.

Chapter Three

The Islamic World

THE CONNECTIONS between Saudi Arabia and the rest of the Islamic world are particularly complex, derived as they are from common religious precepts on one level and hard strategic calculus on another. The "Islamicness" of Saudi foreign policy is not merely a reflection of official ideology, nor is it only lip service. Once again, it is the connection between political realities in Saudi Arabia and developments in the world beyond that makes Islamic concerns an important dimension of Saudi foreign policy.

The Saud family's fundamental claim to legitimacy derives not from its success at military conquest but from its propagation of a particularly pure and austere interpretation and practice of Islam, commonly referred to in the West as Wahhabism after its founder. However much Wahhabi Islam may be ignored in daily life by some Saudis, it is extraordinarily difficult for Saudi leaders to ignore Islamic forces in their own country and elsewhere. Without the aura of legitimacy conferred by Islam, the Saudi regime would enjoy less prestige at home and abroad. As Islam becomes a more assertive force in the world, the Saudis feel particularly anxious to cultivate ties to major Islamic powers. This is both good foreign policy and good domestic politics.

The Islamic theme in Saudi foreign policy is not new. King Faisal, anxious to check radical Arab nationalism led by Egypt's President Nasser, called for Islamic unity in late 1965. This was not a noteworthy success, as few countries responded to the Saudi call. Shah Muhammad Riza Pahlavi of Iran did visit Saudi Arabia in November 1968, but he was unwilling to acknowledge the Saudis as leaders of a conservative Islamic movement, and in any case by then the threat from Nasser's Egypt had receded as a unifying force among conservative Islamic countries. A decade later, however, a richer and more assertive Saudi Arabia once again sought to play a role of leadership in the Islamic world, this time with considerably more success.

Apart from the claim to legitimacy that derives from support for Islam, the regime has a special status in the Muslim world as the guardian of the two most holy sites of Islam, Mecca and Medina. It was here that Islam was born, the Holy Quran was set down in writing, and Muhammad embarked on his mission as God's final prophet.

One of the five obligations undertaken by every Muslim is to make the pilgrimage to Mecca at least once in a lifetime. This places a special burden on the Saudis to ensure that the million or more pilgrims who come each year can be accommodated and worship, while not carrying with them too many subversive ideas.[1] The task of organizing the pilgrimage is immense and virtually paralyzes the top levels of government during the month when the pilgrims arrive. The security services worry that political adversaries will use the cover of the pilgrimage to infiltrate into the country. Political leaders are obliged to devote considerable time to receiving visiting heads of state, for whom the pilgrimage is good politics back home and a chance to seek Saudi aid with or without invitation.

The success of the Islamic revolution in Iran, as well as the struggle of the Afghan Muslim guerrillas against the Soviet invasion of their country, have reminded the world that Islam can be a potent political force. Too much has been made in the West of the idea of an Islamic "resurgence," but there is no doubt that the vocabulary of Islam is increasingly used in expressing political demands in the Middle East and elsewhere. In addition Muslim intellectuals are trying to develop alternatives to the capitalist and socialist models of society imported from the West. Whether or not these efforts will produce much more than apologetics and a nostalgia for the past is uncertain, but for the moment Islam is the subject of serious political debate. As a result of this assertiveness among Muslims, much of the world is now paying some deference to "Islamic" pronouncements on world problems. Some American politicians speak naively of an Islamic alliance to confront Soviet expansion in the Persian Gulf. All of this has heightened the incentives for Saudi leaders to play up the Islamic dimension of their foreign policy. The Saudis took pride and credit in getting the Islamic conference held in Islamabad, Pakistan, in early 1980 to condemn the Soviet invasion of

1. David Edwin Long, *The Hajj Today*, pp. 104–12.

Afghanistan. Similarly, the Saudis have been outspoken in trying to persuade Western and Latin American governments to remove their embassies from Jerusalem and to denounce the Israeli annexation of East Jerusalem. In both cases the Saudis have eagerly assumed the mantle of Islamic leadership.

Early in 1981 the Saudis lavishly hosted a session of the Islamic conference in Taif. It was long on symbolism and short on substance but left the Saudis with a feeling of leadership in the Islamic world. Nowhere else, after all, could nearly all the world's Muslim leaders pray together in the holiest shrine of Islam.[2]

Relatively few issues unite virtually all Muslims as has the issue of Jerusalem. More often the Islamic world is as disorganized and divided as any other region of such great cultural and political diversity. On a day-to-day basis, then, Saudis often couch their foreign policy in terms of general Islamic principles. The world view of Saudi leaders is certainly shaped by Islamic and Arab culture, so such themes come naturally. This does not mean, however, that relations with Islamic countries have been particularly tranquil. For example, Saudi Arabia has not found coexistence with its largest non-Arab Islamic neighbor, Iran, all that comfortable.

Iran

Under the shah's rule, Saudi-Iranian relations were characterized by distrust and some sharp disagreements as well as by cautious cooperation on regional security issues. In the shah's favor were his ties to the West, his opposition to Soviet influence, and the deterrent role his armed forces played against Iraq. He was also a successful reigning monarch at a time when such were in short supply. By the mid-1970s the shah tried to overcome his distaste for the unsophisticated Saudi leaders, just as they tried to hide their resentment of his arrogance and condescension. The shah and Crown Prince Fahd tried particularly hard to transcend their initial prejudices. The security services began to exchange information regularly on Soviet threats, terrorism, and South Yemen.

Whatever reassurance the Saudis may have felt from the shah's military prowess was offset by a fear that Iran's power could be turned against Saudi interests and that the Iranian arms buildup might draw the Soviet Union more deeply into Iraq. The Saudis were not particu-

2. Only the leaders of Iran and Libya did not attend.

larly pleased when Iran seized three small islands in the Persian Gulf that had been linked to the Arab sheikdoms along the coast, nor did the Saudis approve of Iran's quiet support of Israel, including the provision of most of Israel's oil. Saudi Arabia was not, however, in a position to stand up to Iranian power on either of these issues.

On questions of oil, Iran and Saudi Arabia were also often at odds. Iran under the shah sought to keep its oil production and prices high. The Saudis tended to be somewhat less hawkish on prices and were reluctant to cut their own production when Iran sought to expand its share of the market. Nonetheless, by the last year or two of the shah's reign the two countries were generally following parallel policies on oil, as well as on other matters.

The fall of the shah and the establishment of the militant Islamic Republic of Ayatollah Ruhollah Khomeini came as a particularly rude shock to the Saudi leadership. The change of regime in Tehran not only rekindled all the latent suspicions between Iranians and Saudis but also brought to power a man who had explicitly argued that Islam and hereditary kingship were incompatible, a threatening message, to say the least, in Riyadh.[3] In addition Khomeini claimed to speak in the name of all Muslims. The Shiite minority in Saudi Arabia, numbering some 200,000, showed some responsiveness to the message of their coreligionist in Iran, Ayatollah Khomeini. In November 1979 and again in February 1980 disturbances broke out among the Shiites in the town of Qatif in the Eastern Province. Other Saudis were receptive to Khomeini's attacks on corruption and Western values, although few of them sympathized with the violence and excesses of the first phase of the Iranian revolution.

By early 1980 the Iranian regime was regularly broadcasting propaganda in Arabic to Saudi Arabia in the name of the Islamic Revolution Organization in the Arabian Peninsula. One broadcast began with the Quranic verse: "Kings despoil a country when they enter it and make the noblest of its people its meanest."[4] The broadcast went on to say:

When the people have self-confidence and high morale, they will begin to demand their rights and oppose the authorities' policy and conduct. Indeed, it is this which the corrupt monarchies fear most. This is why they always

3. For Khomeini's views on kingship, see Nikki R. Keddie, "Iran: Change in Islam, Islam and Change," pp. 527–42. Also see Christine Moss Helms, *The Cohesion of Saudi Arabia*, pp. 109–10.

4. Surat al-Naml, verse 34. Radio Tehran, in Arabic, March 14, 1980, in British Broadcasting Corporation, "The Middle East," *Summary of World Broadcasts* (March 17, 1980), p. A1.

attempt to trample upon the people's dignity and morale, oppress them and subject them to ignominy in order to prevent the people from ever contemplating opposition and confrontations and to make them yield and subjugate themselves to the ruling authorities. This is the nature of monarchy, which is rejected by Islam. This is what our people in the Arabian Peninsula are suffering under Al Saud's rule.[5]

In the face of these attacks the Saudis adopted a reserved posture. They praised the new regime for its Islamic principles, remarking that Saudi Arabia was also founded on Islamic values. Saudi spokesmen rejected comparisons between the shah's rule and their own. Note was made of hostile statements from Iran, but those were dismissed as "unauthorized." Gradually the attacks subsided and some diplomatic contacts took place.

Publicly the Saudis spoke of their hope for stability in the area. Privately they mentioned their fear that the chaos in Iran could lead to greater leftist influence and eventually Soviet domination. Against these fears Iran's new posture of support for the Palestinians against Israel came as small comfort. When war broke out between Iraq and Iran in September 1980, Saudi Arabia discreetly sided with Iraq but also sought to stay out of the direct conflict.[6]

Pakistan

Although the Saudis were unable to do much directly to influence events in Iran after the shah's fall, they did react to the changing power balance in the region by mending their fences with Iraq as well as with two other Islamic countries, Pakistan and Turkey. Pakistan, in addition to being one of the largest Muslim countries, plays an important strategic role in the Persian Gulf–Indian Ocean region. Until recently Pakistan, along with Turkey, Iran, and Great Britain, was part of the Central Treaty Organization and received substantial economic and military aid

5. Ibid.
6. On September 25, 1980, Baghdad reported that King Khalid had called Iraqi President Saddam Hussein offering support in the "pan-Arab battle and conflict with the Persians, the enemies of the Arab nation." (Release, Iraqi News Agency, Baghdad, September 25, 1980, in Foreign Broadcast Information Service [hereinafter FBIS], *Daily Report: Middle East and Africa*, September 30, 1980, p. E10.) The same day the Saudis announced that the king had spoken to Saddam Hussein to "express his interest and his good fraternal feelings." Release, Saudi Press Agency, in ibid., September 26, 1980, p. C1.

from the United States. For the Saudis, Pakistan has been a buffer against Soviet expansion in their direction.

As U.S.-Pakistani relations began to deteriorate in the late 1970s, and as the Soviet threat loomed ever larger after the invasion of Afghanistan in December 1979, the Saudis moved to strengthen their own ties to Pakistan. The main Saudi contribution to Pakistan was the promise of financial aid, along with political support for the Islamic regime of President Zia ul-Haq. In return Pakistan could be counted on to follow the Saudi lead on Islamic issues, to adopt a firm anti-Israeli stance, and potentially most important, to provide Saudi Arabia with security assistance in the form of ground troops and technicians. In August 1980 it was widely reported that Saudi Arabia had discussed the possibility of providing as much as $1 billion in aid annually in exchange for large numbers of Pakistani ground forces and advisers, to be stationed primarily in the South Yemen border area. Although these reports were premature, by early 1981 about 1,200 Pakistani noncombat forces and advisers were in Saudi Arabia, with plans for an eventual total of as many as 10,000 military men, including some combat troops, half to be located at Tabuk and the rest in the south. This development seemed consistent with the Saudi policy of diversifying sources of support for the kingdom's security.

These arrangements were apparently discussed in a series of meetings between King Khalid and Crown Prince Fahd on the Saudi side and President Zia. The use of mercenary forces in the Middle East is hardly novel, and Pakistani forces have a reputation for professionalism and for being tough fighters.[7] They are of course Muslim—the Saudis reportedly insisted that no Pakistani troops should be Shiites—but they are not Arab and will presumably not be tempted to interfere in Saudi internal politics. In brief, in the case of Pakistan the Saudis may try to wed the Islamic and strategic dimensions of their foreign policies in ways that could have a direct bearing on Saudi security.[8]

7. Some concern has been raised about the reaction of the Saudi professional military, and of Defense Minister Sultan ibn Abd al-Aziz in particular, to the prospect of having large numbers of Pakistani soldiers protecting the kingdom. This political sensitivity no doubt accounts for Saudi unwillingness to confirm that these arrangements have been made. The question has been raised of who will have authority over the Pakistani troops—Fahd, Sultan, or perhaps Abdullah ibn Abd al-Aziz.

8. At the time of Crown Prince Fahd's visit to Pakistan in December 1980 a Saudi newspaper noted in an unusual aside that Pakistan is "working to develop the first Islamic and Arab nuclear bomb." *Ar-Riyadh*, December 8, 1980.

Afghanistan

Because of geographical proximity, if for no other reason, the Saudis have taken an interest in developments in Afghanistan. Like many others, they saw Afghanistan as a buffer state that helped to prevent Soviet expansion toward the gulf. In April 1978, when a Marxist regime seized power in Kabul, the Saudis were alarmed and urged Washington to react. To say the least, U.S. passivity perplexed them.

When the Soviets sent 80,000 troops into Afghanistan in December 1979 and installed a puppet regime under Babrak Karmal, the Saudi attitude was one of "we told you so." The immediate danger appeared to be that pressures could be exerted on Pakistan and Iran to be more accommodating to Soviet interests. To prevent this, and to raise the costs of the Soviet occupation, the Saudis played a significant role at the Islamic conference in Pakistan in January 1980 in mobilizing Muslim sentiment against the Soviet invasion in Afghanistan. In accordance with the recommendations of the Islamic conference, Saudi Arabia finally broke diplomatic relations with the "illegal" government in Kabul in April 1981.

In addition to these diplomatic efforts, the Saudis were widely reported to be providing some financial aid to the Afghan resistance movements. If so, this would again represent a case where Saudi strategic concerns and Islamic sensibilities have overlapped. The combination of these two motivations is enough to ensure Saudi involvement.

Presumably in the hope of adding incentives for the Soviets to remove their troops from Afghanistan, the Saudis have hinted that they would consider normalizing relations with Moscow after Soviet withdrawal.[9] The Saudis are realistic enough, however, not to harbor illusions that Afghanistan will soon be free, but they nonetheless are unwilling to accept the new status quo.

In Islamic political circles a common theme is that both superpowers threaten Islamic interests, the United States for its support of Israel and

9. Foreign Minister Saud al-Faisal has said: "So, much as we appreciate the Soviets' backing of the Arab cause and the Palestinian issue, we are extremely anxious and disturbed by the occupation of Afghanistan. Once the Soviet Union achieves this consistency in its policy [that is, withdraws from Afghanistan] in the region, I think that any inhibition that exists in the Third World, of which my country is a member, and in the Islamic world about evolving and developing good relations with the Soviet Union will be removed." *Monday Morning* (Beirut), July 21–27, 1980.

the USSR for its occupation of Afghanistan. Increasingly the Saudis have begun to speak of both big powers in quite similar terms. For example, Foreign Minister Saud al-Faisal said on the eve of Secretary of State Alexander M. Haig, Jr.'s first visit to Saudi Arabia: "The great powers do not have friends. We deceive ourselves if we believe that our relations with the great powers are based on friendship. The great powers have their particular interests and strategies, and their relations with other countries are based on these interests and strategies."[10] Since the Soviet invasion of Afghanistan, this has become typical of the rhetoric of Muslim political leaders in general and of Saudis in particular.

Turkey

Turkey is more remote from Saudi thinking than Pakistan, and the personal ties at the level of the top leadership are much less intimate. As much as the Saudis may be pleased to see signs of Islamic assertiveness in the secular republic of Turkey, their main concern is strategic, not ideological. Turkey is an important member of the North Atlantic Treaty Organization, a participant in Islamic conferences, and has shown increasing deference to Arab sensibilities on the Palestinian question in recent years.

In 1980, as the Turkish economy came under great strain, the Saudis were prepared to respond generously with economic assistance. This suggests that the Saudis appreciate Turkey's strategic location. If the Soviet Union, for example, were to threaten the Persian Gulf, one of the closest and most reliable staging areas for any American response might be Turkey. Whether or not the Saudis explicitly work this into their foreign policy thinking, their support for the Turkish economy in 1980 helped anchor Turkey to the Western alliance at a particularly crucial moment. In return, Turkey has downgraded the importance of its relations with Israel. Nonetheless, the Saudis generally view Turkey as beyond the reach of their influence.

Somalia and the Horn of Africa

One other Muslim country that has been of deep concern to Saudi Arabia is Somalia. Formally a member of the Arab League, impoverished

10. *Al-Majallah* (London), April 4–10, 1981.

Somalia has little to recommend it to outsiders other than its strategic location. That, plus its Islamic and somewhat tenuous Arab credentials, have led the Saudis to attach great significance to Somalia.

For Saudi Arabia the Horn of Africa is an area of vital interest. Closure of the Bab al-Mandab Strait at the southern entrance to the Red Sea could seriously jeopardize Saudi access to foreign goods vital to development and prosperity and would disrupt oil exports that go through the Suez Canal in small tankers. A major Soviet presence in either Somalia or Ethiopia is therefore viewed by Saudis as directly threatening to their own security.

Up until the mid-1970s one might have expected Saudi Arabia to see Ethiopia as a natural ally. After all, the Ethiopia of Haile Selassie was pro-Western, conservative, and monarchical as well as one of the largest countries on the African continent. By contrast, neighboring Somalia was poor, small, and deeply beholden to the Soviet Union. By 1972 the USSR had managed to gain military access to air and naval facilities at Berbera.

Despite the logic of close Saudi-Ethiopian relations, the chemistry was just not right. The Christian emperor and the Wahhabi king were suspicious of one another. The Saudis resented the second-class treatment of the Muslims in Eritrea, a province they believed should become an independent or autonomous state. In the Somali-Ethiopia conflict over the Ogaden plateau region, the Saudis also found it difficult not to side with their Somali coreligionists. Consequently, with few exceptions, the Saudi-Ethiopian connection was reserved at best and often marked with considerable hostility. Israel's "special relationship" with Ethiopia reinforced Saudi distrust of Christian Ethiopia.

If Haile Selassie raised doubts in Saudi minds, his successor, Mengistu Haile Mariam, was infinitely worse. An avowed Marxist, he broke with the United States in April 1977, invited the Soviet Union into Ethiopia, and welcomed some 15,000 Cuban troops to help repel the Somali invasion of the Ogaden and to suppress the rebellion in Eritrea. For the first time the Soviet Union had a strong position in the most powerful state in the Horn of Africa, and it was only a matter of time before Ethiopia and South Yemen began to forge political and military links.

As the Saudis witnessed Soviet power expanding into the Horn and across the Red Sea to Aden, they were particularly anxious to ensure that Somalia would split with Moscow and turn to the West for arms and diplomatic support. In addition the Saudis stepped up their assistance to the non-Marxist Eritrean liberation groups, reportedly coordinating some of these efforts with Sudan. It is no exaggeration to say that the Horn of Africa ranked alongside the Arab-Israeli conflict as the Saudis' main preoccupation in 1977–78.

Despite Somali recklessness in invading the Ogaden in summer 1977, the Saudis argued strongly with Washington that the Muhammad Siad Barre regime in Mogadishu was deserving of generous support. When the United States refused to supply arms to Somalia until Somali troops had withdrawn from the Ogaden, the Saudis were baffled. They had tried to take some credit for weaning Siad Barre away from Moscow, just as they had when Sadat expelled the Soviet advisers in July 1972. But in this case the United States seemed slow to respond and unappreciative of the opening provided them in Somalia. In later years this reluctance of the Carter administration to aid Somalia was frequently mentioned by the Saudis in their list of grievances.

In the case of Somalia strategic considerations once again seemed to outweigh Islamic sensitivities in shaping policy. But the two were nonetheless mutually reinforcing. When only the Islamic dimension is present, the Saudis tend to adopt a much more relaxed attitude. For example, other large Muslim countries, such as Bangladesh and Indonesia, have benefited from some Saudi economic assistance, and there is little reason to doubt that Islamic considerations do play a part in Saudi aid decisions, especially in Africa. Nonetheless, for all the rhetoric in which Saudi foreign policy is expressed, it seems clear that perceived interests and strategic calculus generally count for much more than religious affinity in guiding Saudi decisions.

Conclusion

The Saudis appear to have come to realize that Islamic solidarity may prove to be as fragile a notion as Arab unity. Therefore, faced with specific choices the Saudis seem to weigh their security concerns first, their ideological preferences second. And while the Saudis take an active interest in both Arab and Islamic issues, it is still the Arab region that is of much more direct preoccupation than the Islamic world as a whole. For example, the Saudi leadership talks of the Arab League's Mutual Defense Agreement as the proper context for considering gulf security, not the broader Islamic conference. Nonetheless, at a time of heightened Islamic consciousness, the Saudis will go to considerable lengths to be in a position of leadership on issues of special importance to Muslims such as Jerusalem, the Palestinians, and assistance to the Afghan guerrillas. This is particularly true when Iran is trying to preempt the position of the leading spokesman for Islamic causes.

Chapter Four

The Superpower Rivalry

SINCE WORLD WAR II much of international political life has been colored by the rivalry between the two nuclear superpowers, the United States and the USSR. Saudi Arabia, although initially outside the arena of direct confrontation between Washington and Moscow, has increasingly felt encircled by the Soviet Union while at the same time often being at odds with the United States. This is a far cry from the idealized image of a special U.S.-Saudi relationship rooted in common interests and buttressed by shared values.

The United States

In the minds of many Saudis and some Americans the foundations of the U.S.-Saudi connection were laid in 1945 when President Franklin D. Roosevelt met with King Abd al-Aziz on the American cruiser *U.S.S. Quincy* anchored in the Great Bitter Lake north of the city of Suez. This was one of the rare trips outside the Arabian Peninsula for the Saudi king, the others being a visit to Basra in Iraq in 1916 and a meeting on a British destroyer off Bahrain in 1930.

The ailing American president's meeting with King Abd al-Aziz symbolized the growing involvement of the United States in Saudi affairs. Oil and Palestine were primary reasons. The war convinced American officials that oil was of vital strategic significance. Secretary of Defense James V. Forrestal became a leading proponent of this view, warning prophetically that "within the next twenty-five years the United States is going to be faced with very sharply declining oil reserves and because oil and all its byproducts are the foundations of the ability to fight a modern war, I consider this to be one of the most im-

47

portant problems of the government. I don't care which American company or companies develop the Arabian reserves, but I think most emphatically that it should be *American*."[1]

In addition to their interest in Saudi oil, American officials, and especially the president, hoped to gain Abd al-Aziz's support for a peaceful settlement of the Palestine problem. But Abd al-Aziz proved to be adamant in his opposition to a Jewish state in Palestine, and it was Roosevelt who implied that his own views were flexible.[2] In a commitment that was to be repeated often in the next three years, the president assured Abd al-Aziz that he would not help the Jews against the Arabs and would not take any steps that were hostile to the Arab people.[3] In addition he promised consultations on the Palestine problem before making any final decisions.

Apart from oil and Palestine, the U.S.-Saudi "special relationship" from the beginning included financial aid and strategic interests. As early as February 1943 the United States had declared Saudi Arabia to be eligible for lend-lease assistance. At the time, this was seen as a necessary step for bolstering the weak Saudi economy as well as a means of securing the American stake in Saudi oil. Before long the Arabian American Oil Company (ARAMCO) was producing substantial amounts of oil and Saudi income was on the rise. In late 1950 the principle of splitting pre-tax profits on a fifty-fifty basis was established, and this greatly increased Saudi income. In 1950 the Saudis received $56 million in oil revenues from ARAMCO; in 1951 that figure reached $110 million. Despite the loss to the U.S. Treasury resulting from the ruling that royalties paid to Saudi Arabia could be credited as income taxes, the U.S. government approved this means of subsidizing the Saudi economy.[4]

During this same period Saudi Arabia came directly under the U.S. security umbrella. While never formally allied with the United States,

1. Forrestal to Secretary of State James F. Byrnes, August 1, 1945, quoted in Aaron David Miller, *Search for Security*, p. 145.

2. At an earlier date Abd al-Aziz had preferred not to become involved at all in the Palestinian problem. (See H. StJ. B. Philby, *Arabian Jubilee*, pp. 204–20.) But by the time he met Roosevelt the Arab world was much more focused on the issue, and thus Abd al-Aziz took a more forceful stand.

3. Miller, *Search for Security*, p. 130.

4. Leonard Mosley, *Power Play*, p. 195. Also see the testimony of Ambassador George C. McGhee in *Multinational Corporations and United States Foreign Policy*, Hearings before the Subcommittee on Multinational Corporations of the Senate Committee on Foreign Relations, 93 Cong. 2 sess. (Government Printing Office, 1974), pp. 86–99.

Saudi Arabia did allow the U.S. Air Force to exercise temporary "unrestricted air traffic rights" at the Dhahran airfield beginning in 1946.

If the U.S.-Saudi relationship could have been frozen in the early 1950s, it would have come close to the ideal of the special relationship. King Abd al-Aziz had personally lent his prestige to the American connection. American oil companies were the exclusive concessionaires for the richest oil fields in the world. The Saudis were fervently anticommunist, to the point of allowing their territory to be used as part of the U.S. global network of strategic bases. In return the Saudis gained unprecedented wealth and a powerful protector.

From the Saudi perspective the United States became a less predictable and reliable friend during the late 1950s. Even earlier there had been differences over Israel. Inter-Arab pressures on Saudi Arabia to cease cooperating with an ally of Israel had contributed to Saudi hesitation to renew the lease of the airfield at Dhahran to the U.S. Air Force in 1956, although eventually a five-year extension was agreed upon. Apart from Israel, on other matters of concern to the Saudis the United States was often supportive. For example, in the Buraymi Oasis dispute the United States urged a diplomatic solution, a position the British viewed as unfriendly to their interests.[5]

From 1958 to 1963 the United States appeared to be courting President Nasser of Egypt, and this created new strains in U.S.-Saudi relations. American recognition of the Republican regime in North Yemen in 1962 came as something of a shock to the Saudis, for it appeared to align Washington with Nasser on an issue of great consequence for Riyadh.[6] If nothing else, the Yemen episode demonstrated that the U.S.-Saudi relationship was vulnerable to inter-Arab political developments. And the suspicion must have taken root that the United States attached more importance to the largest and strongest Arab country, Egypt, than it did to oil-rich Saudi Arabia.

Despite these tensions growing out of the early phase of the Yemen civil war, King Faisal was able to restore relations with Washington to a high level of confidence after 1964. This trend was helped by President Kennedy's willingness to send fighter aircraft to Saudi Arabia after Egyptian attacks on Saudi territory. Faisal was respected by Americans

5. The Buraymi Oasis issue came up in President Dwight D. Eisenhower's meeting with King Saud ibn Abd al-Aziz in January 1957. See Dwight D. Eisenhower, *Waging Peace, 1956–1961*, pp. 118, 195–96.

6. See John S. Badeau, *The American Approach to the Arab World*.

as a serious and competent leader, unlike his brother and predecessor, Saud, who was viewed as extravagant, corrupt, and unpredictable. Faisal's commitment to cautious reforms and modernization was wel-come in Washington. His growing stature in Arab world affairs, espe-cially after Nasser's defeat in 1967, also helped to foster a new atmo-sphere in the Arab world that might be helpful to the United States.

Only on the issue of Israel did the Saudis seem adamantly opposed to U.S. policies. But even there Faisal was in the habit of warning his more assertive Arab brethren that oil and politics should not be mixed. The brief experiences in both 1956 and 1967 of embargoing oil shipments to Israel's allies had not been successful in any case, since non-Arab oil was readily available to make up any shortfall.

Oil as a Resource

The international energy situation began to change suddenly in the early 1970s, just as the Arab-Israeli conflict was building toward another explosion. The combination of these two developments had a dramatic effect on the Saudi relationship with the United States.

By 1970 the energy market was unusually tight. Oil consumption had been growing rapidly, American petroleum production had peaked, spot shortages had set the stage for demands for price increases that were particularly hard for small independent producers to resist, and pressures by producing countries to assume control of oil company operations in their countries were succeeding. Already a sellers' market was develop-ing, and OPEC was beginning to flex its muscles. Between 1970 and mid-1973 the selling price of Saudi crude oil doubled from $1.39 to $2.55 a barrel. Total Saudi oil income in 1972 was about $2.7 billion. (See ap-pendix A, table A-1.)

Against this background King Faisal began in early 1973 to warn publicly that an outbreak of war between Israel and her Arab neighbors was inevitable unless the United States took immediate action to pressure Israel to relinquish captured Arab lands. More ominously Faisal stated that the "oil weapon" might be used in the event of hostilities. For Saudi Arabia, these were unusually strong positions, and the fact that the warnings were issued in public added to their novelty. But to Faisal's chagrin, Washington paid little heed.

When war did erupt on October 6, 1973, Saudi Arabia was more involved than ever before. A small number of troops were sent to the

Syrian front as a symbol of Saudi commitment. Substantial sums of money were made available to Egypt and Syria. And after some delay, the oil weapon was unsheathed. On October 17, shortly after the United States had begun to airlift arms to Israel and had announced a $2.2 billion aid package to Israel, the Saudis announced that oil shipments to the United States would be halted and that total Saudi production would be reduced until Arab rights had been restored. For virtually the first time, the United States and Saudi Arabia found themselves on opposite sides of a major international crisis.

Somewhat against his better judgment, Secretary of State Henry Kissinger, who saw the Saudis as weak and vulnerable to pressure, began to deal with the Saudis as a major player in the Arab-Israeli conflict. He visited Riyadh on virtually all of his Middle East trips. He listened to lengthy lectures on Zionism and communism.[7] Eventually he succeeded in convincing King Faisal to ease the embargo and to restore Saudi production to prewar levels.

By spring 1974 the immediate sense of crisis surrounding oil had subsided; the United States was deeply engaged in seeking a peaceful settlement of the Arab-Israeli conflict; and U.S.-Saudi relations were in good repair. But the posted price of oil had skyrocketed to over $11 a barrel; the average selling price for Arabian light crude exceeded $8 a barrel. This brought an income to Saudi Arabia in 1974 of $22.6 billion and inevitably led other Arab countries to turn to Riyadh for aid. It also meant that Saudi Arabia could begin to spend untold amounts on domestic programs, a development with potentially far-reaching consequences.

Security and Arms Sales

As Saudi financial resources began to grow rapidly, a basic decision was made in Riyadh to modernize and strengthen the Saudi armed forces. At Saudi request, the United States carried out a series of studies of the army, air force, navy, and national guard. Air force modernization began in 1971 with the decision to acquire F-5E aircraft. The navy and national guard were soon to follow suit in the next two years.

Up until 1970 the Saudis had not made serious efforts to develop their military might. It was widely believed that the royal family was reluctant to place much power in the hands of military men. After all, the recent history of the area amply provided examples of monarchies being

7. Edward R. F. Sheehan, *The Arabs, the Israelis, and Kissinger*, pp. 62–77.

removed by reform-minded officers. In order to neutralize the risk of a military coup, the Saudi National Guard, which was recruited from loyal tribes, had traditionally occupied strategic locations near Riyadh, Jidda, and Dhahran, while the army and air force were kept away from the urban centers, often without much ammunition or mobility. This helped prevent political meddling by the military, but it did little to augment Saudi military capabilities.

These practices began to change in the 1970s with large-scale programs of modernization and training. Most of the equipment and services purchased by the Saudis came from the United States. In 1970 only $45 million was spent on U.S. arms and services. By 1973 the figure was $1.15 billion. Following the increase in oil prices in late 1973 the figure for arms purchases for 1974 hit $2 billion and continued to rise in subsequent years. By 1979 over $6 billion in sales agreements were signed with the United States for construction, training, and arms. (Only about one-fifth of these totals went for equipment and one-fifth for training; the rest went for construction.) A simple pattern emerged of military spending growing in close relationship to oil revenues. (See appendix B for more details on the Saudi military program.)

In addition to arms expenditures on an unprecedented scale, the Saudis were sending large numbers of officers for training in the United States. During the decade of the 1970s over 5,000 Saudis from the military and national guard received American training.[8] Since 1951 the United States Military Training Mission (USMTM) has also worked discreetly and effectively with the Saudi armed forces. Within Saudi Arabia the American military presence was comparatively small—a few hundred officers assigned to the USMTM, with another 1,000 or so civilians in defense-related activities by the mid-1970s. But the U.S. Army Corps of Engineers, active in the kingdom since 1965, was rapidly reshaping the Saudi landscape. Projects worth well over $20 billion were planned or under way by 1980. A military encampment near the Iraqi border, named King Khalid Military City, has been estimated to cost $8 billion and will house a population of 70,000 by the late 1980s. Three armored brigades will eventually be stationed there.[9]

8. In 1981 about 2,000 Saudis were receiving military training in the United States. For training and military data, see U.S. Congress, *Saudi Arabia and the United States*, pp. 44, 48–51, 62.

9. Kingdom of Saudi Arabia, Ministry of Defense and Aviation, Directorate of Military Works, "King Khalid Military City" (n.d.).

In brief, during the 1970s the U.S.-Saudi security relationship mushroomed. Expanding oil reserves led to huge increases in purchases of arms. The physical infrastructure of a modern military establishment was acquired, largely from the United States, and thousands of Saudis received professional military training.

Less visible but equally important was the contribution of U.S. military might to the global and regional balance of power. To some extent this provided a security umbrella for the Saudis, although it tended to be both taken for granted and discounted as lacking credibility. In the sensitive area of intelligence cooperation and military advice the United States also sought to contribute to Saudi security.

Despite the magnitude of these efforts, the Saudis entered the 1980s without feeling confident of their own ability to defend themselves, doubting American capabilities and determination, and worrying about circumstances in which American armed forces might be used against, rather than in support of, their interests. Fortunately for American credibility, the Iran-Iraq war of fall 1980, somewhat like the spring 1979 Yemen border crisis, provided an opportunity for the United States to respond to Saudi requests to strengthen their air defense capabilities against external threats by sending AWACS aircraft to help protect Saudi Arabia.[10] This was an important step in reassuring the Saudi leadership that a security relationship with the United States could provide tangible benefits, but it also whetted the Saudi appetite for AWACS aircraft of their own. And if the Yemen experience was any precedent, the benefits to be gained by assisting the Saudis in these crises might well be short-lived.

Economic Ties

If the Saudis have shown some uneasiness about their military ties to the United States, the economic relationship is generally recognized as more clearly beneficial to them. American oil companies have been responsible for the discovery, development, and management of Saudi oil.

10. Four AWACS aircraft were flown to Riyadh in late September 1980 on short notice and remained there to provide continuous radar coverage of the gulf area. These aircraft, combined with other capabilities, give the Saudis between ten and fifteen minutes of warning time in the event of an air attack against their oil fields. Prince Sultan described the AWACS as important to Saudi Arabia "and to others in the Gulf." He minimized the U.S. presence as merely technical, denying that Saudi Arabia was in any way tied by "pacts" to the United States. See his interview with Ahmad al-Jarallah in *As-Siyasah* (Kuwait), December 18, 1980.

Those same companies have pumped the oil, transported it, and ultimately marketed most of it. For Saudi Arabia, this has meant an enormous inflow of wealth.

Oil revenues have not, however, been an unmixed blessing for Saudi Arabia. They have not ensured either development or wealth. If misused, they could upset the social and economic equilibrium of the country.[11] Vast amounts of money are bound to foster corruption and invite charlatans from all over the world who are anxious to profit from Saudi riches. Money by itself would also lose value unless invested wisely, and it could be lost altogether through wasteful development programs.

Having relied on the United States to produce the oil reserves, the Saudis have also turned to the same source for advice and assistance on how best to invest their assets, spend their money, and develop their country. Private American consultants have worked with the Saudis on their successive five-year plans, including the 1981–85 plan to spend nearly $250 billion. American financial experts have advised the Saudis on how to invest their surplus revenues; by 1980 they were earning nearly $7 billion on overseas investments of $80 billion. When added to petroleum-related income, this brought total Saudi foreign exchange earnings in 1980 to over $100 billion. Only the United States, West Germany, and Japan had larger export earnings.[12]

Not surprisingly, U.S.-Saudi trade expanded in parallel with these foreign exchange earnings. In 1979 American companies signed nonmilitary contracts in Saudi Arabia worth nearly $6 billion, or about 35 percent of the total.[13] Actual exports from the United States to Saudi Arabia in 1980 amounted to $5.8 billion; U.S. purchases from Saudi Arabia were more than double that amount. (See appendix A, table A-2.) While the overall level of Saudi purchases from the United States is likely to remain high, American businessmen worry that they are losing their competitive advantage to European and Japanese firms that have stronger backing from their own governments, face few restrictive regulations, and can usually underbid U.S. competitors. U.S. tax laws have made it especially expensive to hire Americans to work abroad, and many of the projects supervised by the U.S. Army Corps of Engineers go to Korean construction companies.

11. See the speech by Minister of Petroleum Ahmad Zaki Yamani to the University of Petroleum and Minerals, Dammam, January 31, 1981, in appendix C.

12. Tom McHale, "Flow of Funds," *Saudi Arabia: A MEED Special Report*, July 1980, p. 88.

13. Ibid., pp. 94–95.

Even if the American share of the Saudi market does slip, the Saudis will nonetheless continue to value the products, the services, and the advice available in the United States. To some extent this will be reinforced by the growing familiarity of young Saudi technocrats with American practices. In recent years thousands of Saudi students have been sent each year to the United States for their university education.[14] Most will probably return to well-paid, if not always very challenging, jobs in government ministries. However ambivalent they may feel about their American experience, they will nonetheless be familiar with the language and methods needed to deal with their American counterparts.

Political Problems: Bases and American Credibility

The security and economic dimensions of the U.S.-Saudi relationship appear to most Americans to benefit the Saudi regime. When differences with Washington do come to the fore, they generally involve political matters. As the Saudis find themselves drawn into an increasingly complex range of issues, the common interests of Riyadh and Washington in resisting Soviet influence in the Middle East and in promoting stability are proving to be an insufficient guarantee of congruent policies. Instead, the Saudis often find themselves somewhat at odds with their closest ally.

Saudi ambivalence toward the United States is nowhere more apparent than on the issue of a U.S. military presence in the Middle East–Persian Gulf area. The official position of the Saudis is that both superpowers should stay out of the region militarily and that no foreign bases should be allowed in the area. Since 1962 the Saudis have been unwilling to allow the U.S. Air Force to make use of airfields in their country. Nonetheless, the Saudis do accept the desirability of an offshore U.S. naval presence in the vicinity of the Persian Gulf, a modest U.S. military presence in such places as Oman and Somalia, a significant American role in the development of the Saudi armed forces, and periodic displays of U.S. military power in Saudi Arabia itself when an immediate threat is clearly perceived. For example, the Saudis have never objected to the small U.S. naval contingent in Bahrain.

14. As of 1980 about 15,000 Saudi students were studying in American universities, most of them on government scholarships. (Only 360 Saudi students were in the United States in 1964.) According to one source, nearly 8,000 Saudi students will return to the kingdom from the United States in 1981. See "Saudis Spend Impressively on Their Students," *Mideast Business Exchange*, June 1980, p. 49.

When confronted with the prospect of substantial U.S. military forces in their own country, however, Saudi leaders are opposed, at least in circumstances short of direct threats to Saudi Arabia. Their reasoning reflects their fears and uncertainties. As some describe it, an American military presence in their country is likely to be either too large or too small to do much good. To deter a direct Soviet invasion of the gulf, one or two American divisions in Saudi Arabia are no match for the forces Moscow can bring to bear in a full-scale war. For smaller contingencies, it would be much more than is needed on a permanent basis. In addition it could serve as a rallying point for forces opposed to the regime, particularly if U.S. policy were seen as hostile to Arab and Islamic interests.

Further, the presence of American troops would expose the Saudis to the charge of cooperating with Israel's ally; it would lead to suspicions that the purpose of the U.S. forces is to seize the oil fields, not to protect Saudi Arabia; and it might lead other countries in the area—Iraq, South Yemen, or Iran—to tighten their ties to the Kremlin. Thus in emergencies the Saudis have preferred to ask for temporary help in the form of AWACS aircraft or a squadron of F-15s—and to purchase such equipment for their own use—rather than pay a significant political price for a permanent U.S. military presence on their territory.

In the final analysis the Saudis seem to believe that the only effective deterrent to direct Soviet military intervention is the global balance of power. If the prospect of nuclear war does not deter the Soviet Union, a few American divisions in the gulf are unlikely to do so. Lesser contingencies can best be dealt with on an ad hoc basis and by building Saudi military power. This somewhat simplistic analysis leads the Saudis to conclude that a U.S. military presence should be small, offshore, unobtrusive, and temporary. This, they maintain, would reduce the risk that such a force would be destabilizing.

On balance, the Rapid Development Force fits the Saudi notion of a possibly useful but not very dramatic form of American military strength. Even so, the Saudis ask themselves whether in fact it would be helpful. Who would it defend? In what circumstances? How quickly? Some skeptics profess to believe it is only capable of seizing control of Saudi oil, not of meeting the Soviet challenge.[15] A more recent theory

15. For articles contributing to such fears see, for example, Robert W. Tucker, "Oil: The Issue of American Intervention," pp. 21–31; Tucker, "Further Reflections on Oil and Force," pp. 45–46; and Miles Ignotus, "Seizing Arab Oil," pp. 45–62.

is that Washington is only trying to strengthen its position in the gulf as a prelude to negotiating some form of condominium with Moscow.

Part of the Saudi attitude toward a U.S. military presence is grounded in the suspicion that the United States is not particularly adept at translating its armed strength into diplomatic leverage. Vietnam was one reminder that American power was limited. More recently the unwillingness of the United States, as seen by the Saudis, to challenge Soviet assertiveness in the Horn of Africa in 1977–78 and in Afghanistan in 1978 and 1980 created an unfavorable impression of American determination. The way the United States treated Pakistan in 1978–79, especially the withholding of arms and economic aid, and Washington's inability to help the shah of Iran in those same years, did not encourage the Saudis to seek U.S. patronage.

In none of these cases did the Saudis have ready-made solutions to recommend to the United States. They did, however, feel threatened by what they saw as unsteady American policies. The United States was unable to convince the Saudis of the rationale for restraint in the Horn of Africa or for its hesitation in helping the shah. Part of the problem, it would seem, was substantive, and part was a serious inability to maintain a strategic dialogue between Washington and Riyadh.

In the period since 1975 the Saudis have only occasionally been pleased with U.S. policies. In 1977–78 the Saudis were initially impressed by President Carter's active pursuit of an Arab-Israeli peace settlement and his willingness to fight hard for congressional approval of the sale of 60 F-15s to Saudi Arabia. In addition the quick U.S. response to Riyadh's requests during the February–March 1979 conflict between North and South Yemen was appreciated, as was the similar action in sending four AWACS aircraft to Saudi Arabia during the fall 1980 Iran-Iraq war.

In nearly every case, however, the Saudis subsequently felt disappointed, either because of lack of follow-through or the emergence of new problems to trouble their relationship with the United States. Little came of Carter's ambitious search for a comprehensive Middle East peace; the F-15s were only approved after serious restrictions on equipment had been imposed; American interest in Yemeni affairs was short-lived; and the AWACS planes became an issue of great political controversy, with Israel mounting an intense campaign against their sale to Riyadh.

Despite reservations and ambivalence born of these experiences, the

Saudis are not prepared to see their security link to Washington severed, particularly at a time when Iran and Iraq may be locked into a protracted conflict. Thus the hope remains among Saudi leaders that a stable and reliable security relationship with Washington can be forged.

U.S. Attitudes toward Israel and the Palestinians

Few issues have caused more disagreements and mutual accusations of bad faith between the United States and Saudi Arabia than the Arab-Israeli dispute. To many Saudis, the unresolved Palestinian question is a source of instability in the Arab world; Israel is seen as a tacit ally of the Soviet Union in its attempts to weaken, subvert, and radicalize the Arab world; and Israel is feared as a military power with the capability of striking at the interests of Saudi Arabia.

The fact that the United States is deeply committed to Israel and provides billions of dollars in economic and military support is something of a mystery to Saudis. They tend to explain away this apparent anomaly by attributing it to Zionist influence in the United States or to some unspoken strategic plan whereby Israel keeps the Arab world weak and divided and thereby helps the United States pursue its oil interests with impunity. Even those Saudis who have a more sophisticated understanding of the U.S.-Israeli relationship find it perplexing that the United States is so heavily one-sided in its approach to the Palestinian problem.

In their most hopeful moments Saudis look to Washington as the only power that can influence Israel. By now the kingdom's leaders seem to be reconciled to Israel's existence, but they are nonetheless chagrined to see Israel in control of 1 million Palestinians in the West Bank and Gaza and of the Muslim holy places in Jerusalem. Thus the Saudis have urged successive American administrations to force Israel to withdraw to the 1967 lines and to return East Jerusalem to Arab control. In addition they have subscribed to the Arab consensus that calls for self-determination for the Palestinians.[16]

16. During his meeting with President Carter in May 1977 Crown Prince Fahd argued in favor of establishing an independent Palestinian state. The Saudi view, he explained, was that the Palestinians should be forced to take responsibility for the decisions affecting their future. He acknowledged that a Palestinian state would have strong incentives to join with Jordan but thought that this should result from the Palestinians' own choice, not be imposed on them. Inexplicably and inaccurately,

A peace settlement involving Israeli withdrawal and a resolution of the political dimension of the Palestinian problem would be seen by the Saudis as a significant step toward bringing stability to the Middle East. The Palestinians, they believe, would cease to be a disruptive force in the area if they had a stake in peace; the Soviets would find fewer opportunities to expand their influence; pressures would decrease to use the oil weapon against the United States; and "moderate" Arab states would be less reluctant than at present to cooperate with Washington on security matters.

It is easy to raise doubts about the precise benefits that might flow from an Arab-Israeli settlement, but it is nonetheless an article of faith for Saudis that their particular problems would be greatly eased if the Palestinian problem were solved. In 1977 the Saudis became enthusiastic supporters of President Carter's search for a comprehensive Arab-Israeli peace agreement. With the means at their disposal, they tried to maneuver the PLO toward a more flexible posture, to keep Sadat and Assad on speaking terms, and to prevent oil price increases. Even the U.S.-Soviet communiqué of October 1, 1977, calling for the resumption of Middle East negotiations in Geneva, was welcomed by the Saudis, despite the symbolic importance of associating Moscow with the diplomatic efforts. Whatever their qualms, they saw the United States pressing hard to define the outlines of a balanced agreement, and they were hopeful of seeing early results.

Instead of a comprehensive peace, the Saudis were surprised by President Sadat's unilateral decision to go to Jerusalem in November 1977. This raised the prospect of a separate Egyptian-Israeli accord, something the Saudis feared. As events unfolded, the United States moved away from its commitment to a broad-based peace, including a homeland for the Palestinians, and toward an Egyptian-Israeli treaty. The Camp David

---

President Carter in 1979 publicly stated that in his talks with Arab leaders, no one had called for the creation of an independent Palestinian state.

More recently Fahd publicly outlined eight principles for an Arab-Israeli peace settlement: full Israeli withdrawal from all Arab territories occupied since 1967, including Arab Jerusalem; the dismantling of all Israeli settlements in occupied territories; freedom of worship for all religions; the right of Palestinians to return to their homes or receive compensation; the placing of the West Bank and Gaza under UN supervision for a transitional period of several months; the creation of an independent Palestinian state with Jerusalem as its capital; the right of all states in the region to live in peace; and a UN guarantee to implement these principles. British Broadcasting Corporation, "The Middle East," *Summary of World Broadcasts* (August 10, 1981), pp. A-1 through A3.

agreements of September 1978 gave the Saudis little reason for encouragement. Despite some vague words about a comprehensive peace, the thrust of Camp David, as it evolved, was toward a separate Egyptian-Israeli agreement without any "linkage" to the Palestinian issue. From the Saudi perspective the peace treaty signed by Sadat and Menachem Begin in March 1979 seemed to confirm their worst suspicions, as did the lack of any noticeable progress in negotiations to settle the future of the West Bank and Gaza.

What worries the Saudis most about the lack of progress toward resolving the remainder of the Arab-Israeli conflict is the possibility that the Soviets and other radical forces will be able to exploit the situation. The threat, as they see it, could come in several forms. One danger is that the Syrians and the Palestinians, left only with a military option for recovering Israeli-occupied territories, will become increasingly dependent on the Soviet Union. In extreme circumstances the Syrians might feel compelled to invite Soviet combat forces, especially air defense units, into their country, much as Egypt did in early 1970. The Syrian-Soviet Treaty of Friendship and Cooperation of October 1980 brought these dangers closer to reality.

Barring direct Soviet intervention in the Arab-Israeli dispute, the Saudis continue to worry about the radicalizing effect in the Arab world of a stalemate over Palestine. The "left" tries to argue that the Arab inability to liberate Palestine is the fault of corrupt regimes beholden to imperialist powers. For example, the Popular Front for the Liberation of Palestine sees the first step toward recovering Palestine as the overthrow of virtually all present regimes in the Arab world, especially the conservative monarchies. The "right" can also use the Palestinian issue to its advantage, pointing to Jerusalem and the duty of Islamic states to devote their resources to its recovery. Extremists of left or right, the Saudis fear, will not hesitate to use subversion and terror to advance their goals. And the Saudis know that they and their oil are attractive targets.

Because of the special relationship between the United States and Saudi Arabia, Palestinians and Syrians can be expected to pressure Riyadh to use its influence in Washington to force concessions from the Israelis. The Saudis know that this is not so easily done, but they cannot show indifference to the Palestinian cause without being accused of collaborating with Israel's allies. The Saudis are reluctant to use the oil weapon, but cannot totally divorce decisions on oil from politics. In their view the United States should help resolve this dilemma by using its undeniable influence with Israel on behalf of a comprehensive peace agreement. If the United States cannot do this, then it will be judged weak; if it refuses, then it will be seen as insensitive to the concerns of its Arab friends.

Apart from political pressures generated by the Palestinian issue through the workings of inter-Arab politics, the Saudi leadership also sees Israel as a potential threat to the kingdom's security. When the Saudis sought to purchase the F-15 aircraft from the United States in 1978, Israeli opposition was intense. Although sixty-two F-15s were eventually sold, Israeli concerns ensured that some munitions and sophisticated equipment would not be provided initially and that the aircraft would not be stationed near the Israeli border.[17]

During the F-15 debate Israelis frequently noted that in any future Arab-Israeli war they would be tempted to launch a preemptive strike against the Saudi air force. The construction of an air base at Tabuk in northwest Saudi Arabia particularly alarmed the Israelis, who insisted that the United States prohibit the stationing of the F-15s at Tabuk. To underscore their determination the Israelis, who have long been concerned with development at Tabuk, frequently overflew the area in 1977–78, occasionally going to such lengths as dropping empty fuel tanks on the runway to demonstrate their capabilities. Needless to say, the Saudis were not amused at these antics and urged the United States to restrain the Israelis.

Finally, though the Saudis rarely mention it, they are embarrassed by the fact that Israel has been occupying a small piece of Saudi territory since 1967. Tiran and Sanafir islands, strategically located in the Strait of Tiran at the mouth of the Gulf of Aqaba, belong to Saudi Arabia but have been under Israeli control since the June 1967 war when they were captured from Egypt, which was temporarily stationing forces on

17. In order to allay congressional fears, on May 9, 1978, Secretary of Defense Harold Brown sent a letter to the chairman of the Senate Committee on Foreign Relations, Senator John J. Sparkman, defining certain restrictions on the F-15s to be provided to Saudi Arabia. The letter specifically stated that the planes "will not have conformal fuel tanks ('fast packs'). . . . Saudi Arabia has not requested that the plane be outfitted with Multiple Ejection Racks (MER 200) which would allow the plane to carry a substantial bomb load. The U.S. will not furnish such MERs. . . . Saudi Arabia has not requested nor do we intend to sell any other systems or armaments that would increase the range or enhance the ground attack capability of the F-15." Brown also noted that the Saudis had assured the U.S. that the F-15 would not be based at Tabuk, the airfield closest to Israel.

them. During the Egyptian-Israeli peace treaty negotiations the status of Tiran and Sanafir was particularly delicate because of the Saudi claim, officially supported by the United States, to the islands. The treaty stipulates that Israel will withdraw from the islands in April 1982, after which they will be part of an area supervised by the United Nations or other international forces.

Oil as a Problem

The issue over which the United States and Saudi Arabia could have the most serious disagreements is oil. Much of the special quality of the U.S.-Saudi connection has grown out of a perceived mutuality of interests over oil. But strains are appearing and can be expected to grow. As a major consumer of imported oil, the United States is deeply concerned about Saudi oil decisions. Not surprisingly, Americans urge the Saudis to keep production high, to restrain prices, and to build substantial spare capacity.

Insofar as the Saudis do respond to these requests they feel they are doing Washington a favor and they expect some quid pro quo. If price restraint by the Saudis simply means larger profits for American oil companies, it will not last for long. And while the Saudis have good reasons of their own not to go along with the demands of OPEC's price hawks, they cannot be expected to produce at maximum capacity indefinitely if the real price of oil is being significantly eroded by inflation.

By now Saudi income needs are quite substantial, but in normal market conditions approximately the same income stream can be generated by cutting production and boosting prices or by expanding production at a given price. Since the Saudis are in such a strong position within OPEC, they come close to holding the key to the international market price of oil if they choose to use all the options at their disposal.

Since 1978 the Saudis, despite some threats and hints to the contrary, have kept production high—between 9 million and 10 million barrels a day through 1981—and have charged substantially less than their competitors. Nonetheless, the price of Saudi oil did double in 1979, with additional modest increases in 1980, before leveling out to $32 a barrel in 1981. If revenue needs alone had been their primary concern, as some contend, the Saudis could have earned in 1980 at least an additional $10 billion without risking the loss of their share of the market.

The kingdom's political leadership has generally chosen not to use the threat of reduced oil production as a blunt form of pressure on the West. But many Saudis, especially the younger generation, see the regime's oil policy as wasteful, short-sighted, and dangerous. They resent the enormous sums of money spent on questionable projects. They deplore ostentatious examples of corruption, especially within the royal family. And some of them fear the unintended consequences of such rapid modernization in a society that is still very traditional and parochial. The United States is blamed in some circles for pushing Saudi Arabia to produce more oil than is good for its long-term interests.

Added to these concerns are the arguments that surplus revenues generated by high levels of oil production are losing value because of inflation. Some fear that investments in the West are not safe, noting the U.S. decision to freeze more than $12 billion in Iranian assets in 1979, and they find it comforting to repeat the questionable proposition that oil in the ground is more valuable than current expenditures on development or investments abroad.

In response to these vigorously argued alternative perspectives, the Saudi leadership has basically pursued a cautious oil policy since 1974. On production, they have tried to meet American and Western expectations, especially during the Iranian crisis and the Iran-Iraq war of 1980. This has resulted in substantial financial surpluses—over $100 billion by 1980—despite the remarkable ability of the Saudi regime to spend most of the country's oil income. On price, the Saudis have generally gone along with OPEC and market pressures, while keeping the price for their oil somewhat below that of their competitors. The Saudis have no interest in pushing prices to the point where alternative energy sources might compete favorably with oil. In addition they know that their long-term interests require a degree of economic health in the industrialized states of the West.

When it comes to the question of developing spare capacity, the Saudis have been slow to act. In the early 1980s maximum sustainable production did not exceed 10.5 million barrels per day, a far cry from the 14–16 million bpd or more that the Saudis and ARAMCO once envisaged. Plans under way in 1981 might bring that level to 12 million bpd by 1985, but not much beyond. This will place an upper limit on the extent to which the Saudis will be able to help meet supply emergencies in the 1980s.

The rationale for the Saudi position not to expand productive capacity is rarely discussed openly. Mention is made of the expense, the technical difficulties, and bureaucratic inefficiency. But the fundamental point seems to be that the Saudis do not want to expose themselves to the pressure that would be directed at them if they could produce 14 million to 16 million bpd of oil. The other members of OPEC would be in constant fear that Saudi Arabia would expand production, forcing prices down and gaining a larger share of the market. They would therefore seek political means of preventing the Saudis from producing at maximum capacity in normal market conditions. By contrast, the United States, Western Europe, Japan, and much of the third world would want the Saudis to produce as much oil as possible. Refusal to increase production, especially in crises, could produce a sharp U.S.-Saudi confrontation, inevitably leading to talk of military action to seize Saudi oil fields. To ward off these conflicting pressures, the Saudis, at least for now, have chosen to go slow with the expansion of their productive capacity. This cautious stance has been reinforced by the anticipated soft market conditions of the early 1980s.

How Special Is the "Special Relationship"?

No country will be more important to Saudi Arabia's future than the United States. The common assumption of the past was that the two countries could count on a stable relationship rooted in mutual interests. But as the relationship has grown in complexity, it has also become a mixed blessing in the eyes of many Saudis. The United States has helped bring wealth and security to Saudi Arabia, but the wealth has been accompanied by dilemmas and pressures that threaten to overwhelm the traditional structures of Arabian society, and security can no longer be automatically derived from tacit alliance with the United States. Within the Saudi leadership, and within the society at large, the American connection will be the object of an intense debate in the years to come.

The Soviet Union

Saudi Arabia has had no formal diplomatic relations with the USSR or with any other communist country since World War II. King Faisal was particularly outspoken in his hostility toward communism as an alien ideology that fostered instability and revolutionary change. He suspected the Soviet Union of encouraging Zionism as a means to weaken and divide the Arab world, noting that the Soviet Union had been one of the first countries to recognize the Jewish state in 1948 and to supply it with weapons to fight for its independence.

Rarely mentioned by Faisal or other Saudis is the fact that the Soviet Union was the first nation to establish diplomatic relations with the Kingdom of Saudi Arabia in 1926, and that those relations have never been broken. Faisal himself made an official visit to Moscow in 1932. The Soviet-Saudi relationship never amounted to much in those years, and on the eve of World War II the Soviets withdrew their diplomats.[18]

As in the case of recognition of Israel, the brief Soviet courtship of King Abd al-Aziz was aimed at weakening the British presence in the Middle East. While little came of these initial contacts, they did reflect a Soviet interest in the Arabian Peninsula and a willingness to deal with regimes regardless of political ideology. In addition, with their own large Muslim population, the Soviets were anxious not to be portrayed as adamantly anti-Islamic.

During most of the cold war era the Saudis aligned themselves closely with the noncommunist powers. Unlike many others in the Middle East, Saudi leaders did not try to play Moscow off against Washington. That was Nasser's game after 1955, and the Saudis tended to see Nasser as a reckless troublemaker.

The Threat

Throughout the 1950s and 1960s the Saudis were particularly worried about the indirect Soviet threat to the region. Radical ideologies— Nasserism, Baathism, socialism and communism—were viewed by the Saudi leadership as disruptive forces that served to advance Soviet interests in the Arab world.

After the 1967 Arab-Israeli war the Saudis had less to fear from Egypt. Inter-Arab politics were no longer so sharply polarized along conservative and radical lines. And King Faisal began to play a more assertive role, drawing on the burgeoning oil resources of his country. Internationally, this was the era of U.S.-Soviet détente, but Saudi Arabia remained wedded to a less sanguine view of Soviet intentions.

18. Stephen Page, *The USSR and Arabia*, p. 17. Philby, in *Arabian Jubilee* (pp. 170–72), recounts some anecdotes from the earliest period of Saudi-Soviet relations. Most striking is his claim that in the early 1930s the Soviet Union sent the Saudis a much-needed shipload of kerosene, for which no payment was ever made. This came at a time when the Soviets were the primary suppliers of petroleum products in the Red Sea area, with shipments from Odessa through the Suez Canal.

For the Saudis, 1970 was a crucial year in crystallizing their views of the Soviet threat to the Middle East. As Egypt and Israel fought an increasingly intense war of attrition along the Suez Canal, the Soviet military presence in Egypt grew rapidly. By midyear Soviet combat pilots and air defense crews were helping to protect Egypt's skies, Egyptian air and naval bases had been turned over to the Soviets, and the Soviets were on their way to being seen as the only major power prepared to side with the Arabs against Israel. These developments confirmed Faisal's belief that the Soviets would seek to exploit regional tensions to gain a military foothold in the region and to drive a wedge between the United States and "moderate" Arabs.

Further evidence that Soviet-induced instability could have a radicalizing effect in the Arab world came in September 1970 with the outbreak of civil war in Jordan. The crisis was precipitated by the Popular Front for the Liberation of Palestine, whose leader, George Habash, was a self-styled Marxist. Before King Hussein was able to restore his authority, Syrian armored units invaded Jordan at the direction of the radical Baathist leadership, and for a brief period it seemed as if only U.S. or Israeli intervention could save the Jordanian monarchy. Coming only one year after the fall of the conservative Libyan monarchy, the collapse of the Jordanian Kingdom would have left the Saudis in a very isolated and exposed position.[19]

Instead, King Hussein defeated his challengers, and Egypt's President Nasser unexpectedly died while trying to mediate the Jordanian-Palestinian conflict. The Saudis, always suspicious of Nasser, were pleased that his successor was Anwar Sadat, one of the few top Egyptian officials whom the Saudis had cultivated over the years and in whom they had some confidence. Above all, they believed him to be much less pro-Soviet than Nasser.

Having sensed direct danger in 1970, and perceiving new opportunities after Nasser, the Saudis tried under King Faisal to use their influence to weaken Soviet influence in the Arab world. In November 1970 the extreme leftist regime in Syria was ousted by the more moderate Baathists under Hafiz al-Assad. Syria seemed to be moving in the right direction and the Saudis offered encouragement and support. Early in 1971 Sadat put down a challenge from a pro-Soviet faction, an act that fur-

19. See William B. Quandt, "Lebanon 1958, and Jordan, 1970," in Barry M. Blechman and Stephen S. Kaplan, eds., *Force without War: U.S. Armed Forces as a Political Instrument* (Brookings Institution, 1978), pp. 257–88.

ther convinced Faisal that Sadat was the best person to back in Egypt. Shortly thereafter, President Numeiry of the Sudan crushed a coup attempt led by the Sudanese Communist party. Sadat rushed Egyptian troops to Numeiry's support. Once again, moderate forces backed by Saudi Arabia prevailed.

Most gratifying of all to the Saudis was Sadat's abrupt decision in July 1972 to expel the Soviet military presence from Egypt. Whether or not the Saudi role was particularly important in providing Sadat with incentives to rid himself of the unpopular Soviets, the Saudis strongly implied to Washington that they deserved part of the credit.

Taken together, this series of developments in the Arab world seemed to indicate a new trend toward moderation, away from the Soviets. Some thought it reflected the growing financial clout of the conservative Arab oil producers, especially Saudi Arabia. Expectations were being raised that a new era of Saudi leadership of the Arab world was beginning and that this would have a clear impact on Soviet influence in the area. Only Iraq and South Yemen seemed to be locked into the Soviet orbit, beyond the lure of Saudi financial inducements.

The October 1973 war had three important consequences for the Saudis. First, it opened the way for an active U.S. diplomatic role in trying to resolve the Arab-Israeli conflict, something the Saudis had long sought as a crucial element in undermining the Soviet position in the area. Second, it set the stage for dramatic increases in the price of petroleum, thereby strengthening even further the Saudi role in inter-Arab affairs and vis-à-vis the United States. Third, it led to the restoration of a U.S.-Syrian dialogue, which the Saudis welcomed as a step toward moderating Syria's radical policies of the past.

By the time of his death in 1975 King Faisal had achieved international recognition as a skillful statesman, a major Arab figure, and a strong opponent of communism. Soviet commentators made it clear that they hoped that King Khalid would be less of an adversary.

The Soviets must have been disappointed by the indications of continuity under Khalid, Crown Prince Fahd, and the outspoken new foreign minister, Saud al-Faisal. In 1976 and 1977 the Saudis were active in trying to forge a moderate Arab consensus. Saudi aid was also being offered to anti-Soviet regimes in Africa, such as Zaire, and even to the anti-Marxist Angolan forces under Jonas Savimbi. As the Soviets tried to enhance their position in revolutionary Ethiopia, the Saudis provided aid to Eritrean rebels and to Somalia. In the case of Somalia the Saudis sought to convince Siad Barre to break with the Soviets and turn to the West. When he did so in 1977, the Saudis were quick to take credit and to urge U.S. military and economic assistance to Somalia.

President Carter met with Foreign Minister Saud al-Faisal in the fall of 1977. Most of their discussions focused on the prospects for reconvening the Geneva peace conference, but toward the end of the conversation Saud raised the question of U.S. aid to Somalia. He stressed the importance of growing Soviet influence in Ethiopia and mentioned the presence of 15,000 Cuban troops there. Carter replied that there were no Cuban troops present and that the United States could not help Somalia as long as Somalia was carrying out acts of aggression against Ethiopia in the Ogaden. Saud al-Faisal expressed the fear that Soviet influence would return to Somalia unless the United States stepped in. Carter demurred, noting that this was one of the few times the United States and Saudi Arabia had disagreed on an issue.

Before long a new source of discord arose that was to bring to an end a period of Saudi activism in foreign policy. On November 19, 1977, as much of the world looked on in disbelief, Anwar Sadat met with Israel's Prime Minister Menachem Begin in Jerusalem to talk about peace between their two countries. The Saudi attempt to forge a united front embracing Egypt, Syria, Jordan, and the PLO was in shambles. To the Saudis it appeared as if Sadat had decided on a separate peace, which would leave the Palestinian problem unresolved, the Arab world divided, and Saudi Arabia in a particularly awkward position. As time went by, these Saudi fears seemed to be coming true, and in response they edged away from Egypt, reduced their visibility in regional affairs, opened channels to Iraq, and waited for the dust to settle.

Meanwhile Soviet adventurism appeared to be on the rise. A communist regime seized power in Afghanistan in April 1978. South Yemen, under the leadership of the revolutionary Abd al-Fattah Ismail, seemed intent on subverting North Yemen and spreading revolution throughout the peninsula. Soviet bases were being built in Ethiopia and South Yemen, all as part of what the Saudis feared to be a determined effort by the Soviets to encircle them.

With the successful conclusion of the Camp David talks between Egypt and Israel in September 1978, the Saudis saw U.S. policy moving away from the search for a comprehensive settlement of the Arab-Israeli conflict toward endorsement of a bilateral agreement on Sinai. Washington had not consulted the Saudis in advance but nonetheless seemed to expect Saudi support for Camp David. It was not forthcoming, and the Saudis instead aligned themselves with the other Arab states at Baghdad in November 1978 in opposition to Sadat.

Operation Charm

As the Soviets watched the mounting tensions between Washington and Riyadh, they apparently sensed an opportunity to make overtures of their own to the Saudis. In a major article in the *Literary Gazette*, Igor Belyayev, a noted Soviet expert on Middle East affairs, wrote in friendly terms about Saudi Arabia.[20] He spoke of Saudi "non-alignment" and the opposition of the Saudis to Camp David and concluded that there were "no implacable conflicts" between Moscow and Riyadh. He went on to express the hope that Khalid might be less anti-Soviet than Faisal, and spoke positively of Fahd, despite his pro-American tendencies. A few weeks later, many of these same themes were repeated by Radio Moscow, including the point that communism was not incompatible with Islam or monarchies.[21]

Shortly after these overtures from the Soviets, Foreign Minister Saud al-Faisal mentioned the "positive" Soviet role in the area.[22] Fahd also referred to the "importance" of the Soviet role but said that talk of diplomatic relations was premature.[23]

The next flurry of commentary on Soviet-Saudi relations came in early 1980 shortly after the Soviet invasion of Afghanistan, which the Saudis had sharply condemned. Twice in January 1980, interviews with Fahd were published in which he spoke of the USSR. He emphasized the importance of recognizing the reality of Soviet power. "I would like to tell you that we have recently observed a positive development in the Soviet Union's policy. It began through its information media with the expression of some views indicating that it behaves as though it understands us. . . . On our part we began dealing with it even indirectly in a reasonable way." Fahd went on to say that economic and trade relations were good and that "in a short time we will reach the desired

20. Igor Belyayev, "Saudi Arabia: What Next?" *Literaturnaiia Gazeta*, January 31, 1979, in FBIS, *Daily Report: Soviet Union*, February 2, 1979, pp. F7 through F11.
21. Radio Moscow, in Arabic, February 22, 1979, in FBIS, *Daily Report: Soviet Union*, February 26, 1979, p. F9.
22. Interview with Salim al-Lawzi, editor of *Al-Hawadith* (London), March 2, 1979, p. 21.
23. "The Saudis Play Their Hand," *Newsweek*, March 26, 1979, p. 37.

level." Asked about diplomatic relations, Fahd said that public opinion must first be prepared. "However, we are sure that this will take place at the appropriate time."[24]

A few weeks later Fahd again talked about the Soviet Union, this time with a somewhat different nuance. "We do not compete with the Soviet Union in any way. Nobody can use us as a tool. In the circumstances we cannot but admit that the Soviet Union is a major power and that we want no problems with it. A frequent error is to highlight Saudi Arabia as the only state that can resist the Soviet Union and fight it everywhere. This is a mistake, and we do not want to nominate ourselves to a rank we cannot obtain."[25]

The Soviet response came later in the spring. In the *Literary Gazette*, Yevgenii M. Primakov, Central Committee member and Middle East specialist, mentioned with concern that the United States was encouraging the condemnation of Soviet policy in Afghanistan as a way of trying to weaken Saudi relations with the USSR.[26] *Izvestiya* picked up the same theme of the U.S. "policy of disorientation" aimed at influencing "certain representatives of the Saudi ruling circles, who have been talking increasingly frequently about the 'Soviet threat' which allegedly exists for their country." In fact, the article asserted, it is the United States that threatens to seize Saudi oil and that keeps tensions high in the area.[27]

In July Foreign Minister Saud repeated his country's condemnation of Soviet intervention in Afghanistan but added that an end to the Soviet occupation would remove all inhibitions in Saudi Arabia to the development of good relations with the Soviet Union.[28]

Gradually, it seems, the Saudis are responding to Soviet overtures

24. Interview with Talal Salman in *As-Safir* (Beirut), January 9, 1980, in FBIS, *Daily Report: Middle East and North Africa*, January 16, 1980, p. C32. This part of the interview was omitted from the text read over Riyadh radio. According to Saudi sources, the interview was actually given before the Soviet intervention in Afghanistan, which may explain why this section was omitted from the January 1980 broadcast.

25. Interview with Chief Editor Milhim Karam in *Al-Bayraq* (Beirut), January 26, 1980.

26. Dialogue between Primakov and I. P. Belyayev in *Literaturnaiia Gazeta*, March 12, 1980, p. 14.

27. V. Kudryavtsev, "Policy of Disorientation," *Izvestiya*, April 6, 1980, in FBIS, *Daily Report: Soviet Union*, April 14, 1980, p. H7.

28. See Saud al-Faisal's interview with Mona es-Said in *Monday Morning* (Beirut), July 21–27, 1980.

and are talking of the possibility of opening some form of diplomatic contacts. Messages are frequently passed by the Soviets through intermediaries such as the PLO. Foreign Minister Saud has confirmed that Saudi and Soviet diplomats meet regularly in various regions of the world as part of an ongoing dialogue between Riyadh and Moscow.[29]

A recurring theme in these exchanges is reportedly that the Soviets share the Saudi interest in regional stability and that there would be much to talk about of mutual interest. The Saudis see this as a not very subtle way of reminding them that South Yemen and other Soviet clients can make life unpleasant and that the Soviets could be helpful if the Saudis were to make some political concessions. Top Saudi leaders have had occasional meetings with Soviet diplomats. When asked about the Soviet goal in the Middle East, one Saudi official said: "The answer is simple: our oil. . . . At this moment, we do not expect an invasion, but we do expect the Soviets to use their power to maneuver themselves into a position to make arrangements for a guaranteed oil supply."[30] How the Saudis react to these anticipated Soviet pressures for accommodation will be in large measure a function of their relationship with and confidence in the United States.

Europe and Japan as Alternatives

As much as the Saudis may fear Soviet expansion and depend on the United States for ultimate security, they are not eager participants in the superpower struggle for influence in the Middle East. In public the consistent Saudi line has been that both superpowers should keep their military forces out of the area. In recent years the Saudis have articulated elements of what might be viewed as a nonaligned posture, differing with the United States on Camp David while condemning the Soviets for aggression in Afghanistan.

The most tangible sign that the Saudis are anxious to demonstrate a degree of independence of the United States comes primarily in their dealings with other industrialized powers, not in flirtations with Moscow. European and Japanese companies have been avid participants in

29. Interview with Abd al-Karim Abu an-Nasir, *Al-Majallah* (London), April 4–10, 1981.

30. David B. Tinnin, "The Saudis Awaken to Their Vulnerability," *Fortune*, March 10, 1980, p. 56, quoting Prince Turki al-Faisal, head of Saudi intelligence services.

the Saudi economic boom, often with strong support from their governments. In 1978 the European and Japanese share of Saudi imports amounted to nearly 60 percent of the total with the U.S. share remaining fairly steady at just over 20 percent.[31]

More worrisome to Americans than the European and Japanese competition in the Saudi commercial market has been the Saudi propensity in recent years to turn to European sources for arms. The French, for example, held serious talks in 1980 concerning the possible sale of nearly $3.5 billion in equipment and services to the fledgling Saudi Navy. In addition the French provided tanks for two armored brigades and would very much like to sell the Mirage 2000 or 4000 to the air force. Other European arms suppliers have been less successful, although the Saudis have shown some interest in the German Leopard tank and the Tornado fighter aircraft.[32]

Questions have been raised about the contribution that these arms purchases make to Saudi security. At some point limits on Saudi manpower could preclude further expansion of the armed forces, and the purchase of major components of the navy from the United States and France would complicate rational force planning and strain limited human resources. Nonetheless, the Saudis have been determined to diversify their sources of arms, primarily as a symbol of political independence, but perhaps also as a hedge against uncertainty in the event the U.S.-Saudi relationship goes sour. In any event, the ability to turn to Europe for arms will help to ensure that the Americans cannot be entirely unresponsive to Saudi military requests without some risk.

Finally, Europe and Japan have also become havens for surplus Saudi petrodollars. The Japanese in particular have eagerly sought to attract Saudi funds for investment. While the Saudis have attempted to diversify away from investments in the United States and in the Eurodollar market, alternatives for placing very large deposits abroad are limited.

31. Robin Allen, "The U.S. Connection," *Saudi Arabia: A MEED Special Report*, July 1980, pp. 89, 96.

32. The Germans have been reluctant to sell arms to the Middle East. While discussions were under way in 1980 concerning the possible Saudi purchase of Leopard tanks, Saudi Arabia agreed to a $2.25 billion loan to Germany to help finance the current account deficit. (*Mid East Markets* [London], January 26, 1981.) As of mid-1981 Saudi Arabia was West Germany's largest creditor, with outstanding loans of $5.8 billion. "Bonn Puts Credits before Oil," *Saudi Arabia: A MEED Special Report*, July 1981, p. 14.

The United States remains the primary market for Saudi funds, and the dollar is the currency in which most Saudi investments are held.

Unlike some Middle East countries, most notably Iraq, the Saudis will have difficulty in trying to keep their distance from both superpowers while meeting essential economic and security needs from Europe and Japan. The degree of dependence on the United States for arms and technology is too great to be suddenly reversed. Nonetheless, Saudi ties to these modern industrial powers, especially in the economic area, can be expected to grow. They, after all, are eager to offset their enormous oil import bills by selling goods and services to the Saudis.

As an additional sweetener, the Europeans and Japanese are generally predisposed to adopt a more pro-Arab position on the Palestinian question than is Washington. It is not lost on the Saudi leaders in Riyadh that a large arms purchase from France will convey the message to Washington that Saudi political interests should not be ignored. In their most optimistic moments the Saudis may hope that their European ties will serve as an indirect form of leverage on U.S. Middle East policy. To date there is little evidence that this carries much weight, but the hope doubtless remains. In any event the European connection is useful in its own right; in some instances, such as cooperation on internal security, relations can be conducted outside the blaze of publicity, which is not always the case when dealing with Washington.[33]

33. In response to a request from Interior Minister Prince Nayif, the French reportedly sent a small four- or five-man antiterrorist team to help advise the Saudis during the Mecca incident (see chapter 6). During the final drive to suppress the dissidents, according to some sources, the French advisers accompanied Saudi troops into the underground rooms where Juhayman bin Muhammad bin Sayf al-Utaiba and his followers were holding out. The French assistance, although helpful, was not crucial to the eventual Saudi success, but the French have received much credit nonetheless. On the official level the French have never acknowledged playing any role at Mecca, and the Saudis appreciated this discretion. One book published in France purports to detail the French role in Mecca. See Jean-Claude Bourret, *G.I.G.N.— Opération impossible* (Paris: Editions France Empire, 1981). See also "Les trois français qui ont sauvé la Mecque," *Paris Match*, May 29, 1981, pp. 3 ff.

Part Two

Coping with the Threats:
The Saudi Political System

Saudi Arabia seems destined to confront serious external challenges during the 1980s. Much depends on how the Saudi regime handles these threats. Inevitably questions about Saudi foreign and defense policies lead to questions about the nature of the Saudi political system and its capacity to deal with both domestic and external problems.

In the aftermath of the Iranian revolution it became fashionable to write off the Saudi regime as vulnerable to the same pressures that unseated the shah. Apologists for the Saudis were quick to point to the many differences between Iran and Saudi Arabia, leaving the reassuring impression that the Saud family was immune to the revolutionary virus spreading around it.

The debate over Saudi stability has been largely sterile because of the partisanship of most protagonists. And yet the issue is of sufficient importance that it is worth trying to identify the strengths and weaknesses of the Saudi regime and the strategies available to it for coping with the challenges of the 1980s. To that end, part II of this study examines the structure of authority in Saudi Arabia, the internal pressures for change, the problems most likely to arise, and typical patterns of response. Finally, several recent cases of Saudi foreign policy decisions are analyzed, including decisions on oil production and pricing.

Chapter Five

The Structure of Authority

SAUDI ARABIA does not fit easily into the conventional models of political systems. It is a monarchy, but the king is only one among several key personalities who participate in most important decisions. It is a family enterprise, but the family itself is not united and commoners are anxious to gain power. It is an Islamic state, but secular influences are everywhere present. It is an authoritarian government, but access to rulers is comparatively easy and citizens' demands for individual redress of grievances are often met. It is a society avidly seeking the comforts of the modern world, but traditional elements such as tribes remain influential. It is a country in which unbelievable wealth coexists alongside pockets of subsistence-level poverty.

Part of the difficulty in categorizing Saudi Arabia is that the kingdom has been undergoing a peaceful political, social, and economic revolution since at least the early 1970s. Leadership and institutions have changed. Oil wealth has provided immense resources to a country that as recently as the mid-1960s was nearly bankrupt. Education has spread with remarkable speed, and the physical landscape of the country in some places has been altered beyond recognition. While the past is still a useful guide to some present-day realities, few precedents exist for much of what is taking place in Saudi Arabia.

Dynastic Rule

For most of the past 250 years the Saud family, the Al Saud, has held sway in at least part of the Arabian Peninsula. (See appendix D.) It has had its ups and downs over the years, but since the beginning of this century the family has managed to extend its power to an unprecedented extent.

Unlike some regimes in the Middle East, the Al Saud have roots in the social and political history of the country, especially in the central Najd region. This is not to say that the Al Saud enjoy uncontested legitimacy. They do not. But the Saud dynasty has two centuries of history behind it in trying to establish its claim to rule. There are many leaders in the Middle East whose credentials have been less impressive, including the former shah of Iran.

Much of the success to date of the Saud family has been due to a number of remarkable political leaders. The founder of the present Kingdom of Saudi Arabia, Abd al-Aziz (1902–53), had a genuine talent for knitting together the diverse elements of the Arabian Peninsula into a modern state. He was realistic enough to know when to exercise restraint in the face of external dangers, and he was skillful at mixing force and positive inducements to outmaneuver his rivals. He made good use of Islam but did not become a captive of its most rigid interpreters or its most fanatic proponents.[1] By marrying into many tribes of the peninsula, he forged alliances with other powerful families and left as his legacy to the kingdom a royal family that numbered in the thousands. (See appendix E for partial genealogy.)

If Abd al-Aziz was a man of recognized ability, his successor, King Saud ibn Abd al-Aziz (1953–64), was much less skillful. Confronted with serious challenges from outside and the need for internal reforms, Saud presided over the mismanagement of Saudi resources to the point of endangering the state. By 1958 other members of the family began to circumscribe the king's powers, demonstrating that the senior princes can wield great influence, to the point of deposing an unpopular or ineffectual ruler.

Fortunately for the regime, Saud's brother, Faisal ibn Abd al-Aziz, was both experienced and widely respected. With the support of other sons of Abd al-Aziz, and in particular Muhammad and Fahd, Faisal assumed increasing responsibilities as prime minister and foreign minister. Saud briefly resisted, but in 1964 he was forced to abdicate in favor of Faisal.[2]

The transition from Saud to Faisal was a major test of the family's ability to deal with crises. Several lessons can be drawn. First, it is essen-

1. See H. StJ. B. Philby, *Arabian Jubilee;* and Christine Moss Helms, *The Cohesion of Saudi Arabia.*
2. Ralph Braibanti and Fouad Abdul-Salam Al-Farsy, "Saudi Arabia," pp. 3–43; and William Rugh, "The Emergence of a New Middle Class in Saudi Arabia," pp. 7–20.

tial for the king to retain the support of other senior princes. Second, blatant corruption and incompetence will not be tolerated indefinitely. Third, the family moves slowly to make changes in the system of rule, trying to preserve the facade of unity to the outside world. Fourth, external events can play a major role in domestic policies, as in the case of Saud's inability to compete effectively with Egypt's President Nasser.

Faisal's reign, from 1964 to 1975, was marked by an unusual degree of stability. This was partly because of Faisal's abilities and character and partly because the threat from Nasser's Egypt declined after 1967. Oil revenues were also on the rise, but rapid modernization had not yet had a particularly disruptive influence.[3]

Faisal's major contributions were the restoration of the Saudi economy and of Saudi prestige in the Arab and Islamic worlds by setting Saudi Arabia on a cautious path of reform and modernization, as well as the establishment of close ties with the United States. By the time of his assassination in 1975 some steps had also been taken toward strengthening modern institutions, most notably a number of ministries, the cabinet, the armed forces, the national guard, the monetary agency, and the intelligence services. Saudi capabilities for dealing with the outside world were increasing, as were the dangers from abroad.

Faisal's long experience with foreign affairs—he was foreign minister from 1930 to the time of his death, with only one brief interruption—meant that other members of the family were comparatively inexperienced in dealing with events abroad. Kamal Adham, Faisal's Turkish-born brother-in-law, had been in charge of intelligence and had handled many sensitive issues for the king. But to a remarkable degree, Faisal shaped Saudi foreign policy during his reign.[4]

No Saudi ruler, however, can make decisions in a vacuum. Consensus has been the watchword in the royal family, and public sentiment, especially on Arab and Islamic issues, must be taken into account. These constraints became even more important after Faisal, partly because no other Saudi leader commanded as much respect and also because the country's stake in foreign affairs was rapidly growing, thus increasing the controversy over how Saudi Arabia should play its part and use its resources.

3. Willard A. Beling, ed., *King Faisal and the Modernization of Saudi Arabia.*
4. One of King Faisal's closest advisers on foreign policy was Rashad Farawn, a Syrian who had served as King Abd al-Aziz's personal physician and adviser. Farawn has remained a respected adviser to King Khalid and is often the only one outside the royal family who is present when the king meets with foreign leaders.

Political life within the royal family is shrouded in secrecy.[5] But from what can be known, recent history seems to provide two very different patterns of authority. Under both King Abd al-Aziz and King Faisal, power was concentrated in the hands of the monarch himself. This was particularly true in foreign affairs, although Abd al-Aziz delegated some of his authority to Faisal, reserving for himself the conduct of relations with Saudi Arabia's most immediate neighbors.

Under Kings Saud and Khalid the structure of authority has been more diffuse. Saud's behavior led to active opposition from within the family, resulting in his eventual deposition. In this case splits in the family were deep, but nonetheless the tensions were handled with a sensitivity to preserving the position of the Al Saud. Even the "Free Princes" who established themselves in Cairo in the early 1960s eventually drifted back to Saudi Arabia and in some cases were given positions in the government.

When King Faisal was assassinated in March 1975 by an alienated nephew, the family immediately closed ranks and proclaimed Khalid the new ruler and Fahd crown prince and deputy prime minister.[6] By temperament, Khalid has not been inclined to take an active interest in affairs of state, although he had frequently accompanied Faisal on trips abroad. Nor has his health been particularly good. But he has been admired as an honest man, and he has maintained good relations with the traditional forces in the country. Saudis often speak of the king with sympathy and respect.

If Khalid has been more than a figurehead, he has also been much less than an effective leader. Still, he has embodied many of the appropriate characteristics of a Saudi ruler, unlike King Saud, and he has therefore won support and been shown deference. On some issues, including

5. Three essays on Saudi political dynamics, each written from quite different perspectives, are well worth reading: Michael Collins, "Riyadh: The Saud Balance," pp. 200–08, which describes the various power centers in the country and how the family keeps the heterogeneous system in balance; Ghassane Salameh, "Political Power and the Saudi State," pp. 5–22, which analyzes the social structure of the country and politics within the royal family; and A. Vasil'yev, "Saudi Arabia Between Archaism and Contemporaneity," pp. 19–21, for a surprisingly nonideological view of Saudi politics from a Soviet journalist. All three conclude that the short-term prospects for stability are fairly good.

6. The following day Saudi citizens were invited to swear allegiance to the new king in Riyadh. The family's proclamation naming Khalid was signed in order of seniority by the one surviving brother of Abd al-Aziz, Abdallah, and the four eldest of Abd al-Aziz's sons, Muhammad, Nasr, Sa'd, and Fahd, and then other members of the family.

foreign policy questions, he has weighed in with views of his own. For a brief period it was widely believed that Khalid was putting his distinctive stamp on Saudi foreign policy, but by 1978–79 his health had further deteriorated and he seemed largely uninterested in day-to-day policies.

Senior Princes

In the absence of strong leadership from the king, Saudi foreign policy has become the province of several of the senior princes.[7] Something of a division of labor has appeared, a development that corresponds with the growing complexity of Saudi interests but also makes the task of coordinating and implementing consistent policies more difficult.

For most of the period since Faisal's death Fahd has been the single most important figure in shaping Saudi foreign policy. This is not to say that he always gets his way or that his mandate covers the whole range of Saudi concerns. But with respect to U.S.-Saudi relations and oil price and production decisions, Fahd has played the major role since 1976–77. In some circles he has been referred to as pro-American, which is a great oversimplification and can be very misleading. Nonetheless, Fahd appears to value the relationship with the United States and seems to believe that Washington can be persuaded to support Saudi Arabia without threats and confrontation. In his dealings with Washington, Fahd is often indirect, elusive, and soft-spoken. He never directly brandishes the oil weapon and seems aware of the risks of doing so.

In inter-Arab politics, Fahd is a centrist, seeking consensus and trying to avoid Saudi Arabia's isolation. He is less anti-Egyptian than many Saudis but was personally offended by Sadat's unilateral initiatives and his frequent attacks on the Saudi royal family.[8] With Sadat's death in October 1981, Fahd will probably cautiously seek to improve ties with Egypt, especially if Husni Mubarak succeeds in consolidating power.

Apart from Khalid and Fahd, three other senior princes, also sons of

7. The best guides to the members of the royal family are Brian Lees, *A Handbook of the Al Sa'ud Ruling Family of Saudi Arabia;* Philby, *Arabian Jubilee,* apps. 1, 2, 3; and "The Royal House of Saud," *Financial Times* (London), March 20, 1978, for details on the thirty-two surviving sons of Abd al-Aziz.

8. Fahd was particularly angry at Sadat for giving an interview to a Kuwaiti journalist in which Sadat referred to Fahd as a "donkey." Fahd found this hard to believe until he purchased the tape of the interview from the journalist and heard Sadat's own voice uttering the offensive phrase.

Abd al-Aziz, have played a part in foreign policy decisions: Abdallah, Sultan, and Nayif. Abdallah is head of the national guard, second deputy prime minister, and next in line after Fahd to become king. Abdallah is a half brother of Fahd. His mother came from the Shammar tribe in the north.

Some observers see Khalid, with his Jiluwi background, supporting Abdallah as a way of offsetting the influence of the Sudayris, represented by Fahd, Sultan, and Nayif.[9] Indeed, Saudis often describe both Khalid and Abdallah as "men of the desert" with a deep love of hunting and falconry. It is thus probably correct to see Khalid and Abdallah as personally close, but the political significance of this should not be exaggerated.

Abdallah has taken a special interest in internal affairs, as befits his position as head of the national guard, a position he has held since 1963. He spends considerable time with traditional elements of the society, especially tribal leaders who provide troops for the guard. He has also played an important part in Saudi relations with various Arab states, especially Syria, Jordan, and Morocco. He has traveled in the Arab world and was involved in mediating the Syrian-Jordan dispute in December 1980. He is reported to maintain close ties to Syrian President Assad and to Assad's powerful brother, Rifaat.

On occasion Abdallah is mentioned as heading an anti-American faction of the royal family. While he may be less committed to the U.S.-Saudi "special relationship" than Fahd, there is little evidence to support the view that Abdallah is much different from other members of the royal family in his basic foreign policy views. Indeed, there is considerable reason to believe that he is enough of a political realist to want to develop his own channels to communicate with Washington.[10]

9. King Abd al-Aziz had seven sons by Hussah bint al-Sudayri. These powerful brothers are often referred to as the Sudayri Seven. Fahd, born in 1921, is the eldest and serves as crown prince and first deputy prime minister; Sultan, born in 1924, is minister of defense and aviation; Abd al-Rahman, born in 1926, is a successful businessman; Nayif, born in 1933, is minister of interior; Turki, born in 1934, served as deputy minister of defense for some time before entering private business; Salman, born in 1936, is governor of Riyadh; Ahmad, born in 1940, is deputy minister of interior. Although Khalid's mother was a Jiluwi, her mother was a Sudayri. King Faisal was linked to four of the great families of Saudi Arabia: his mother was from the Al Shaykh; his three wives were, in order, from the Sudayri, Jiluwi, and Thunayan families.

10. See interviews by Meg Greenfield and James Hoagland with Princes Fahd and Abdallah, *Washington Post*, May 25, 1980.

Arabs who have dealt with Abdallah invariably describe him as pleasant and sincere, even possessing a sense of humor, but they do not attribute to him much dynamism or depth. In addition they view his public reticence as an obstacle to his being widely accepted as a strong leader in a culture that values rhetoric and forceful personalities.

Sultan, the minister of defense and aviation, is the next of the senior princes generally considered to be eligible for the kingship. The family has not formally decided that he should be next in line after Abdallah, but he certainly expects to be crown prince if Abdallah becomes king. By most accounts he very much wants to be king himself some day.

Unlike many Saudis, Sultan is rather outspoken and extroverted. He is an activist who wants to see Saudi Arabia play an important role in Middle East politics. As minister of defense since 1960, he has overseen the expenditure of enormous sums on the military, and this has provided him with opportunities to strengthen his position and to help those loyal to him. He oversees an immense patronage network and has a reputation for generosity. Much of his power depends on his ability to provide for the armed forces, and thus he inevitably becomes a proponent of pressing the United States for sophisticated weaponry. Fahd, who shows less enthusiasm for rapid military modernization, has generally gone along with Sultan's requests.

In addition to his dominant voice in U.S.-Saudi security relations, Sultan has been the principal figure dealing with North Yemen. As much as anyone, he has been responsible for the ups and downs of Saudi policy toward the Yemens. Perhaps because of his concern for Saudi security and for the Yemens, Sultan is an articulate proponent of the view that the Soviets are trying to encircle Saudi Arabia. The Soviets have taken him to task publicly for his unfriendly views.[11]

As minister of interior, Prince Nayif has less formal responsibility for dealing with events beyond Saudi Arabia's frontiers. But no clear line can be drawn to divide Saudi foreign and domestic policies, just as no obvious demarcation exists between the spheres of influence of the senior princes. Nayif has taken a special interest in the gulf states and Iraq.[12] He maintains links to leftist factions in Lebanon and has been

11. V. Kudryavtsev, "Policy of Disorientation," *Izvestiya*, April 6, 1980, in FBIS, *Daily Report: Soviet Union*, April 14, 1980, p. H7.

12. Prince Nayif declared at the conclusion of a visit to Kuwait in late November 1980: "The security of Kuwait is the security of the Kingdom of Saudi Arabia and this calls for a joint treaty for Gulf security." *Al-Siyasah* (Kuwait), November 27, 1980, in FBIS, *Daily Report: Middle East and Africa*, December 1, 1980, p. v.

mentioned as one of the few members of the royal family to have had any direct dealings with the Soviets. The French have shown a special interest in Nayif, and he has sought French assistance in strengthening Saudi police capabilities, including counterterrorist training. It was reportedly through Nayif that the French were asked to provide modest assistance during the November 1979 Mecca incident.

From this sketch of the senior members of the royal family, there appears to be some diffusion of responsibility in foreign policy.[13] Fahd, with the king's support, is the dominant figure. When serious policy differences have arisen, the family has gone to great lengths to prevent internal quarrels from surfacing. Decisions may be postponed or compromises forged to preserve the facade of consensus.

If Fahd becomes king, he may try to be more assertive in setting the broad lines of Saudi foreign policy. This could produce some resistance from others in the family, but the patterns of the past provide little reason to expect serious splits unless Fahd tries to govern without regard for the views of others in the family. Periods of stress seem to bring the senior princes closer together rather than to exacerbate their differences. In early 1979, at a time when Saudi Arabia was very worried about events in Iran and Yemen as well as by the Egypt-Israel peace treaty, Crown Prince Fahd was absent from Saudi Arabia for about one month. While Fahd recuperated in Spain, Abdallah and Sultan assumed more responsibility in foreign affairs and demonstrated a reassuring capacity for working together. Ultimately, it seems, the senior princes are aware that they cannot afford to allow their differences to go too far. Consensus is not just a traditional virtue. It is also the key to the Saud family's survival.

Junior Princes

Apart from Khalid, Fahd, Abdallah, Sultan, and Nayif, a number of junior princes, as well as a few commoners, play some part in the formulation and implementation of Saudi foreign policy. Although it is likely that the younger generation, both royal and nonroyal, will seek a greater voice in policymaking during the 1980s, to date they have had very little

13. Prince Salman, governor of Riyadh and one of the Sudayri Seven, is very close to his full brother Crown Prince Fahd. He often travels abroad with him and is believed to have some influence on foreign policy issues.

influence over major decisions. Power still resides for most purposes in the hands of the sons of Abd al-Aziz.

Of the junior princes, Saud al-Faisal and Turki al-Faisal, sons of Faisal, and Bandar ibn Sultan, son of Sultan, have begun to assume positions of responsibility for foreign affairs and national security. Unlike their fathers, they are Western-educated, quite cosmopolitan, and very articulate in explaining Saudi foreign policy concerns to Western audiences.

Saud al-Faisal, who has served as foreign minister since 1975, is particularly skillful in addressing American public opinion and has done well in international conferences, such as the Islamic conference in Pakistan in January 1980, which condemned the Soviet invasion of Afghanistan. Greatly influenced by his father and carefully tutored by Kamal Adham, Saud has nonetheless developed a style and outlook that are distinctively his own. For example, he is particularly insistent on the centrality of the Palestinian issue, which he frequently defines as the most serious threat to regional stability. He, more than many Saudis, tries to link Saudi oil policies to the Arab-Israeli conflict. While his rhetorical stance on this issue is sometimes stark, he also has demonstrated an understanding of the complexities of issues.

Saud al-Faisal's willingness to stand up to the United States on the Palestinian question has given him some genuine popularity in Saudi and Arab circles. Among younger Saudis, he is seen as something of a spokesman for nationalist views. On key issues such as oil production, however, he has yet to show much direct influence.[14]

Saud's brother, Turki al-Faisal, became head of the Saudi intelligence services in 1978, a position previously occupied by his mentor Kamal Adham. Unlike his brother, Turki has not developed much of a public personality, but he is highly intelligent, analytical, and much respected by those who have dealt with him. He has been sent on a number of discreet diplomatic assignments and is one of the few Saudis who has tried to explain his country's policies to the Western world. During the lengthy debate in early 1978 over the sale of sixty F-15 aircraft to Saudi Arabia, Turki was sent to Washington where he performed admirably

14. Crown Prince Fahd does not seem to share Saud's aversion to military cooperation with the United States, as demonstrated by the Saudi request for AWACS aircraft in late September 1980 when Iraq and Iran opened hostilities. This is the type of decision that Saud, who was in the United States at the time, would most likely have opposed.

in meetings with congressmen, journalists, and administration officials. His rational and balanced explanations of Saudi security requirements made a positive impression and helped to ensure congressional support for the controversial sale.

Joining Turki in the F-15 effort was his cousin, Bandar ibn Sultan, a pilot in the Saudi Air Force. Bandar also received high marks for his lobbying skills, and during that period he learned much about Washington politics. He returned to the United States in 1979 to complete his pilot training and to get a master's degree in international politics. Because of his engaging and extroverted personality, as well as his connections, he made extensive contacts throughout the administration and in Congress. He played squash with the chairman of the Joint Chiefs of Staff, met with the president, and cultivated the Washington press corps. From his Washington townhouse, at the touch of a button on his private phone he could be in direct contact with Fahd and Sultan.

Bandar returned to Saudi Arabia in fall 1980 to resume his responsibilities with the air force but remained interested in assuming a direct role in foreign policy. It will be worth watching how the Saudi political system accommodates the demands of such an assertive and active individualist. The initial Saudi reaction to his highly visible performance in Washington was to remove him from the limelight for a cooling-off period. But he was soon back in Washington during much of 1981 to help press the Saudi case for AWACS and to deal directly with President Reagan. It is not clear, however, that the Saudis are quite ready for a flamboyant figure in the foreign policy arena. In any case he is still quite young and age counts in Saudi politics.

One other member of the royal family has begun to receive attention as a spokesman on security issues and foreign policy from within the military. Fahd ibn Abdallah, the able head of air force operations, comes from the al-Kabir branch of the Saud family.[15] He has been very active in promoting the interests of the air force, as in the case of the F-15 sale and the request in mid-1980 for additional sophisticated military equipment. In 1981 he negotiated some of the details of the AWACS sale with Washington. His branch of the family is well represented in the armed

15. The Saud al-Kabir are the descendants of Saud ibn Faisal, an elder brother of King Abd al-Aziz's father, who ruled in Arabia between 1871 and 1875. In the early phase of Abd al-Aziz's attempt to consolidate his leadership, members of the al-Kabir branch of the family (known as the Araif) opposed him and sided with ibn Rashid. Eventually the two branches of the family were reconciled and Abd al-Aziz's sister Nura married Saud, the father of Muhammad Shaqran .

forces and through him is now reportedly seeking a political voice as well. His grandfather, Muhammad Shaqran, as the oldest member of this senior branch of the family, reportedly ranks second after King Khalid in royal protocol.

Technocrats

Apart from these members of the royal family who exercise responsibilities in the foreign policy arena, a number of ministers have technical competence and ambitions to shape future policies. Best known in the West is Ahmad Zaki Yamani, minister of petroleum and mineral resources since 1965.[16] With more than fifteen years of experience in his job, Yamani knows the international energy picture extremely well. On technical issues his voice doubtless carries much weight. But on crucial issues of pricing and production it is less obvious that he plays a decisive role. A careful review of his frequent public declarations reveals that they are not a particularly good guide to Saudi oil behavior, nor is there a great deal of internal consistency. If Yamani does carry weight, it is likely to be by reinforcing Fahd's inclinations to keep production at fairly high levels and to keep prices a bit below the OPEC average.[17] He does not appear to side with the "conservationist" school among the technocrats, although he frequently talks of the pressures on Saudi Arabia to cut production. At the same time, he has persistently tried to devise a common price strategy for OPEC that would require Saudi Arabia to be prepared to use its spare productive capacity to enforce price discipline.

In 1975 the Council of Ministers was significantly strengthened by the inclusion of a number of young, technically competent ministers. They had in common that they were all Western-educated and not members of the royal family. They also tended to be critical of indiscriminate spending on development projects, seeking to apply standards of rationality to the Saudi budget. On foreign policy issues, the technocrats, as they are commonly called, tend to be nationalistic and insistent

16. Yamani's predecessor was Abdullah Tariki. See Stephen Duguid, "A Biographical Approach to the Study of Social Change in the Middle East: Abdullah Tariki as a New Man," pp. 195–200.

17. See Yamani's remarks at the University of Petroleum and Minerals, January 31, 1981, in appendix C. Some close observers of Saudi politics maintain that Yamani is not particularly close to Crown Prince Fahd.

that Saudi Arabia not be taken for granted by the West. On both economic and political grounds, they usually favor lower levels of oil production and less deference to American preferences. They argue that oil left in the ground will appreciate in value more rapidly than investments abroad. In general they do not believe that Saudi Arabia should produce much more oil than is necessary to cover its own internal development needs. Despite such reservations, however, these are the same men who will be presiding over a five-year development plan (1981–85), which will spend at least $50 billion annually.

While there are variations of opinion among the technocrats, who apart from the Council of Ministers have no institutional base for advancing their views, they nonetheless represent a serious group with an impact on economic and financial decisions, if not yet on foreign policy across the board. Among the best known representatives of this group are Hisham Nazir, minister of planning; Ghazi al-Qusaibi, minister of industry and power; Muhammad Aba al-Khayl, minister of finance and national economy; Abd al-Aziz al-Qurayshi, head of the Saudi Arabian Monetary Agency; Muhammad Abduh Yamani, minister of information; Sulaiman Abd al-Aziz al-Sulaim, minister of commerce; and Faisal al-Bashir, deputy minister of planning. All seem loyal to the royal family, but inevitably they would welcome a broader sharing of power. These are not potential coup-makers, but they can be expected to be articulate spokesmen for a nationalistic foreign policy and for reciprocity in relations with the United States. As such, they seem more in tune with the views of Prince Saud than with the older generation of princes.[18] With their concern for corruption and waste, they also have something in common with the religious conservatives.

In the realm of Saudi foreign policy formulation, power is tightly concentrated in the hands of a few senior members of the royal family. On specific issues younger princes may have some voice, along with a few key ministers and senior military officers. Less visible within this inner circle, however, are religious leaders, the Ulama.

The Ulama

Most studies of Saudi Arabia attribute considerable importance to the Islamic religious leaders, the Ulama. The ascendancy of the Saud

18. Aba al-Khayl, however, has close personal ties to Minister of Defense Sultan.

family in Arabian Peninsula society over the past two centuries is widely believed to stem from the alliance in 1744 between the founder of the Al Saud dynasty, Muhammad ibn Saud, and Muhammad ibn Abd al-Wahhab, head of what came to be known as the Al al-Shaykh. Even today the Al al-Shaykh are represented in government, although not in positions directly touching on foreign policy.[19] It is hard to escape the conclusion that the Ulama have little influence over the conduct of the kingdom's external affairs.

Nonetheless, the Ulama do help set the rules of social behavior; they influence the educational system; and they help ensure an Islamic orientation in Saudi policies, at least on the public level. During moments of uncertainty, such as the transition from Saud to Faisal, and again at the time of Faisal's assassination, the support of the Ulama for changes decided upon within the family provides an aura of legitimacy.[20] The royal family has deftly managed to identify the Ulama so closely with the regime that any criticism of the rule of the Al Saud is portrayed as a challenge to Islam itself.

The Saud family has generally sought to accommodate the Ulama and to enlist their support for major policy initiatives. King Abd al-Aziz, as is frequently recounted, won over the Ulama to the introduction of the telephone in Saudi society by demonstrating that the Holy Quran could be communicated by such modern means. More recently, when Faisal and the shah met in Riyadh in 1968, both leaders included in their entourage many prominent Ulama.[21]

Before the Mecca incident in November 1979 the Ulama had urged the political authorities to show leniency toward a group of young religious zealots who had been arrested in 1978 for inciting people against the regime. Once released, these extremists resumed their agitation and on the first day of the new Islamic year, 1400 Hegira, they seized control of the Grand Mosque in Mecca. Again the regime sought the formal support of thirty-two religious scholars before using force against the dissidents.

19. The ministers of justice, agriculture, and higher education in 1981 were from the Al al-Shaykh. So was King Faisal's mother.

20. The Ulama played an important role in legitimizing the removal of King Saud and his replacement by Faisal in 1964. See "Documents," *Middle East Journal,* vol. 18 (Summer 1964), pp. 351–54. The Ulama referred to growing differences between Saud and Faisal and the consequent danger of civil strife and chaos (*fitna*) that "could almost have occurred as a result of them." (Ibid., p. 352.)

21. See Hermann F. Eilts, "Security Considerations in the Persian Gulf," pp. 103–04.

These examples suggest that the Ulama, at least in areas touching on security and foreign policy, have some role in setting limits on the regime's behavior, on influencing the style of public discourse, and on enforcing a strict Islamic interpretation of events in public. But the Ulama as such are not a powerful force in influencing Saudi foreign policy, in determining strategies of development and oil production, or even in the direction of Saudi aid to Islamic countries. They are, however, given some leeway and funds to pursue missionary work in North Yemen and in Africa. Unlike the clergy in Iran, the Saudi Ulama do not have autonomous means of support, depending instead on the regime for financial resources, not on the community of believers. As influential as they may be in enforcing certain social codes, they are unlikely to have decisive influence over Saudi foreign policy in the future. Nor will the Ulama, acting on their own, pose much of a threat to the regime. They could, however, play a role in legitimizing any challenge to the regime.[22]

22. A good source that reflects the Ulama's views is the journal *Al-Da'wah* (Riyadh). Although the Ulama's views may have limited influence, they do find expression.

Chapter Six

Pressures for Change
and Problems for the Future

DESPITE its conservative outward appearance, Saudi Arabia has been undergoing dramatic social, economic, and political changes since the consolidation of the state under Abd al-Aziz in the 1920s and 1930s. During the 1970s in particular, the pace of change was extremely rapid, raising questions about whether oil revenues and forced modernization might not prove to be destabilizing. The experience of neighboring Iran was frequently mentioned to highlight the unsettling consequences of modernization.

When Saudis complain, sometimes nostalgically, about the unpleasant aspects of sudden wealth, they nonetheless do not seem anxious to turn back the clock very far. Some members of the older generation remember the anarchy and general insecurity of bedouin society. Many recall the poverty, sickness, and illiteracy that was the lot of most inhabitants of the Arabian Peninsula a generation ago. Like many others, Saudis seem to want the benefits of science and technology while preserving something of their own traditions and identities. Nowhere in the world has it been easy to strike a balance, and Saudi Arabia is no exception.

Some of the pressures of change are likely to come from within the royal family itself. During King Saud's reign family members worried about Saud's profligacy and his inability to meet Nasser's nationalist challenge. Corruption and backwardness were weakening the regime and Radio Cairo's anti-Saudi propaganda could find a receptive audience. Faced with these dangers, the family circumscribed Saud's powers, placing in Faisal's hands increased authority. Saud fought back briefly by trying to identify himself with the reform-minded progressives. Finally, when Faisal assumed full powers in 1964 he announced a ten-point plan of modernization. Characteristically, Faisal moved slowly, while Fahd, as minister of interior, was reported to favor a more rapid pace of change. The result was that modest reforms were deliberately introduced by the regime once the dangers of inaction had been made clear.

The Mixed Blessing of Oil Wealth: Development and Corruption

Differences reportedly still exist in the family concerning the appropriate pace of Saudi development. Fahd and Sultan are usually identified with the "modernizers." Abdallah is thought to be somewhat more conservative. The technocrats often find themselves in a curious position. They favor social and political reforms—education, health, bureaucratic efficiency, less corruption, more sharing of power—but some are opposed to the indiscriminate, breakneck pace of development that marked the second Saudi Five-Year Plan (1976–80). They resent the inflated prices, the poor quality of work, the lack of real planning, and the general wastefulness of Saudi expenditures.[1] Thus some would argue for fewer grandiose projects and more social investments, including the training of Saudi manpower to take the places of some of the skilled foreign workers in the country.

It is primarily from the ranks of the professionals and technocrats that complaints are heard about corruption. It is not that they are poorly remunerated. Nor are they immune to the desire for sudden riches. But they resent the privileged position of some members of the royal family who use their connections to make enormous fortunes. No one begrudges Saudi businessmen their normal profits and commissions, as generous as those may often be, but when a prince earns over $100 million in a single transaction, then eyebrows are raised and gossip spreads. The explosion of petrodollar wealth has had a corrosive effect on values throughout the oil-rich countries, and once again Saudi Arabia has not been able to escape the virus.

Demands for Political Participation

Wealth comes from connections, from wheeling and dealing, by good luck, by the regime's munificence—but not primarily because of hard

1. For further discussion of these topics, see the series of articles by Karen Elliott House in the *Wall Street Journal*, June 2, 4, 8, 10, 16 and 18, 1981; Eric Rouleau, *Le Monde*, April 29 and 30, May 2, 3, and 4, 1981; and Pranay B. Gupte, *New York Times*, March 23, 24, and 26, 1981.

work, dedication, or probity. There are few incentives for young Saudis
to learn a technical skill, to become trained industrial workers, to acquire academic knowledge. With the exception of a few top people in
the ministries of government who are as able and hardworking as their
counterparts anywhere in the world, one finds comparatively few Saudis
who are using their talents to develop their country.

A pervasive lethargy and passivity seems to characterize the Saudi
bureaucracy, apart from the overworked, excessively busy people in
charge. Delegation of responsibility is difficult to institute, and as a
result, decisions are virtually all channeled to the top of the bureaucratic
pyramid. Loyalty is rewarded more than competence. Frustrations
abound as the pressures for responsiveness from government exceed the
capacity of the system to react. The constraint is not financial resources
—although the Saudis have occasionally overspent the budget—but
rather the lack of human resources.

Saudi society provides few means for assessing public sentiment or
for allowing organized political activity. There are no legal political
parties or trade unions. There is no free press and no opinion polls. There
are no elections or mass demonstrations.[2] There are, however, some traditional channels for the redress of specific individual grievances. For
example, most Saudi leaders still hold the *majlis*, which provides ordinary
citizens with a chance to bring their problems directly to the attention
of rulers. Petitions are received and may be acted on. At the national
level the functioning of the *majlis* is bound to be rather perfunctory, but
in the provinces it remains an essential element of governing along with
the courts, which dispense justice in accordance with a strict interpretation of Islamic law. But the *majlis* is not a forum for discussing constitutional reform or limits on the power of the royal family. It cannot
satisfy the expectations of the young, educated groups in the population
who seek a role in shaping policy, not just occasional access to those
with power who can dispense or withhold favors.

What can Saudis do if they want to advocate large-scale change in
the nature of the political system? What can a Saudi do to influence the
choice of who will rule his country? Very little, apart from those who
are members of the inner circle of the family. Organized political oppo-

2. Mosques, other than the Grand Mosque, are sometimes places where politics
can be discussed and the Friday sermons may have political content. After the Mecca
incident in November 1979, there were reports that some mosques were kept closed
except at prayer times.

sition is virtually unknown. Exiles try to rally opinion against the regime from abroad,[3] and there are occasional rumors of discontent in the armed forces.[4] But no serious challenge to Al Saud rule has come from within the country since King Abd al-Aziz put down the rebellion in the late 1920s of his militant Islamic supporters, the Ikhwan.

The Mecca Incident

Many would argue that the Mecca incident in November 1979 and the Shiite disturbances in the Eastern Province in December 1979 and again in February 1980 are danger signals that should not be ignored. And there is reason to believe that the regime itself was alarmed by these outbursts of violence, even if by Middle East standards they were limited in scale.

The Mecca affair was largely the work of a small band of religious zealots, coupled with a few leaders who had tribal and personal reasons for opposing the House of Saud. The history of Islam is filled with comparable protest movements, including the Wahhabis themselves, who have used Islamic theological argumentation to advance political interests. In this case the leader of the group was a young man named Juhayman bin Muhammad bin Sayf al-Utaiba from the powerful Utaiba tribe.[5]

3. The best known of these exiles was Nasir al-Said, head of the Arabian Peninsula People's Union. Fahd refers to him in an interview with Chief Editor Milhim Karam in *Al-Bayraq* (Beirut), January 26, 1980. For Nasir al-Said's comments in support of the seizure of the mosque in Mecca, see "Saudi Opposition Leader: 'The Mosque Incident Was Part of a People's Revolution,'" *MERIP Reports*, no. 85 (February 1980), pp. 16–18. In late 1979, reports circulated that Nasir al-Said had been abducted from Beirut and killed. The Saudis have denied any role in his disappearance.

4. The only verifiable challenge to the regime from the armed forces took place in 1969 when a number of dissident air force officers plotted to overthrow Faisal. The plot was uncovered early, the conspirators arrested, and some were subsequently allowed to return to civilian life. More recent reports, such as those circulated in the *International Currency Review*, vol. 11, no. 6 (1980), pp. 51–67; and in the *London Currency Report*, December 17, 1979, seem to be primarily disinformation.

5. The Utaiba tribe consists of two main branches, the Rawaqah and the Burqa. During Abd al-Aziz's rise to power, he was opposed by the Burqa faction of the Utaiba. Juhayman, however, came from the Rawaqah branch, and his father had supported Abd al-Aziz. The best press accounts of the Mecca incident are found in the *New York Times*, February 25, 1980, and the *Financial Times* (London), April 28, 1980.

Juhayman had a checkered and undistinguished past until 1972, when he entered the Medina theological college and initially came under the influence of Shaykh bin Baz, the rector of the college until King Faisal eased him out of that position. There, Juhayman's intelligence and strength of personality drew students, including non-Saudis, to him. As he gained a following, he began to challenge some of the accepted theological interpretations, using alternative bodies of tradition (*sunna*) to question many aspects of Saudi society, including the compatibility of monarchical rule with Islamic precepts.

By the mid-1970s Juhayman and his group of Salafiyya, or reformers, were openly preaching in mosques for a strict adherence to Islam, a repudiation of Western ways, an end to education for women, and other inflammatory topics. They were easily recognized by the long beards they wore in sharp contrast to typical Saudi style. In June 1978 Juhayman and ninety-eight of his followers were arrested. But after brief detention they were released under pressure from the Ulama, especially Shaykh bin Baz, who saw them as misguided but nonetheless sincere Muslims who should not be persecuted for their beliefs.

With the Islamic revolution in neighboring Iran in 1978–79, the Saudi rulers were more worried by Khomeini's challenge than by their own homegrown fundamentalists. Each year the pilgrimage brings a million or more foreign Muslims to Saudi Arabia.[6] The security services are stretched to the breaking point during this period, and in 1979 there was particular concern that followers of Khomeini would cause trouble during the pilgrimage. As a result, little attention was directed to Juhayman and his followers. Without much notice from the Saudi authorities, they began to print pamphlets in Kuwait, to purchase arms from sources in Saudi Arabia, and to plan for a dramatic act to symbolize their protest, which would coincide with the beginning of the new Islamic year.

On November 20, 1979, Juhayman and 225 of his followers, heavily armed and well-provisioned, seized control of the Grand Mosque in Mecca. The Saudi leadership was caught by surprise. Crown Prince Fahd was in Tunis at a meeting of the Arab League. For days confusion reigned and rumors abounded. The government said little in public, which added to the mystery surrounding the events.

As soon as the mosque was seized, the Saudi leadership sought the support of the Ulama for using force to break the siege. The Ulama

6. David Edwin Long, *The Hajj Today*, p. i.

agreed but set conditions that would limit damage to the mosque and would minimize casualties, especially among the many hostages being held.

With these strictures guiding their efforts, elements of the Saudi police, national guard, and regular armed forces all entered the fray.[7] They found a dedicated, well-armed, and fanatical group opposing them. The mosque itself provided excellent cover. Short of destroying the structure, the Saudis were obliged to fight room by room to gain control.

The process of containing, then eliminating, the Mecca threat tells something about Saudi capabilities and attitudes. First, there was indisputably an intelligence failure. The group was known but was not taken seriously. Its plans for Mecca were not detected. Second, the Saudis moved slowly to crush the challenge, partly because of the setting but also because of uncertain leadership. Third, the Saudis feared that Mecca might be part of a larger plot, including a threat to the oil fields. Key military units were rushed to the Eastern Province and to Medina, where no disturbances actually took place. Fourth, the initial assumption among Saudis was that the group was foreign, or at least foreign-inspired. In fact, after intensive interrogation of the survivors, the Saudis concluded that no foreign government was implicated.

During the two weeks the incident dragged on, life in Jidda, Riyadh, and other major population centers continued much as normal. Security forces were not particularly in evidence. Saudis discussed the Mecca affair and were irritated with their government for withholding information and for misleading public opinion, but there were no demonstrations of solidarity with the Mecca insurgents. For some who shared his dissatisfaction with developments in Saudi Arabia, Juhayman made an unforgiveable mistake in using force to seize the Grand Mosque. Such sacrilege did much to undermine his proclaimed religiosity and sincerity and that of his followers.

In the end the Mecca affair was a shock to the Saudi establishment, tarnishing its prestige internationally and leading to a spate of stories about instability in Saudi Arabia. Following Mecca, there was a bit of

7. Shortly after the Mecca affair Fahd referred in an interview to the fact that his full brothers Princes Sultan and Nayif were in charge at Mecca. He made no mention of Abdallah and the role of the national guard, which apparently did not perform well in the first few days. See Fahd interview with Salim al-Lawzi in *Al-Hawadith*, January 11, 1980, in FBIS, *Daily Report: Middle East and North Africa*, January 15, 1980, p. C7.

soul-searching, some talk of cracking down on corruption,[8] and a revival of the oft-mentioned plan to form a Consultative Council (*Majlis al-Shura*). The governor of Mecca, an ineffectual man in any case, along with a few senior military officers, was removed from his position.[9] Greater deference was paid to conservative social strictures, and the new Five-Year Plan was designed to emphasize social investments rather than new massive construction projects. But more than a year after Mecca little of consequence had changed. There was no Consultative Council. Power remained in the same hands. And Mecca was generally viewed in retrospect by the Saudi leadership as an isolated incident of little importance.

Shiites: A Repressed Minority

Somewhat more alarming to many Saudis than the Mecca incident were the disturbances by Shiites in Qatif in late 1979 and early 1980. Shiites are concentrated in the Eastern Province, especially around the Al-Hasa Oasis.[10] Numbering some 200,000 to 300,000, the Shiites have often been treated as second-class citizens by the Wahhabi rulers, many of whom have shown antipathy for Shiites on religious grounds.[11]

The Iranian Revolution and Khomeini's incessant call for uprisings in the name of (Shiite) Islam inevitably had some effect on the Shiites

8. The *New York Times*, April 16, 1980, carried a long article by Philip Taubman on corruption in Saudi Arabia. Fahd's son, Muhammad ibn Fahd, was prominently mentioned for his well-known role in the telecommunications contract that netted him at least $100 million. Adnan Khashoggi, a very wealthy businessman, was also noted, and shortly thereafter the Saudis informed foreign firms that they should not make use of Khashoggi's services when bidding for contracts.

9. Fawwaz ibn Abd al-Aziz, the governor of Mecca, had been one of the Free Princes who had gone to Cairo in the early 1960s and had subsequently been reintegrated. He was not viewed as an effective governor, however.

10. See F. S. Vidal, *The Oasis of Al-Hasa*.

11. The Wahhabi hostility toward Shiites should be understood as part of a more general antipathy toward *shirk* (the association of anyone or anything with God). See Christine Moss Helms, *The Cohesion of Saudi Arabia*, pp. 82–84, 95–102. In practice the Saudi rulers generally tolerated the Shiite community as long as it did not cause problems or engage in offensive religious rituals in public. Persecutions in the 1920s, however, led to some migration of Shiites from the Eastern Province. It is striking to find Crown Prince Fahd's seeming tolerance in 1980 in calling for an Islam without denominations, to be defined through discussions with Sunni and Shiite Ulama. Interview with Talal Salman in *As-Safir* (Beirut), January 9, 1980, in FBIS, *Daily Report: Middle East and North Africa*, January 16, 1980, p. C25.

of Saudi Arabia. On two occasions violence flared in Qatif on a significant scale. The Saudi National Guard was not particularly subtle in its
application of force. Some Saudis, however, urged a more accommodating policy, emphasizing social and economic reforms. There was talk of
naming a new governor for the Eastern Province, but no immediate
action was taken.[12]

In late 1980, however, King Khalid visited the area and met with
delegations of Shiites. During the often tense month of Muharram,
there was no repetition of Shiite agitation in 1980 as there had been the
preceding year.[13] Nonetheless, pressures for change from the Shiites
will continue, and external events, especially those in Iran, will have a
direct bearing on developments in the Eastern Province.

Potential Problems

Saudi Arabia, like many states in the developing world, faces a stag-
gering number of internal and external problems in the years ahead.
But on at least some counts the Saudis are more fortunate than most.
With foreign exchange earnings in 1980 of more than $100 billion,
Saudi Arabia had a per capita annual income of over $20,000. While
Saudi leaders will have choices to make concerning the distribution and
investment of this vast wealth, they will be spared the more common
economic difficulties of third world countries. It may be fashionable to
talk of the destabilizing effects of too much money, but few would
trade the dilemmas of wealth for the burdens of poverty.

Oil revenues will be the main Saudi instrument for meeting the challenges of the 1980s. Social problems will be subjected to the solvent of
money. Political support, if not loyalty, will be sought by distributing

12. The governor of the Eastern Province has traditionally been from the Jiluwi
branch of the Saud family. The governor at the time of the 1979–80 disturbances was
Abd al-Muhsin ibn Jiluwi, widely regarded as a weak man who has done little for
his constituents. In 1981 Crown Prince Fahd was named head of a special committee
to oversee the expenditure of some 1 billion riyals on development projects in the
Eastern Province.

13. During 1980 high-level Saudi officials spent considerable time in the Shiite
areas investigating grievances. They concluded that the Shiites felt neglected, were
reluctant to accept loans from the government, and disliked the governor of the
province. Before the Shiite holy month of Muharram 1980, the authorities released
Shiite prisoners who had been held since the earlier disturbances in return for promises of good behavior. The unpopular Amir of Qatif was also replaced.

wealth. Arms, advisers, and even soldiers can be bought from abroad. Scientists, workers, technicians, and teachers can all be hired. The enmity of adversaries may be softened by generous doses of aid. American protection may be secured against Soviet pressures by adroit use of oil diplomacy.

Not all Saudi problems, however, can be handled by flooding them in petrodollars. What, then, are the issues most likely to tax the capabilities of the Saudi political system, and what are the chances that the regime will be able to survive the decade of the 1980s?

Leadership and Succession

First there is the question of whether the royal family can continue to provide acceptable leadership for the country. The Al Saud has been the backbone of the political system. It is a large clan, with as many as 5,000 male members. It has produced strong leaders, as well as many incompetents. But the quality of those in positions of power has generally been impressive. The family's instinct for survival has led to a weeding out of the least able of the princes from the hierarchy of power, often relegating them to the less prestigious task of making money.

One danger the Saud dynasty faces is internal divisions. To date the family has managed its internal problems, such as the Saud-to-Faisal transition, with noteworthy skill. Conflicts and factions have clearly existed, but they have not been allowed to weaken the hold of the family on the reins of power. Only rarely have senior princes criticized each other in public—the Free Princes episode in the early 1960s, involving several of the sons of Abd al-Aziz criticizing the regime from Cairo, being the exception—and there is little reason to expect that whatever differences may exist between Fahd, Abdallah, and Sultan, for example, will lead to sharp internecine struggles.

Of all the potentially divisive issues in the family, that of succession to the kingship is the most dangerous. No Islamic monarchy has successfully worked out rules of succession. Historically, this has often meant that the death of a king opened an era of uncertainty. No claimant to the throne enjoyed automatic support simply because of age or kinship ties. Instead, a ruler would have to win the support of powerful groups to establish his legitimacy as monarch. And just as consent of the senior members of the family and the Ulama could provide legitimacy, the withdrawal of that consent could bring down a monarch, as with King Saud in 1964.

Having been through the unpleasant episode with Saud, today's senior princes have tried to reach agreement on the next stages of succession. The current presumption is that the order of succession should be set by seniority among the sons of Abd al-Aziz. Upon Faisal's death, Muhammad, who had waived his right to rule, was skipped over, and the next eldest son, Crown Prince Khalid, became king. Fahd, the next eldest, became crown prince and deputy prime minister in charge of day-to-day governing.

Few question that Fahd will become king after Khalid, but it took some time for the family to agree that Abdallah would follow Fahd. That has now been decided, but Sultan's position in line after Abdallah remains uncertain.[14]

Barring an unforeseeable dramatic development, the sons of Abd al-Aziz should still be ruling Saudi Arabia through the 1980s. But at some point in the 1990s power will inevitably pass to a younger generation. This could be the moment of interfamilial quarrels over succession. There will be many plausible claimants among the grandsons of Abd al-Aziz and perhaps from collateral branches of the family, such as the Saud al-Kabir. Faisal's sons are among the best educated and most experienced, but their position is only as strong as the support they can find within the family and among the power centers of the country. If there is a risk of interfamilial rivalries weakening the regime, it is more likely to occur when power passes from one generation to the next, not while Fahd, Abdallah, Sultan, and a few of the other older sons of Abd al-Aziz are still alive.

Social Problems: Students, Foreign Workers, Western Influences

If splits in the family are unlikely to be the cause of the Al Saud's undoing in the 1980s, what are the main dangers? Some would argue that social unrest, exacerbated by rapid economic change, could have revolutionary consequences, as occurred in Iran. After all, tens of thousands of young Saudis are studying abroad and are being exposed to new, possibly dangerous, ideas.[15] They can hardly all be expected to return

14. Sultan's claim based on age to be next in line for the kingship after Abdallah has been challenged by Abd al-Muhsin and Mishal, sons of Abd al-Aziz, both of whom have asserted that they are as old as Sultan.

15. An investigation of the effect on young Saudis of studying in the United States indicates that the most noticeable change of attitude is a somewhat more positive view of the role of women in society. See Abdullah Saleh Al-Banyan, *Saudi Students in the United States.*

to the carefully controlled Saudi environment without feeling deep frustrations. In career terms, they are likely to be as qualified as many who are in power, but they will find fewer opportunities for advancement within the bureaucracy. Not all of them will be content with the alternative of making money. Some will agitate for more political participation.[16] For the moment there is little for politically minded Saudis to look forward to other than jobs in the bureaucracy and opportunities to become rich in the private sector. Political parties and public debate are virtually unthinkable, leaving the discussion of political issues confined to small groups of friends and family members. While it is difficult to detect deep-seated unrest with the current restrictive political environment, one can assume a high level of frustration among some sections of the population.

Another source of social tensions is likely to be the large community of foreign workers, numbering some 1.5 million to 2 million in 1980. The largest group consists of Yemenis, between 500,000 and 750,000 workers, who fill the lowest ranks of the labor force. Most seem apolitical, but they are nonetheless closely watched by Saudi security forces. No serious incidents have been reported. But if South Yemen, for example, were ever to decide on a concerted policy of subversion against Saudi Arabia, the large Yemeni work force could provide useful cover for its agents.

Apart from the Yemenis, Egyptians and Palestinians fill important posts in education and the bureaucracy. They tend to be of middle-class origins and are generally careful not to engage in political action. They nonetheless represent currents of opinion found elsewhere in the Arab world, some of which may be considerably more nationalistic and secular than the official Saudi ideology. On balance, however, there is little reason to fear the destabilizing presence of these skilled Arab workers.

The Westerners in Saudi Arabia probably constitute the most socially disruptive community. Formerly concentrated in the ARAMCO compound near Dhahran and the diplomatic enclave in Jidda, Americans and Europeans can now be found in large numbers in Riyadh as well. Some 40,000 Americans live in Saudi Arabia, many still with ARAMCO, but others as military advisers and technicians and many as businessmen.

In recent years the Saudis have gone to great lengths to keep the Western presence from being particularly visible—women cannot work

16. This is the theme of "Poor Little Rich Nation: Open Letter to Saudi Arabia," by Hayyan ibn Bayyan (pseud.), in *The Nation*, April 4, 1981.

or drive, Christian religious services cannot be held openly, pictures of unveiled Western women are not allowed in Saudi publications—but nonetheless the signs of Westernization are everywhere. Video cassette recorders have flourished, allowing Saudis to see Western films in the privacy of their homes that could never be seen in public or on Saudi television. Western fashions have made their way to Saudi Arabia, and strong pressures can be expected from the younger generation, especially from women, to relax the strictures on veiling. The consumption of alcohol in private is substantial but is totally forbidden in public. It is this gap between public morality, which is strictly defined by Saudi religious authorities, and private behavior, sharply influenced by Western habits, that lends such an air of unreality to Saudi life. Hypocrisy is probably more frequently decried by Saudis than financial corruption. The double standard provides conservatives with a target. Those who seized the Grand Mosque in Mecca were also vehemently opposed to the creeping Westernization of Saudi Arabia, including education for women and the large American community in the country.

Even Saudis who have lived in the West often seem to resent the intrusion of Western values into Saudi society. Thus an issue exists, exacerbated by the size and visibility of the Western community, which is ripe for exploitation by religious conservatives. Part of the Saudi opposition to American bases in their country stems from their unwillingness to play host to many more thousands of Americans.

Although the presence of so many foreigners in Saudi Arabia does appear to create social tensions, foreign workers are indispensable to the Saudi economy. Increasingly the Saudis are turning to non-Arab, non-Western workers, especially Koreans, Pakistanis, and Filipinos, to do semiskilled jobs. They are apolitical, work hard, and do not seek to remain in the kingdom. For all the problems the foreigners cause the Saudis, however, it is not from this sector that the regime need feel directly threatened.

The Military

This leaves one remaining source of potential danger to the regime, the military establishment. Middle East history is littered with examples of monarchies that have been threatened or toppled by the armed forces. This occurred in Egypt in 1952, Iraq in 1958, and Libya in 1969 and there were nearly successful coup attempts in Jordan in 1957 and in

Morocco in 1970 and 1971. But Saudi Arabia has never experienced a serious challenge from the military, with the exception of an amateurish conspiracy in the air force in 1969.[17] Is Saudi Arabia immune from the Middle Eastern disease of politicized military officers seeking power?

Part of the Saudi success in avoiding military coups stems from an acute awareness of the danger. The royal family has gone to great lengths to keep control over the Saudi armed forces, often by taking measures that do little to enhance the capabilities of the Saudi military. For example, until the mid-1960s Saudi Arabia spent little on its armed forces. Several parallel military units were formed, including royal guards to protect the king, a national guard for internal security, an army, air force, and small navy to deter external aggression, and border guards to deal with minor incursions across the borders. Each component had its own command structure, generally linked to different members of the royal family. Senior officers were usually drawn from the Saud family, with rewards for loyalty more than for competence. The national guard in particular was largely composed of tribal units that had shown loyalty to the Al Saud. Armored forces were kept far away from the main cities.

The withdrawal of British forces from the Persian Gulf in 1971, the rapid arming of Iran, and doubts about American power combined in the 1970s to convince the Saudis that they needed to modernize their archaic military structure. After 1973 oil wealth made it possible to purchase the most sophisticated equipment and to create the physical infrastructure for a modern armed force. Modernization also entailed advanced training for Saudi officers, with increasing attention being paid to technical competence.

After a decade of military modernization the Saudis entered the 1980s with very modest armed forces. The army consisted of about 30,000 men, the air force about 14,000, and the navy only 2,000. The national guard totaled some 20,000, but only four battalions had been modernized, with four more planned for 1982–85.

The inventory of equipment for the armed forces was impressive, although not startling by regional standards. (See appendix F.) But the Saudis had not yet taken the step of fundamentally reorganizing the armed forces to enhance combat capabilities. The old habit of building

17. See two leftist accounts, based on secondary sources, of Saudi opposition groups, including the 1969 plot by Nasserite officers: Fred Halliday, *Arabia Without Sultans*, pp. 47–78; and Helen Lackner, *A House Built on Sand*.

in checks and balances persisted, and political considerations continued to prevail over standards of military rationality. The result was that the military posed little immediate challenge to the regime, but it also provided little security to the country in the event of external aggression or even serious domestic problems.

The danger in this situation is that Saudi officers will in time become frustrated by the political constraints imposed on them. They will demand more authority, more autonomy, and the logic of managing a complex modern military establishment will be on their side. They will insist on more professional training, more exercises, more coordination among the various security branches. If the political authorities are recalcitrant, they will be blamed for neglecting the security of the country. If they acquiesce, they will be placing power in the hands of men whose corporate interests and identity may lead eventually to intervention in politics, as has occurred everywhere else in the Middle East.

There is nothing inevitable about a military coup in Saudi Arabia. In fact, the regime has a number of strategies available for reducing the risks. But the military is bound to be taken seriously by the senior members of the family, and a complex political game will surround the Saudi military buildup. The Saudi leader who can best identify himself with the military will be in a strong position of influence on many foreign policy issues. Pressures from the military will be difficult to resist, particularly demands for sophisticated weapons. In time, the logic of military modernization will have created a nucleus of army and air force officers who will have the capability to seize power for themselves. Whether they will be tempted to do so or not is impossible to answer, but one can be certain that the Saudi military will play a growing role in the shaping of Saudi foreign policy.[18] At a minimum they will constitute an influential interest group seeking arms, prestige, and influence. Less probable but still possible would be a bid by young officers for power, perhaps in support of one or another faction of the royal family. If the United States is unable or unwilling to provide Saudi Arabia with the military equipment and technology it seeks, the armed forces can be expected to become advocates of closer ties to European countries at the expense of the U.S.-Saudi "special relationship."

In brief, the military will push the political leadership to advance

18. Serious problems could arise if the political leadership were to order the military into some action that exceeded Saudi capabilities. A humiliated armed forces could turn on the politicians, as occurred in Egypt in 1952.

Saudi security interests, to use Saudi oil wealth to strengthen the military, and to enhance Saudi prestige as an independent and powerful Middle East country. If the political leadership fails to respond to their desires, there is some possibility that professional officers, encouraged perhaps by religious conservatives and restless technocrats, will seek power for themselves or will take sides in an interfamilial dispute, perhaps throwing their weight behind the younger, more nationalistic princes. If a unifying theme is needed, the defense of Islamic values against corruption and excessive Western influence would find a wide appeal in the country.

Prospects for Stability

In politics the concept of "stability" can mean both the absence of abrupt change and predictability. In these terms Saudi Arabia appears to be a poor candidate for stability in the 1980s. Change will certainly continue, no doubt with some surprising consequences, and Saudi policies will not be fully predictable.

Nonetheless, it would be a serious mistake to see Saudi Arabia as fundamentally unstable. The kingdom will almost certainly not experience the kind of revolutionary upheaval that swept Iran in 1979. Nor is a change of leadership likely to produce the kind of sharp foreign policy reversals witnessed in Egypt when power passed from Nasser to Sadat.

Rather than try to classify Saudi Arabia as inherently stable or unstable, or to force artificial comparisons with other countries, it seems to make more sense to analyze the kinds of internal and external developments that could produce significant changes in Saudi foreign policy. In particular, under what circumstances might Saudi Arabia move sharply away from the United States toward nonalignment? What, if anything, might lead Saudi Arabia to an aggressive policy of using oil as a weapon against the West?

First, it is important to note that policy shifts toward nonalignment and the use of the oil weapon could take place without a political upheaval in Saudi Arabia. Indeed, they might be part of the regime's strategy to defuse domestic discontent with the traditionally pro-Western tilt of Saudi policy. Still, the likelihood of major discontinuities in policy would increase with a change of top-level leadership.

Leadership changes in the 1980s will certainly take place, but probably not because of serious disputes within the royal family. The most difficult problems would occur if Fahd or one of his brothers were to try to rule without consulting the rest of the family, or when the younger generation, the grandsons of Abd al-Aziz, begin to contend for the top positions of power.

If the family is unlikely to split, can it be overthrown? Because of its size and its involvement with key sectors of society, the Saud family will not be easily ousted from power. Mass uprisings on the Iranian model seem highly unlikely, even though widespread discontent may exist.

If revolution is ruled out, what about the more common Middle East phenomenon, the military coup? No one can be sure where the reform-minded majors and colonels may be in the Saudi armed forces. The regime shows signs of being aware of the dangers from this quarter, and elaborate measures are taken to keep the military out of politics. Still, the means for seizing power do exist within the armed forces. And some pretext could easily be found or manufactured to make a coup appear to be a patriotic or religious duty.

The military coup, then, must be taken seriously as a threat to the Saudi regime. But it is not inevitable. Its probability would increase if there were prolonged factional fighting within the family; if corruption and hypocrisy generated widespread political discontent; or if the armed forces were humiliated in battle with a neighboring country.

With these points in mind, one should resist the temptation to try to predict how long the Saudi regime will remain in power. Suffice it to say that the regime will be obligated to change, to adapt, and to improvise if it is to continue. Deference will have to be shown to the nationalistic views of the young, the educated, and the technocrats. The military will have an important voice in Saudi politics. And the traditional pillars of the system, the tribes, the Ulama, and the family elders, will also have to be accommodated.

Unfortunately for the United States, any Saudi regime in the 1980s will from time to time feel obliged to show its independence of Washington, especially if American policies in the region are seen as hostile to Arab and Islamic interests. Virtually any regime will also ask for arms, while most likely refusing to offer military facilities to the United States. This will inevitably cause some strains in the relationship.

With respect to oil production and pricing, no regime is likely to be much more cooperative than Saudi Arabia under Khalid and Fahd has been. If anything, another leadership would probably cut production somewhat and be less restrained on prices, but the range of choice is limited even here.

In conclusion, stability in the sense of no change in the basic makeup of the political system seems to be a reasonably good bet for the coming years, at least until the mid-1980s. By the 1990s, pressures for substantial changes can be expected, and Saudi leaders will doubtless respond in some fashion. It would be rash, however, to predict the demise of the Saud family entirely anytime in the indefinite future.

Nonetheless, stability in the sense of unchanging policies cannot be assumed. Strong pressures exist on Saudi Arabia to move toward a non-aligned nationalistic posture. This can be offset to some degree by effective American and Western diplomacy, but the pressures themselves are unlikely to subside. What their effect will be may depend as much on what happens in Washington as on decisions made in Riyadh.

In short, unless the United States succeeds in developing a coherent and consistent Middle East policy, one should not expect consistency or predictability from Saudi Arabia. The impact of American policy is as much an uncertainty in assessing Saudi stability as any of the other elements in the equation, and it is also one beyond Saudi control. Little wonder that the Saudis feel vulnerable and ambivalent about their ties to Washington.

Chapter Seven

The Ingredients of Decision: Recent History

SAUDI FOREIGN POLICY decisions are made by a small group in private and with little public discussion or explanation. Nothing in Saudi political culture encourages open debate of issues, least of all those touching on the country's security. No concept of public accountability exists. Even when someone is removed from office for incompetence or mistakes, there is rarely any account of the reasons. "Poor health" is offered as the excuse for any number of personnel changes, and no one, of course, pays much heed to such declarations.

Secrecy breeds a heavy dose of skepticism, even cynicism, among some Saudis and the kingdom's critics in the Arab world. Rumors abound. Lack of evidence is never a conclusive reason for rejecting an interpretation. Political discourse is filled with wildly conspiratorial interpretations of events.

Amid all this the Saudi public stance is Sphinx-like, or at best defensive. The veil is rarely lifted on the inner workings of the family. Those who try to penetrate the inner sanctum are viewed as enemies, and those who talk too freely are seen as unfriendly, if not dangerous. Quite simply, Saudi leaders believe it is no one's business how decisions are made. This is literally a family matter. Inquisitive foreigners are dismissed as dangerous gossips, perhaps agents, and Saudi citizens know better than to pry.[1]

At best, secrecy helps to preserve a facade of family unity. It could even encourage frank discussion of issues in the knowledge that the outside world will not learn of discord. And in the conduct of foreign policy it is not, after all, wise to advertise all one's intentions and maneuvers. So secrecy has its defenders. But it also allows failures and mistakes

---

1. The Saudi reaction to the film *Death of a Princess* revealed this extreme sensitivity.

to pass unnoticed or unpunished. It creates an apathetic public and alienates much of the bureaucracy. It feeds the culture of conspiracy and manipulation that pervades Middle East politics. And it leads to a strong sense of frustration among educated Saudis who want to participate in the political life of the country.

Consultation and Consensus

Despite the veil of secrecy, it seems as if the time-honored principles of consultation and consensus are still practiced in Saudi decision-making, at least on some issues. Faisal probably felt less need to consult and could count on shaping the family consensus in foreign policy matters, but his successors, lacking his authority and good judgment, have been obliged to spend more time discussing issues, letting time pass until the senior members of the family have come to terms.

The process has its drawbacks. It can be slow. It can produce results that represent a lowest common denominator. It is not well-designed for the rapid tempo of crises. It places a premium on interpersonal relations, not the merits of a policy position. But in the Saudi context, some of these drawbacks may be strengths. Politics is a highly personalized affair, and the unity of the family is the key to the survival of the Al Saud. Consultation ensures that the various factions in the family, as well as some outsiders, feel they have a stake in the system. If key persons are not given a hearing, they may go public with their grievances, as occurred with the "Free Princes" in the early 1960s. This is not only embarrassing. It can be politically risky.

Consultation and consensus are probably better adapted to dealing with internal Saudi matters than to foreign policy. In the international arena, the Saudi style of making decisions is often slow, reactive rather than assertive, elliptical rather than direct. This leads foreign powers to misread Saudi intentions on occasion. It also produces expectations that Saudi positions can be altered by pressures or inducements. Most important, it tends to preclude a strong position of leadership for Saudi Arabia in the Arab and Islamic contexts where decisive, forceful expression of policies would be more respected than the cautious Saudi style.

What happens if there is no readily discernible consensus? Then, it seems, there is a propensity to defer, delay, and avoid issues, or at best to straddle them by taking positions that appear to be self-contradictory. For more than a decade, for example, Saudi leaders have talked of instituting a Consultative Council, but it has never been clear what the council would do or who would participate. These are potentially controversial issues. They require positive answers. In practice it has been easier to delay. Commissions have been formed, reports written, predictions of imminent action made, and yet nothing has resulted from all this. Some day such a council will perhaps be formed, but only after the key figures in Saudi Arabia have been assured that it poses no threat to their power. By the time it sees the light of day, it is virtually certain to have been rendered powerless. In brief, the current system holds little promise of broadened political participation.

Other controversial issues lead to a denial that any problem exists. For example, many foreigners have been concerned about the vulnerability of Saudi oil fields to sabotage or attack. When asked, most Saudis will avoid the issue. In private they may acknowledge that they are worried, but since no easy solution can be found, a public stance of denial is adopted. This has the virtue, perhaps, of not advertising one's vulnerabilities and not alarming the Saudi public, but it may also have the effect of preventing serious discussion of the issue altogether.[2]

Indecision and Principled Stands

The net effect of the Saudi style of making decisions is to rob the leadership of the capacity for decisive, sustained leadership in foreign policy. The Saudis are more likely to react to events, to launch trial balloons, to temporize when controversial issues arise, and to panic in crises. Since systematic contingency planning is almost antithetical to the Saudi style, crises can produce a sudden reaction that reveals the Saudi sense of vulnerability. When South Yemen attacked border positions in North Yemen in early 1979, the Saudis demanded American action on a

2. Before the outbreak of the Iran-Iraq war there was little protection of the oil fields. Thereafter, two Saudi National Guard battalions were sent to Dhahran, where permanent quarters for them were being built. In addition, hardened shelters for Saudi Air Force F-5Es and F-15s were being built at Dhahran air base by 1981.

large scale. Again, when Iran and Iraq went to war in September 1980, the king and Crown Prince Fahd asked for rapid American assistance. Once the immediate sense of danger receded, in both cases the regime reverted to a posture of relative unconcern and detachment. In neither case were the Saudis able to develop sustained initiatives to deal with these threats on their doorsteps.

When crises occur further afield and the risks seem more manageable, the Saudis are better able to function effectively to shape events. For example, recurring problems in Lebanon may find the Saudis quietly trying to patch together face-saving compromises liberally laced with financial inducements. This discreet role of consensus building is much more congenial to the Saudis than overt displays of leadership or highly visible personal diplomacy. There is no prospect for a Saudi version of Egyptian President Sadat's unilateral decision to travel to Jerusalem to make peace with his Israeli enemies in the full blaze of publicity.

This tentativeness and caution produces a certain disconnectedness in Saudi foreign policy. Issues come and go with a degree of unpredictability. Suddenly requests may be made for urgent decisions on long-standing military requests. Just as suddenly an issue may drop from the agenda. Expectations may be raised that the Saudis are on the verge of using their financial muscle to produce some diplomatic coup, then nothing may happen for months. One day rumors will abound that the Saudis have received assurances that the PLO will accept UN Security Council Resolution 242, with its implied recognition of Israel's legitimacy as part of an overall Arab-Israeli peace settlement, and then the PLO reiterates its normal policy of rejection. Vague promises may be made that the Saudis will use their moderating influence at the next Arab summit, and then the resulting resolutions turn out to be as extreme as ever.

Americans and Arabs who complain about such Saudi behavior will receive a withering rebuttal, often replete with a full account of their own deficiencies. The Saudis will point to the quiet, subtle transformations that have taken place in the Arab world as a result of their patient efforts. They deplore the Western desire for public relations coups, preferring the low-key, patient pattern of diplomacy. They profess to take a long view, rather than trying to achieve instant success. Self-assured and sometimes self-righteous, they do not take kindly to criticism of their foreign policy.

To their credit, the Saudis have been guided by several constant principles, even if their day-to-day application may raise questions. And many critics have indeed been unfair to the Saudis, who after all do not constitute a superpower with unlimited capabilities. For most of the past decade or two the Saudi regime has repeatedly warned that the Arab-Israeli conflict was dangerous, explosive, and urgently needed U.S. diplomatic efforts to defuse it. Jerusalem has also been consistently mentioned by the Saudis as a top priority concern in any Arab-Israeli accommodation. The Saudis have repeatedly warned that the Soviets will seek to extend their influence in the Middle East by manipulating local conflicts, first and foremost the Palestinian issue. In addition the Saudis have often argued that oil supplies from the gulf cannot be taken for granted by the West. Reliable oil supplies, they have maintained, require a certain type of political and security environment in the region and an adequate pricing formula. They have pointed to reduced consumption in the West as the key to moderate oil prices. Whether one agrees with the Saudis or not on these various points, one can hardly accuse them of not making their views known and sticking to them.

This suggests that on the level of broad principles one can expect considerable continuity and predictability in Saudi policies. Problems arise in translating principles into concrete actions. Here the particular characteristics of Saudi decisionmaking are likely to produce delays, equivocation, ambiguity, defensiveness, and a lack of follow-through. Much of this is attributable to the uncertainties of the Saudi foreign policy environment. Some of it is deeply rooted in the political culture.

The Arab-Israeli Conflict

To hear the Saudis talk about their foreign policy, no issue is of greater importance than the Palestinian question. On a symbolic level the cause of the Palestinians has acquired centrality in Arab, Islamic, and third world contexts. The Saudis, who seek to play an important role in each of these arenas, inevitably become champions of the Palestinians. At a pragmatic level the Saudis see the perpetuation of the Arab-Israeli conflict as dangerous to their own security, primarily because of the effect of the dispute on regional instability and radicalization. Finally, as

Arabs and Muslims, the Saudis genuinely view Zionism as a particularly unacceptable form of Western colonialism. In their eyes the Palestinian issue is a clear case of right versus wrong.

Up until the early 1970s the Saudis had remained comparatively aloof from the Arab-Israeli conflict, limiting their role to statements of principle and subsidies to some of the Arab participants in the struggle.[3] The October 1973 war brought the Saudis directly into the arena as they took the lead first in wielding the "oil weapon" on behalf of the Arabs, then in ending the embargo in spring 1974. Thereafter the Saudis remained on the sidelines of Kissinger's "shuttle diplomacy," encouraging American initiatives but playing little role in shaping the substance of any of the three disengagement negotiations that emerged in 1974 and 1975.

The Saudis were not particularly pleased with the results of Kissinger's efforts, especially the Sinai II agreement of September 1975. This latter accord caused a breach in Arab ranks, placing Egypt and Syria at odds. Caught between Sadat and Assad, the Saudis felt acutely uncomfortable. Sadat was the most moderate Egyptian leader the Saudis could hope for, and yet he was unpredictable and prone to act unilaterally. Assad was also a vast improvement in Saudi eyes over his predecessors, and the Saudis were reluctant to side with either Cairo or Damascus as the dispute widened. Instead, in late 1976 the Saudis sought to heal the breach in an uncharacteristic display of Saudi political and financial muscle.

In November 1976 the Saudis invited Sadat and Assad to Riyadh for a reconciliation meeting. Arab ranks were to be closed in preparation for dealing with the newly elected administration of Jimmy Carter. With Saudi urging, several important gains were made. The bloody civil

3. See, for example, Philby's account of King Abd al-Aziz's caution in the early 1930s upon being urged to play a more active role in resolving the Palestinian conflict: "His answer was characteristic of an attitude which, progressively developing from that day to this, has largely undermined the potential leadership and initiative in Arab affairs which might have been his, and has contributed to the present-day situation in which his unwillingness to take a decisive line of his own on matters of general concern to the Arab world outside his own sphere has relegated Sa'udi Arabia to a position of relative insignificance as an ordinary member of the Arab League, or of one of its mutually dissident camps . . . ; and he was already showing a tendency to become a middle-of-the-road man, unwilling to offend the British and other World Powers or to incur criticism from the Arab press or public opinion." H. StJ. B. Philby, *Arabian Jubilee*, p. 122.

war in Lebanon was brought to a temporary standstill, with Syria's dominant position being accepted. In return, Egypt and Syria called off their public quarrel and agreed to cooperate in any new Middle East peace initiative. As further incentive for the United States to adopt a balanced policy, the Saudis undertook to moderate price increases of oil at the next OPEC meeting in December.

The Carter administration responded positively to these Saudi moves. Carter sent a personal friend, John C. West, former governor of South Carolina, to Jidda as ambassador, thus assuring the Saudis of direct access to the White House. During the early months of the Carter administration, the Saudis were consulted on and informed of the policy of working for a comprehensive Arab-Israeli peace. Carter's willingness to grapple with the ticklish Palestinian issue was welcomed by the Saudis. Crown Prince Fahd visited the United States in late May 1977, and in subsequent months the Saudis worked to get the PLO to moderate its views so that Palestinians could join the negotiations.

By August 1977 the makings of a deal seemed near. If the PLO would accept UN Resolution 242, even with some reservations, the United States would begin official talks with PLO representatives. The Saudis were delighted at this prospect. But in the end the deal failed to materialize. The PLO, under heavy Syrian pressure, was unwilling to take the step of accepting the UN resolution. The Saudis felt embarrassed and betrayed but could do little to change the reality of the situation.

From September 1977 onward the Saudis watched with apprehension as the initially promising U.S. initiative came to a halt. The gap between the Syrian and Egyptian positions on reconvening Geneva grew large, and Saudi efforts were no longer enough to bridge the difference. Then, in early November the Saudis were caught by surprise as Sadat announced his intention of visiting Jerusalem to discuss Middle East peace directly with Israeli Prime Minister Menachem Begin. Sadat had neither consulted nor informed the Saudis of his plans. His willingness to meet the enemy in Jerusalem was particularly offensive to the Saudis.

As Sadat set off on his historic journey, the Saudis retreated to the sidelines to see what would come of this. Their fear was that Arab ranks would again be split, with Saudi Arabia caught in the middle. From a Saudi perspective a separate Egyptian-Israeli peace agreement would do little to reduce the instability of the area, nor would it help undercut Soviet power. On substance, the Saudis found themselves closer to the views of Syria, Jordan, and the Fatah wing of the PLO than to Egypt. Nonetheless, the Saudis did not immediately join with Sadat's critics. But they did become less active in trying to shape an Arab consensus with which the United States could deal effectively.[4]

During much of 1978 the Saudis hoped that Sadat would turn his initiative back toward a comprehensive Middle East peace. But they feared that under U.S. pressure and faced with Israeli intransigence he would settle for the return of Sinai. Rather than try to influence Sadat's policies the Saudis chose instead to concentrate on consolidating their military relationship with Washington by pressing for an early decision to sell them F-15 jet fighters. While this issue occupied center stage, Saudi interest in Arab-Israeli diplomacy seemed to flag.

Up until the Camp David summit meeting in September 1978, the Saudis continued to hope that Sadat would resist the temptation to strike a separate agreement with Israel. But the results of the summit confirmed their worst fears. Two unrelated agreements emerged. One dealt in detail with the Sinai. The other dealt in generalities with the Palestinian question, envisaging only a vaguely defined "autonomy" for the inhabitants of the West Bank and Gaza, not Israeli withdrawal from occupied territory.

American efforts to paint Camp David in a positive light were met with skepticism. While saying little in public, the Saudis expressed their disappointment in private. And pressures mounted to condemn Sadat and Camp David. The Saudis were caught between their friendship for Washington and their Arab commitments. Shortly before an Arab summit meeting scheduled for Baghdad in November 1978, a top Saudi official gave the impression to American officials that Saudi Arabia would prevent any harsh denunciation of Sadat or Camp David. Some read this to mean that Saudi Arabia would even support the negotiations and use influence to bring Jordan and the Palestinians into the process.

When the results of the Baghdad summit became known, American officials were furious at the Saudis. The communiqué condemned Sadat, Carter, and Camp David. Fahd had felt obliged to go along with tough rhetoric, managing only to prevent a complete break of economic and

4. During his brief visit to Riyadh in early January 1978, President Carter consulted with the Saudis on a formula supporting the right of the Palestinians "to participate in the determination of their own future," a phrase that came to be known as the Aswan formula and was eventually incorporated into the Camp David accords.

diplomatic relations with Egypt.[5] In their defense the Saudis argued that the results of the conference would have been much worse without Saudi influence, and that by remaining part of the Arab consensus the Saudis could hope to moderate opposition to U.S. policies in the future.

The simple lesson of Baghdad seemed to be that the Saudis, when forced to choose between their Arab commitments and a controversial U.S. policy such as the Camp David agreements, would not hesitate to side with the Arab position. American anger was of less concern than isolation in the Arab world over an issue as emotionally charged as the conflict with Israel.

U.S.-Saudi relations went through a rough period between the Baghdad summit in November 1978 and the conclusion of the Egypt-Israel peace treaty in March 1979. This coincided with the collapse of the shah's regime in Iran, an event that raised doubts in Saudi minds about the value of their American connection.

In a somewhat clumsy attempt to patch up relations, the Carter administration invited Fahd to Washington, but the date set was shortly after the signing of the Egypt-Israel treaty. Fahd, already sensitive about his pro-American reputation, wanted to avoid the implication that he endorsed the treaty. Thus the visit was canceled, with Fahd's health being mentioned in some circles as the reason. This led to articles in the American press that were highly unflattering to Fahd, and the Saudis assumed they were deliberately planted by the administration.[6]

Against this background the Arab League met to consider what actions to take against Sadat for his separate peace with Israel. Once again, some American officials clung to the hope that the Saudis would play a moderating role. This time the results were only slightly ambiguous. Saudi Arabia supported Egypt's expulsion from the Arab League and agreed to end diplomatic and economic relations with Cairo. But the Saudis did not agree to a total ban on contact with Egypt, nor would they cancel previous aid commitments. They would not expel Egyptian workers from Saudi Arabia or suspend airline services.

Saudi willingness to continue funding Egypt's purchase of fifty F-5E aircraft was of particular importance to the United States. The Saudis

5. According to one highly placed Saudi source, Yasir Arafat's behavior at the Baghdad summit was very aggressive toward Saudi Arabia. He reportedly talked of the PLO's responsibility for protecting the Islamic holy places and the pipelines—both within Saudi Arabia!

6. See James Hoagland, *Washington Post*, April 15, 1979.

had initially agreed to provide $300 million, then $525 million, to cover most of the costs of the program. Washington pressed for additional funds, and by late April 1979 agreement had been reached that Saudi Arabia would finance the bulk of Egypt's F-5E program. Then, on May 1, 1979, Sadat gave a major speech in which he viciously attacked Saudi Arabia and its leaders. This led the Saudis to withdraw their offer. The F-5E deal, which represented the only remaining Saudi aid program to Egypt, collapsed. America's two closest friends in the Arab world were no longer on speaking terms.

What lessons can one draw from the record of Saudi policy toward the Arab-Israeli conflict in recent years? First, the Saudis have not been very successful in getting their way. They were not able to use their financial leverage over the PLO to bring about a change in Palestinian policy toward peace with Israel. They were unable to mediate the differences between Egypt and Syria over the Geneva conference. They were unable to prevent Sadat from concluding a separate peace with Israel. They could not deter the United States from throwing its weight behind Sadat and Begin.

Second, the Saudis have clearly seen their interests best served by remaining part of the Arab consensus on the Palestinian issue. Whether by conviction or pragmatic calculation, they have chosen to stay in step with the other Arabs on this issue, even at the expense of straining relations with Washington and breaking entirely with Cairo.

Third, Saudi policy on the Palestinian issue went from an activist phase in 1976–77 to a more passive stance after Sadat's trip to Jerusalem. This suggests that Saudi Arabia is reluctant to try to exercise strong leadership on such a sensitive issue, especially when there is little prospect of shaping a common Arab position.

Fourth, the Saudis were unwilling to use the oil weapon in any overt way to try to influence U.S. policy on the Arab-Israeli conflict during this period. In 1976–77 the Saudis deliberately stuck to a moderate position in an attempt to win American favor. From late 1978 onward, when Iranian production dropped, the Saudis kept their output above 9.5 million barrels per day, except in spring 1979, when they cut production to 8.5 million bpd, perhaps to show their displeasure with the Egyptian-Israeli peace treaty. Saudi Arabia continued to charge somewhat lower prices for its oil than other OPEC members did throughout 1979–80. Although there may well have been good economic reasons for this behavior, the point to be made is that the Saudis did not regularly manipulate oil supplies in an attempt to influence U.S. policy toward the Arab-Israeli conflict. The 1973–74 experience, and perhaps the cutback of spring 1979, suggest that in extreme circumstances the Saudis will use oil as a political weapon, but generally they have shown a strong reluctance to engage in sustained attempts to pressure the West by withholding oil.

The F-15 Controversy

Beginning in the early 1970s the Saudis invited the United States to help draw up plans for the modernization of their military forces. At the time, the Saudi Air Force was small and ineffectual, consisting primarily of British Lightning interceptors.

The 1967 Arab-Israeli war, as well as the attrition campaign along the Suez Canal in 1969–70, had graphically demonstrated the importance of air power. The American-made Phantom F-4 acquired almost legendary status as the Israelis displayed the uses to which it could be put. The less dramatic performance of air forces in October 1973 did little to reduce the appetite of such newly rich potential consumers as the Saudis.

The United States initially tried to steer Saudi Arabia away from the offensively configured F-4, which the Saudis had shown interest in as early as 1967, recommending instead that they purchase the simpler F-5E fighter-bomber. The Saudis agreed, but with the expectation that the F-5E program would be a transition to a more sophisticated aircraft at a later date.

As a test of the Nixon-Kissinger commitment to Saudi Arabia in spring 1974, just as the oil embargo was ending, the Saudis urgently requested approval of the Phantom F-4. After considerable hand-wringing in Washington, approval in principle was granted. Having gained symbolic satisfaction, the Saudis never raised the F-4 issue again. Already they had their sights fixed on the new generation of U.S. combat aircraft—the F-14, F-15, F-16, and even the F-18, which was then only a concept on the drawing board.

A U.S. Air Force survey team reviewed all these aircraft with the Saudis. The F-14, purchased by the shah somewhat earlier, was too complex. The F-16 was attractive, but it was primarily designed for air-to-ground operations, and the Saudis preferred an interceptor to replace their aging Lightnings. The F-15 seemed to be the best plane for the task.[7]

While wrestling with the question of which plane to purchase to replace the Lightnings, the Saudis also sought to enhance the capabilities of the F-5Es by adding Sidewinder air-to-air missiles and Maverick air-to-ground missiles. The Ford administration approved the request, but in the face of strong congressional opposition the numbers were cut significantly below what the Saudis had sought. This was the first serious sign of congressional concern over Saudi arms purchases.

Toward the end of the Ford-Kissinger period the Saudis were told privately that the administration would agree to sell the Saudis the advanced aircraft of their choice—in other words, the F-15 or the F-16. But since 1976 was an election year the Saudis were urged not to press the issue further until after November. With this promise in hand, the Saudis hoped for President Gerald R. Ford's reelection. Instead, they were confronted with Jimmy Carter and his fervid advocacy of arms control.

During most of 1977 the Saudis concentrated their foreign policy efforts on encouraging a forceful U.S. role in promoting a comprehensive Middle East peace settlement. A formal request for sixty F-15s was made in May, but the Saudis did not press for an immediate response.[8] But after Sadat's trip to Jerusalem in November 1977 the Saudis were uneasy about the direction of American policy. Thus when President Carter made a brief stop in Riyadh between visits to Tehran and Aswan in early January 1978, the Saudis insisted on an early decision on the advanced aircraft they felt they had been promised. They reminded the president that they had been told they could have the aircraft of their choice. The F-15 was the plane they had settled on. Carter said he would remain bound by President Ford's commitment but that the details—number, delivery schedules, price—remained to be worked out. The Saudis made it clear that they wanted quick action.

Unfortunately for the United States, the Saudi request came at a time of unusually sensitive Arab-Israeli diplomacy. The Carter administration was trying hard to modify the positions of the Israeli government on

7. The F-15, like the F-5E, also had two engines, which the Saudis strongly preferred to the single engine F-16.

8. During his May 1977 visit to Washington, D.C., Fahd asked President Carter to grant Saudi Arabia "exempt" status so that arms sales to the kingdom would not be subject to any ceiling. The Israelis made a similar request. Both were denied.

two key points: the continued building of Israeli settlements in occupied Arab territory and Begin's refusal to acknowledge that Israel's commitment to UN Resolution 242 entailed an obligation to withdraw from at least some of the West Bank and Gaza in the context of a peace agreement. This effort was producing sharp Israeli resistance, and Israel's friends in the United States were warning against U.S. pressure. This was hardly an ideal time for Carter to endorse the Saudi request for F-15s.

To blunt the domestic reaction to the Saudi F-15 deal, Carter decided to proceed with a long-standing Israeli request for F-16s, as well as to act on an Egyptian expression of mild interest in the F-5E. Fearing that Congress would turn down the Saudi deal while approving the other two, Carter resorted to a unique device of submitting the three cases as a single package to Congress. Unless all were approved, he stated, he would withdraw the entire package. The Israelis were furious. Congress was irritated. And public controversy swirled around the "Middle East arms package" for much of February and March 1978.

In submitting the Saudi request to Congress, Carter asked for sixty F-15s, with delivery to begin only in 1981. To help win congressional favor the Saudis engaged the help of professional lobbyists in Washington, most notably Frederick G. Dutton, a former assistant secretary of state for congressional affairs, and sent some of their most articulate younger leaders, especially Princes Saud al-Faisal, Turki al-Faisal, and Bandar ibn Sultan, as well as Ministers Qusaibi and Yamani, to present the Saudi case to Congress and American public opinion.

Somewhat surprisingly the White House pulled out all stops to gain support for the F-15 sale. Senators, congressmen, and staff aides were endlessly briefed, as were reporters. When questions were raised by the pro-Israeli lobby about the sale, the administration was quick to respond.

Despite all these efforts the administration could not be sure of congressional support unless certain restrictions were placed on the F-15s. The Saudis found this extremely distasteful. From their point of view the F-15s were a legitimate request. The U.S. Air Force had agreed that Saudi Arabia required an advanced interceptor. The Saudis were prepared to pay for the planes with their own resources, unlike the Israelis and Egyptians. Why, if Israel and Iran could have their pick from the U.S. arsenal, was Saudi Arabia placed in an inferior position?

Reluctantly the Saudis acquiesced in Carter's request for reassurances on the F-15s. The aircraft would not be based at Tabuk, an air base in northwest Saudi Arabia within range of Israel. Nor did the Saudis intend to purchase bomb racks that would enhance the offensive capabilities of the F-15 or conformal external fuel tanks to extend the combat radius of the aircraft. These assurances were conveyed to Congress in a letter signed by Secretary of Defense Harold Brown on May 9, 1978. On May 15 the Senate approved the sale of the sixty F-15s to Saudi Arabia by a narrow margin of 54 to 44.

The Saudis learned a great deal about the American political process from the F-15 experience. It was not particularly reassuring, even though the end result was gratifying. During the controversy the Saudis had been repeatedly attacked in public, and questions had been raised in the American press about their stability, their reliability, their intentions toward Israel, and their support for the PLO. The chairman of the Senate Foreign Relations Committee, Frank Church, had been particularly outspoken in his criticism of the Saudis. If they needed any evidence that the "special relationship" between Washington and Riyadh was not quite as special as that governing U.S.-Israeli ties, the F-15 fight was a vivid reminder.

From this episode one can conclude that the Saudis used the F-15 case to try to consolidate U.S.-Saudi relations at a moment when Sadat's initiative raised doubts about the direction of American policy. This need for reassurance reflected political debates in Saudi Arabia over the value of the Washington connection. Once a decision was made to press the F-15 case, the Saudis were very impatient.

In terms of their concern that Carter continue to work for a comprehensive Middle East peace, the Saudi demand for the F-15s in early 1978 was largely counterproductive. After fighting the F-15 issue through Congress, Carter was less able and less inclined to press Begin further on the Palestinian question. Perhaps the Saudis did not see this connection. Perhaps they thought Carter could win both battles. Or perhaps they attached greater value to their own security needs, as they saw them, than to the ambiguous ongoing Arab-Israeli diplomacy.

The sequel to the F-15 decision tells much about the divergence of U.S. and Saudi perceptions. Many Americans felt that the F-15 sale should guarantee Saudi cooperation with U.S. peace efforts, including Camp David. One enthusiastic American official reported that Fahd would not be able to deny Carter any request he might make, so deep was his gratitude for the president's efforts on behalf of the F-15 sale.

But for the Saudis, the sale simply gave them what they had been promised, and only after a rather humiliating ordeal at that.

By mid-1980 the Saudis were again apprehensive about U.S. policy in the region. The Camp David process had predictably stalled; the Soviets were in Afghanistan; the Islamic Republic of Iran was trying to export revolution; and the U.S. rescue attempt to recover the hostages held in Tehran had failed. In this setting Prince Sultan met with Secretary of Defense Brown in Geneva to press the case for five additional items of military equipment. Included in the request were the bomb racks and fuel tanks that had earlier been proscribed, along with items such as the sophisticated AIM 9-L air-to-air missile, aerial refueling tankers for the F-15, and AWACS aircraft.

Brown urged Sultan to postpone the requests until after the November 1980 elections. Many Americans were mystified at the timing of the Saudi bid for arms and at the inclusion of items that they had specifically said they had no intention of requesting. The reason for the Saudi action, it seems, was not only the desire for U.S. reassurance but also a need to respond to pressures from the assertive head of the air force, Fahd ibn Abdallah, who pointedly stated that he had never said anything about not wanting bomb racks or external fuel tanks for the F-15.

For several months the issue died down. Then, hot on the campaign trail, Jimmy Carter said he would never agree to sell bomb racks to the Saudis for the F-15s. This infuriated the Saudis, who thought there was a tacit agreement with Brown to let the matter rest until after the elections. A Defense Department official was sent to soothe the Saudis but was told that a yes-or-no answer on all five requests was required in ten days. This was obviously impossible for Washington, and Carter's defeat put off the moment of truth in any case.

President Ronald Reagan thus inherited from Carter the problem of responding to the Saudi requests. In one of its earliest foreign policy decisions the new administration decided to sell the fuel tanks, the AIM 9-L missile, five AWACS aircraft, and seven KC-135 refueling tankers. No immediate decision was made on the bomb racks. With this decision, Washington hoped to win Riyadh's cooperation on security issues and to deflect Saudi pressures for rapid movement to resolve the Palestinian question. Opposition in Congress to the AWACS sale in particular, however, threatened to undermine the administration's strategy and raise once again questions in Saudi minds about American reliability.

Conclusion

By tradition and by history the Saudis are not particularly well prepared to conduct the kind of complex foreign policy that will be required of them in the 1980s. A cautious, reactive, often secretive policymaking process is ill-adapted to the world of oil diplomacy, arms races,
Arab-Israeli clashes, and superpower rivalry.

Gradually the Saudis have begun to develop a foreign policy bureaucracy, an intelligence service, an aid program, a military establishment,
and an oil policy. But crises can still catch the regime poorly prepared.
Military modernization has not yet produced much usable strength.
And arms requests are still made to test the U.S.-Saudi relationship as
much as they are a part of a coherent design.

The Saudis no doubt feel more at home with inter-Arab politics and
with other Islamic countries then they do with the American-European
diplomatic tradition. Our legalistic, document-oriented style of diplomacy strikes Saudis as lacking in subtlety and flexibility. Their nuances
often seem to us to reflect vacillation and uncertainty. In brief, the Saudi
style of making decisions adds to the difficulties of managing the U.S.-
Saudi relationship. Both parties have a long list of complaints.

Chapter Eight

Saudi Oil Decisions

SAUDI ARABIA's primary means for advancing its national interests is its oil production. Thus decisions on production levels, prices, and investment in future capacity take on extraordinary importance. In addition, they are one of the few concrete, public manifestations of the Saudi political process. Yet even though the record of oil production is readily available, it remains difficult to interpret the motivation behind Saudi oil decisions. As usual, the Saudis themselves are not particularly forthcoming in describing their own motivations.

Economics or Politics?

Two schools of thought exist concerning Saudi oil behavior. One places primary emphasis on economic factors. For example, Saudi domestic and foreign expenditures require a certain level of production to generate needed revenue. In addition, price moderation in comparison to other OPEC members is rational behavior in light of the size of Saudi reserves and the near total dependence on oil as a source of wealth. These factors, often mentioned by Western economists, suggest that it is in Saudi interest to produce substantial quantities of oil at comparatively moderate prices.

But economic analysis can also argue for producing less oil (probably at higher prices), avoiding the accumulation of huge financial surpluses, and counting on future price increases to make oil in the ground a worthwhile form of investment for the future. This is the argument often made by Saudi technocrats who believe Saudi revenue needs could easily be met by producing as little as 5 million to 6 million barrels per day instead of the level of 8 million to 10 million bpd that has prevailed in recent years. The difference between these two economic perspectives is largely accounted for by sharply contrasting expectations of the future world energy market.

The second major school of thought places primary emphasis on political considerations as determining Saudi decisions. Since politics can cover a multitude of sins, it is hard to deny its influence entirely, but to make the case that politics is decisive one must point to Saudi behavior that clearly runs contrary to economic self-interest. This is particularly difficult to do when economists can plausibly account for both high levels of production at moderate prices *and* lower levels of production at higher prices.

The Saudis themselves often emphasize the political dimensions of their oil decisions. They argue that insofar as Saudi Arabia is producing at levels that generate a very large financial surplus, or is selling oil at prices well below those that the market will sustain, this is done out of political considerations. These may include providing incentives to the West to bring pressure to bear on Israel, a favorite theme, or a concern for the health of Western industrial societies that could become susceptible to Soviet pressures if the world economy were to be severely shaken by oil shortages.

The problem with the economics versus politics dichotomy is that it is too simplistic to account for the available evidence. Any careful look at the record leads to the conclusion that political and economic factors have become intertwined in unusually complicated ways. Few persons appear to be involved in the decisionmaking process, with Crown Prince Fahd playing the central role. Other members of the Supreme Petroleum Council who may be consulted on oil decisions are Saud al-Faisal, Yamani, Hisham Nazer, Aba al-Khayl, and al-Qurayshi.[1]

On some issues, such as prices, the Saudis are heavily influenced by world market conditions. They cannot charge more than buyers are prepared to pay, nor can they be expected indefinitely to accept much less for their oil than do their competitors. Supply and demand may work imperfectly in setting world oil prices, but they are not irrelevant.

With respect to oil production levels, the Saudis have some latitude to make periodic adjustments in order to influence prices. But the range of choice is bounded by a ceiling and a floor. At the upper end of the

1. See David E. Long, "Saudi Oil Policy," pp. 83–91.

spectrum the Saudis have not developed the capacity as of 1981 to produce more than 10.5 million bpd at a sustained rate. On several occasions, especially in late 1978 and again in late 1980 and early 1981, Saudi production reached its maximum level. (See appendix G.)

Since 1973, average Saudi production on a quarterly basis has never dropped below 7 million bpd and has generally been in the range of 8 million to 9 million bpd. When world market conditions have been slack, as in 1974–76 and in most of 1978, Saudi production has run around 7 million to 8 million bpd. In 1977, and since the Iranian revolution in early 1979, production has exceeded 9 million bpd, with only brief exceptions. Only in the first three quarters of 1980 and in the first eight months of 1981 did Saudi Arabia keep production above 9.5 million bpd in a soft market situation, and by September 1981 the Saudis cut back to about 9 million bpd.

Thus in practical terms Saudi leaders in recent years have exercised only modest latitude in setting production levels once market and technical factors were taken into account. If the preferred Saudi level of production is assumed to be 8.5 million bpd, as is claimed, variations of about 1.5 million bpd on either side of that figure represent the realistic range of market-induced and politically motivated decisions.

Of all the Saudi oil decisions, those involving expansion of future capacity seem most susceptible to political calculus. If the maximization of Saudi wealth and power were primary motivations, expansion of productive capacity would be a top priority. Indeed, when ARAMCO was charged with these decisions in the early 1970s, plans were made to increase capacity to as much as 20 million bpd by the mid-1980s. But as Saudi Arabia took effective control of ARAMCO, these plans were shelved, and today one hears only of intentions to reach a maximum capacity of about 12 million bpd, perhaps by 1985.

Lack of substantial spare capacity means that the Saudis cannot expect indefinitely to exercise strong and consistent price leadership in OPEC. The much-discussed Saudi strategy for OPEC price unity and gradual price increases requires an ability to expand Saudi oil production to prevent other OPEC members from trying to drive prices higher by withholding production. Whether Saudi Arabia will have the capacity to impose its price preferences on OPEC will depend heavily on world market conditions. In 1980 the Saudis were unable to prevent price increases when the Iran-Iraq war disrupted supplies, but in 1981, with ample supplies worldwide, they were able to bring prices down by producing at maximum capacity. In 1981 they came closer to success but even then were unable to get formal OPEC agreement on a price strategy.

Why have the Saudis been reluctant to expand capacity? Some argue that it is expensive. Others note that the Saudis do not need to produce more oil than their current capacity permits. Both points have some truth to them, but they hardly seem decisive. Any model of economic maximization would certainly show that the economic benefits of expanded capacity outweigh the costs. But the Saudi leadership has been reluctant to take action for several reasons. First, such steps are often portrayed as doing a favor to the West, which is not politically popular in the kingdom. Second, expansion of capacity arouses the suspicions of other OPEC members and subjects Saudi Arabia to pressures not to use its capacity to dampen prices. This is particularly true in the soft market conditions of the early 1980s. Third, it exposes Saudi Arabia to Western pressures to increase production in tight market situations. Not having the capacity reduces these political pressures considerably, albeit possibly at the price of weakening Saudi leadership in the world energy market.

Explaining Saudi Oil Decisions

If the simple economics-versus-politics approach to Saudi oil decisions is unconvincing, it becomes necessary to look at a broader range of plausible explanations. Among the most important elements to be considered are the following:

Market conditions. These were generally tight in 1973–74, 1977, 1979, and in late 1980. Shortages were brought about by the production cutbacks associated with the October 1973 Arab-Israeli war, the Iranian revolution, and the Iran-Iraq war. In 1975–76, 1978, and much of 1980 and throughout most of 1981 oil supplies were ample.

Revenue requirements. For both domestic development and foreign aid the Saudi appetite for oil revenues has grown sharply. The second five-year plan (1976–80) entailed outlays of nearly $40 billion to $50 billion in its last years. In 1977–78 and 1978–79 the Saudi budget registered modest current account deficits. In 1980, however, a current account surplus of nearly $35 billion was achieved.[2] The third five-year

2. "Saudi Arabia," *Middle East Economic Digest*, vol. 25 (July 17–23, 1981), p. 40.

plan envisages expenditures of at least $55 billion to $65 billion annually. At $32 a barrel, this would necessitate producing at least 5.5 million bpd. Additional revenue will be required for defense expenditures and foreign aid. Apart from oil income, Saudi Arabia earns over $10 billion annually on its foreign investments. With foreign exchange reserves of over $100 billion in the early 1980s, the Saudis could meet current expenditures for some time by drawing down reserves.

Technical problems. Some of the largest Saudi oil fields cannot be efficiently produced at excessively high rates. In addition, Saudi reserve structure corresponds to a ratio of about 50 percent Arab light crude and 50 percent medium to heavy crude. In early 1978 the Saudis limited the total of Arab light in ARAMCO's production to 65 percent in order to approximate this reserve structure, and efforts have begun to shift toward producing more heavy crude from fields near the Kuwait border.

Internal politics. Conservationists argue for producing less oil to stretch out the useful lifetime of Saudi Arabia's main resource. Nationalists favor using oil as a form of pressure to advance Saudi and Arab interests. Other members of the royal family seem to be more responsive to U.S. concerns but feel the need to show some quid pro quo for moderate oil policies.

Expectations. At what price will new fuels begin to displace oil as a primary source of energy? What is the value of oil left in the ground? What rate of inflation can one expect in the future? What about the value of the dollar? Are foreign investments in the West secure? How much will consumption drop as prices rise? All of these questions can influence the debate over oil policy.[3]

OPEC pressures. The Saudi threat to increase production to keep prices moderate is taken seriously by other OPEC members. Iran and Iraq have the physical capabilities to bring considerable pressure to bear on Saudi Arabia if the Saudis seem to be cutting into their share of the market.

Associated gas. Saudi industrial plans envisage using large quantities of gas at plants in Jubayl and Yanbu. All gas is currently produced in association with oil and is separated from the oil by means of some fifty-eight gas-oil separation plants. If future oil production drops much below 8.5 million bpd, there will not be enough gas to meet the needs of all the industrial plants that are now being built. Nonassociated gas exists in Saudi Arabia but has not yet been developed.

3. See Yamani's remarks in appendix C.

Relations with the United States. Saudi ability to get arms from the United States may be affected by the perception in Congress of Saudi oil policy. When major decisions are pending, price restraint may help ensure political support. A reputation for moderation may also help the Saudis to influence broader U.S. Middle East policy.

The Palestinian problem. The Saudis can try to use their oil resources to reward or punish individual countries for their policies toward Israel and the Palestinians. King Faisal generally opposed the use of the "oil weapon" until 1973, but ever since then the view has persisted that Saudi oil decisions are affected by the overall Arab-Israeli situation. With the growing tendency for the Saudis to sign state-to-state contracts for the sale of oil, often containing restrictive clauses, they can favor such countries as France that have usually been pro-Arab in their broad Middle East policies.

Specific Cases

While each of the explanations above of Saudi oil policy has been offered at one time or another to account for specific decisions, no single clear pattern emerges from the evidence of the past decade. The most interesting recent cases are the following (also see appendix G):

The October 1973 war and its aftermath. Two weeks after the outbreak of the Arab-Israeli war, Saudi Arabia announced an embargo on oil shipments to the United States and the Netherlands, ostensibly because of their support for Israel. The practical effect of the embargo itself was modest, since oil supplies could be switched from other sources. In early November, therefore, the Saudis and other Arab oil producers stated that they would reduce production by 25 percent from September 1973 levels until Israel had withdrawn from occupied Arab territories. In November and December 1973 Saudi production dropped sharply to just above 6 million bpd, helping to create circumstances that led to a doubling in the posted price of oil at the OPEC meeting in late December 1973.[4] It was this cutback in production, not the embargo,

4. All Arab oil producers except Iraq curtailed production in November and December, reaching an average reduction for the last quarter of 1973 of 17 percent compared with September levels. The Saudi reduction was 19 percent. Ali Johany argues that the most important consequences of the October 1973 war for oil prices was the acceleration of the transfer of property rights from the oil companies to the producing countries. (See Ali D. Johany, *The Myth of the OPEC Cartel*, p. 48.) That process had been under way well before the war and had already resulted in

that produced the shortages felt for several months in most industrial countries.

By January the United States was pressing Saudi Arabia to restore production. Nixon and Kissinger made their involvement in the postwar diplomacy conditional on the relaxation of Saudi oil policy. As the disengagement negotiations began, Saudi Arabia promised to return production to normal and to lift the embargo, and shortly before the completion of the Syrian-Israeli disengagement talks the Saudis carried out this promise. This was a case where political imperatives certainly took priority between October 1973 and May 1974. The fact that the Saudis benefited economically does not vitiate the point that oil policy was in this instance largely a function of the Arab-Israeli conflict.[5]

The Doha decision. At the OPEC meeting in Doha, Qatar, in December 1976 most OPEC members called for an immediate 10 percent price increase, to be followed in mid-1977 by another 5 percent boost. Saudi Arabia, joined only by the United Arab Emirates, held out for only a 5 percent increase. By mid-1977, the Saudis agreed to raise their prices by an additional 5 percent to restore price unity, in return for which the other OPEC members agreed to freeze prices for the rest of the year. To back their position, the Saudis kept production high through 1977, averaging about 9.2 million bpd. This helped to produce a soft market in 1978.

---

substantial price increases in 1972. During the October 1973 war posted prices were raised from $3.01 to $5.12 a barrel. By January 1, 1974, they stood at $11.65. It should be recalled that posted prices were used to calculate payments to governments. Actual selling prices to customers were considerably lower.

5. Eliyahu Kanovsky argued in "Deficits in Saudi Arabia" that oil field technical problems account for the drop in production, not political decisions. His source for making this assertion was a Senate report, *The Future of Saudi Arabian Oil Production*, pp. 25–31. According to the report, pressure problems were developing in some Saudi fields during 1973. Some experts believed that excessive pumping was running the risk of damaging the fields. Saudi "conservationists" were also concerned with the rapid expansion of production and its effect on Saudi development. The report mentions the "obvious political dimension explaining ARAMCO's October cutback" (p. 28), but notes that other considerations of a technical nature may have carried weight. The evidence presented does nothing to weaken the argument that the primary motive in making the cuts and then restoring them was political. The fact that the cuts helped to make technical problems more manageable cannot be plausibly used as evidence that the motivation for the cuts was technical, not political. As is often the case, the Saudis are able to serve more than one purpose with their oil decisions. ARAMCO engineers reject the notion that the post-October 1973 war cutbacks were the result of technical problems and tend to dismiss the concern over producing at pressures below the "bubble point" as exaggerated.

Part of the Saudi behavior in this period seems to have been aimed at winning support from the new Carter administration.[6] The Saudis wanted both movement on the Palestinian issue and positive responses to their arms requests. They were also anxious to involve the new administration more actively in the Horn of Africa to counter Soviet incursions. Alongside these political concerns was a desire to exercise leadership in OPEC and to allow for a period of economic recovery in the Western economies on which the Saudis were heavily dependent. In this case politics and economics led to the same policy of high production and relatively moderate prices. It is worth noting that Saudi disappointment over U.S. support for Sadat's unilateral peace initiative did not seem to have contributed to the decline in Saudi production early in 1978. Market forces adequately explain the drop.

December 1978 to July 1979. This is the most difficult period of Saudi oil policy to explain. After Camp David some Saudis argued for a production cut, but by December 1978 Saudi output was at an all time high of 10.4 million bpd. This was largely due to the collapse of Iranian exports. Then, on January 20, 1979, the Saudis suddenly announced a ceiling for first-quarter production of 9.5 million bpd.[7] This came shortly after OPEC had agreed on a graduated pricing formula for 1979 and had the effect of driving spot prices sharply higher. In early February the shah's regime finally collapsed and was replaced by the Islamic Republic of Ayatollah Khomeini. Iran berated the Saudis for producing too much oil at low prices.

6. J. B. Kelly, in *Arabia, the Gulf and the West,* pp. 263–64, implies incorrectly that the United States and Saudi Arabia had reached some form of understanding after 1974 in which the Saudis promised uninterrupted supplies of oil, constant prices, and assurances that surplus revenues in the United States would not be withdrawn. In return the United States allegedly would guarantee the dominance of the Al Saud dynasty. He adds, again incorrectly, that after Fahd's visit to Washington in spring 1977, agreement was reached to increase Saudi production to 9.9 million bpd for the last half of 1977 and to 10.4 million bpd after January 1978, with the excess over 8.5 million bpd to be placed at the disposal of the United States. Without any such agreement, Saudi production remained at about 9 million bpd through 1977, dropped in early 1978 in a soft market, then rose in late 1978 as Iranian production fell. Most important for consumers, prices did in fact remain essentially frozen during all of 1977 and 1978, which in real terms meant a slight decline in the price of oil. Kelly is correct in criticizing those who believe that an agreement such as the one he describes could be made to work. He is wrong, however, in thinking that any such agreement was ever reached or even seriously contemplated.

7. Some analysts believe that this decision was required by technical difficulties of continuing to produce oil at near maximum capacity.

March 1979 was a traumatic month for the Saudis. Barely adjusted to the new reality of the successful Iranian revolution, they were confronted with the conclusion of a separate Egyptian-Israeli peace treaty. In addition, the U.S. press was full of negative articles about the Saudis. At Baghdad in April the Egyptians were expelled from the Arab League and nearly all Arab states broke economic ties and diplomatic relations with Cairo. The Saudis went along with the Arab consensus, much to the anger of official Washington.

In this setting, the Saudis reimposed the 8.5 million bpd ceiling on oil production for the second quarter. This made way for resumed Iranian exports but left the market tight, and spot prices rose. The United States mounted a major effort to get the Saudis to return to 9.5 million bpd, and finally in July Crown Prince Fahd told Ambassador Robert S. Strauss, the new Middle East negotiator, that Saudi Arabia would comply. By then OPEC prices had skyrocketed to over $20 a barrel, although the Saudis remained at $18 for several months. In November they increased to $24, thereby narrowing the gap between their prices and the rest of OPEC.

Saudi revenue needs were perhaps a minor factor in this period. Their fiscal year 1978–79 ended in the spring with a current account deficit, but this could have been met by raising prices or expanding production. Instead, production was cut and for the last half of 1979 they charged substantially less for their oil than other OPEC members. On Arab-Israeli grounds, the Saudis may have wanted to signal their unhappiness after the treaty, and the choice of Strauss to carry the good news in July may have been an attempt to encourage more active U.S. diplomacy. Pressures from Iran also help explain the cut to 8.5 million bpd in the second quarter.

Whatever the precise mix of reasons, the direction of Saudi oil policy for the first half of 1979 was uncertain. This has led some to conclude that the family was unable to reach a consensus.[8] If so, the period of confusion was short-lived. If pressure on Washington was the object, it was unsuccessful. Saudi production cuts, however, did add to the unpredictability in the market that allowed for the huge price hikes in the latter half of 1979. If this period shows anything, it is the vulnerability of Saudi oil policies to competing pressures. In addition one cannot preclude the hypothesis that the Saudi decisions to reduce output were

8. Theodore H. Moran, "Modeling OPEC Behavior," pp. 241–72.

deliberately intended to convey to Washington the kingdom's unhappiness over American Middle East policy.

1980–81. The Saudis defined their policy for 1980 as reunification of OPEC prices, to be followed by agreement on predictable increases that would reflect inflation and currency fluctuations.[9] Thus despite a soft market the Saudis kept production at 9.5 million bpd and sold their oil at $28, while others were selling comparable grades for $32 or more. Private stocks of oil were rapidly expanding and it was frequently predicted that the Saudis would reduce production to 8.5 million bpd.[10]

Early in 1980 the United States was considering resumption of purchases of oil for the Strategic Petroleum Reserve (SPR). There was anxiety, however, that increased demand would push prices higher and that the Saudis might further tighten the market by reducing production to 8.5 million bpd. Secretary of Energy Charles W. Duncan, Jr., after visiting Saudi Arabia in early March 1980, concluded that the time was not right to purchase oil for the SPR. The Saudis did not, as some have reported, threaten a cutback, but American officials worried that they might retaliate.[11]

---

9. Minister of Petroleum Yamani outlined the rationale for his OPEC price strategy in an interview in *Al-Majallah* (London), June 7–13, 1980 (FBIS, *Daily Report: Middle East and Africa,* June 9, 1980, pp. C1 through C3). Yamani argued that OPEC should adopt a price strategy of seeking annual increases equivalent to rates of inflation, fluctuation of currencies, and increases geared to growth rates in the industrial states. He pointed out, however, that the strategy would not work in the event of great shortages or great surpluses. If there is a surplus, OPEC would need a production-sharing plan; if there are shortages, spare capacity would be required. Yamani also noted that Saudi Arabia has a stake in the health of the international economic system. "There are interconnected interests which sometimes require an increase in production above the limit we need to meet our financial obligations."

10. Admiral Stansfield Turner, director of the Central Intelligence Agency, testified before the Senate Committee on Energy and Natural Resources on April 22, 1980, saying: "We expect by this summer that the Saudis may reduce actual output to 8.5 million b/d or lower." (*U.S. Security Interests and Policies in Southwest Asia,* p. 214.) Deputy Secretary of Energy John Sawhill remarked in ibid., pp. 170–71: "Future Saudi production is primarily a political decision. For its own foreign exchange needs, Saudi Arabia has to produce less than 5 million bpd. However, Saudi Arabia has a great interest in the political stability of the West and the stability of our financial markets." See also U.S. Central Intelligence Agency, National Foreign Assessment Center, *The World Oil Market in the Years Ahead,* ER79-10327U (CIA, 1979), pp. 6, 46, for reasons why the Saudis will be reluctant to produce more than 8.5 million bpd of oil.

11. By the time of the Iran-Iraq war worldwide stocks of oil were about 400 million barrels above normal, almost exactly the amount of oil accounted for by the additional 1 million bpd produced by Saudi Arabia since mid-1979.

As events worked themselves out, the United States did not increase purchases for the SPR until later in the fall, and then at a moderate rate of only 100,000 bpd. The Saudis kept production at 9.5 million bpd. In an attempt to unify the OPEC pricing structure, which had virtually collapsed in the preceding year, the Saudis raised their price for Arab light crude to $30 in September. But instead of cutting production back to 8.5 million bpd as anticipated, the Saudis found themselves faced with a new international crisis, the outbreak of war between Iraq and Iran in late September.

In early October 1980 the Saudis announced that production would be increased by nearly 1 million bpd to help make up for lost Iraqi and Iranian production. This brought Saudi production back up to near its maximum sustainable capacity as they entered the OPEC meeting in Bali in mid-December. There, another small price hike occurred; the Saudis raised their price to $32, while others continued to charge several dollars more per barrel for comparable quality.

Throughout the first two quarters of 1981 the Saudis continued to produce at maximum capacity. Prices began to soften, especially for higher-priced crudes. OPEC members complained about Saudi behavior, but to no avail. At the June 1981 OPEC meeting in Geneva, a price freeze for the remainder of the year was announced, but still Saudi Arabia refused to cut production to prevent prices from falling further.

Another unsuccessful attempt at price unity was made in August 1981 at a special meeting of OPEC in Geneva. When OPEC price hawks refused to accept a $34 reference price, the Saudis decided to keep their own price at $32 a barrel but did agree to cut production for September 1981 to 9 million bpd to prevent a sharp erosion of prices.

One lesson from 1980–81, it would seem, is that Saudi Arabia cannot quickly or easily enforce price discipline on OPEC, but in time it can help create market conditions that oblige OPEC's price hawks to cut production or prices. The Iraq-Iran war was a reminder of how quickly oil market disruptions can occur, although loss of output was less than anticipated by many observers. Fortunately world stocks were at an all-time high, consumers did not panic, and several producers, including the Saudis, temporarily raised output. As Iraq and Iran returned to the market in 1981, they pressed Saudi Arabia to cut back production. Up to a point the Saudis can resist such pressures, but eventually production is bound to be adjusted downward once prices have stabilized around $32 a barrel, as occurred in the latter part of 1981.

Lessons

What do these cases demonstrate? First, there is no clear-cut instance in which Saudi economic and political interests have sharply diverged. Even the most politically motivated decisions—the cutbacks in 1973–74—proved to be extremely beneficial economically. Moderation on prices (compared with other OPEC members) may have led to some short-term economic losses but could be justified by longer-term preferences for discouraging the development of alternative fuels on a scale that might replace Saudi production, and by a general interest in a stable international economic order and a strong dollar.[12]

Several myths can be laid to rest. First, oil and politics do mix, as shown most clearly in the October 1973 war. In addition, the Saudis are not "low absorbers." They are quick to learn how to spend their increased revenues.[13] Third, the Saudis have not usually been price leaders in OPEC in recent years. In general the spot market has defined the prevailing price of oil, OPEC has followed the trend of those prices, and the Saudis have gone along with others in OPEC, while keeping their prices somewhat below the full market price for their oil. Fourth, the Saudis have rarely explicitly linked oil decisions to the Arab-Israeli conflict. When they have been most upset over U.S. Middle East policy, they have not demonstrated their displeasure by manipulating oil production, with the important exceptions of October 1973 and possibly the spring of 1979. Fifth, the Saudis do seem to be somewhat sensitive to pressure from their OPEC neighbors, Iran and Iraq, to cut production

12. See Yamani's remarks in appendix C.
13. See especially Kanovsky, "Deficits in Saudi Arabia," pp. 313–59, and Kanovsky, "An Economic Analysis of Middle East Oil"; and Donald A. Wells, *Saudi Arabian Development Strategy*, p. 59. Wells very accurately predicted that Saudi foreign assets would reach $100 billion by 1980, earning some $10 billion in income. In addition, see the speech by Abdul Aziz al-Quraishi, head of the Saudi Arabian Monetary Agency, June 3, 1980, to the International Monetary Conference in New Orleans: "There has always been a natural tendency among the members of OPEC to raise expenditures in line with or in excess of growth in income. For example, the actual expenditures of the second five-year plan in Saudi Arabia were $200 billion, or nearly 40% higher than original estimates. In the case of actual expenditures for the 1979/80 fiscal year, these were 19% higher than original estimates while budgeted spending for the fiscal year 1980/81 will be $75 billion which is 30% more than actual spending in the previous year. The third five-year plan in Saudi Arabia entails expenditures equivalent to nearly $235 billion in constant terms, excluding defense spending, foreign aid and transfer payments."

in times of surplus. Sixth, concerning the expansion of productive capacity, the Saudis have been slow to act, presumably out of a desire not to expose themselves to excessive pressures from abroad.

As in other aspects of their foreign policy, the Saudis reveal by their oil decisions a generally cautious attitude, one sensitive to the conflicting pressures to which they can be subjected. A consensus seems to have emerged in the late 1970s that production should be maintained at levels ranging from 8 million to 10 million bpd, while prices would be set slightly lower than those of other OPEC members.[14] Major investments in expanding future productive capacity have been postponed as too controversial, probably unnecessary, and possibly risky.

While strong nationalistic and conservationist voices can be heard in favor of sharp cuts in Saudi production rates, they have not yet managed to gain decisive influence over policy. For the royal family, political considerations, including the need to minimize pressures and to seek short-term economic gains, seem to be as decisive as long-term economic considerations, which in any event are very difficult to analyze precisely. If Saudi Arabia felt less vulnerable, or if it sought to maximize its power, it might use its oil resources more aggressively. But the Saudis have shown in recent years an awareness of the limits of their power, just as they did in the crucial formative years of the 1920s. Then, as now, it was primarily foreigners, not the Saudis themselves, who viewed the kingdom as an emerging superpower.

14. While economists can argue that the Saudis seek to stay on a preferred price path to maximize long-run returns from their oil, in practice the Saudis seem to have set production levels within predictable limits and have not succeeded in keeping prices on a gradually increasing path. Instead, since 1973 sharp increases have been followed by short periods of modest decline of prices in constant dollars. The Saudis have not engaged in the type of fine-tuning of production decisions that would be required to impose a farsighted price strategy on other producers and consumers. From spring 1979 to fall 1981, for example, the Saudis made only four production decisions: a cut to 8.5 million bpd in March 1979, a restoration of production to 9.5 million bpd three months later, an increase to 10.3 million bpd in fall 1980, and a reduction to 9 million bpd in September 1981.

Part Three

The American Connection

For most of the past generation the United States and Saudi Arabia have engaged in a mutually beneficial relationship. American companies discovered, developed, and marketed Saudi oil, bringing untold wealth to the population of the kingdom and especially to its ruling family. In the process the companies themselves profited greatly, and until the 1970s, at least, consumers also enjoyed oil at modest prices.

Saudi and American interests also converged in the common desire to check the spread of Soviet and radical influences in the Middle East. While differences have frequently emerged over tactics, this shared objective has been a strong element of the U.S.-Saudi dialogue and has led to some attempts at coordinated action.

Finally, Washington and Riyadh have both professed an interest in regional stability. But on this issue policies have often diverged, particularly over the intractable Palestinian problem.

In view of the apparent similarity of interests between the United States and Saudi Arabia, one might expect the relationship to be relatively free of trouble. In fact, however, there has been a persistent undercurrent of tension, occasional sharp disagreements, and periodic crises of confidence.

As the two countries enter the 1980s they will find an increasingly difficult agenda of issues confronting them. Middle East political problems will be extraordinarily complex as a result of the Iranian revolution, inter-Arab disputes, the Palestinian controversy, and Soviet ambitions and power. Questions of oil supplies and prices will assume unprecedented importance. And the security requirements of both countries will add strain to the relationship.

Neither the United States nor Saudi Arabia is particularly well prepared for the scope and complexity of their relationship in the 1980s.

As a result, mistakes will certainly be made, perhaps with grave consequences. While the pressures on Saudi Arabia are likely to grow, it is less certain that the means available to the Saudis to cope with these pressures will be adequate.

The United States can make a difference in two respects: by its regional and global policies it can either aggravate or reduce the pressures; and by its direct relationship with Saudi Arabia it can either strengthen Saudi capabilities or add to domestic burdens. In brief, more than any other country, the United States, by its actions or inaction, will have a decisive influence over Saudi developments in the 1980s.

Chapter Nine

U.S.-Saudi Relations

No one denies that the United States has a direct and continuing interest in the petroleum resources of Saudi Arabia. For the indefinite future the United States and its allies simply cannot do without substantial quantities of oil from Saudi Arabia. If Saudi exports were to be discontinued, the cost to the world economy would be comparable to the Great Depression of the 1930s.[1]

The Substance of U.S.-Saudi Relations

On what terms and with what degree of confidence can the United States and other major oil-consuming countries meet their needs from Saudi Arabia? By the early 1980s Saudi Arabia was the largest supplier of oil to the United States. This was not necessarily a desirable position to be in for either country. While some Americans have benefited from the marginally lower price of Saudi oil, there has nonetheless been discomfort in relying so heavily on a country that has on at least one occasion tried to withhold oil for political reasons.

Energy Policy Problems

Generally lacking a coherent national energy policy of its own, the United States has not always been certain of what it wanted from Saudi Arabia with respect to oil. The list of demands has included high rates of production, moderate and predictable prices, development of spare capacity to help meet emergencies, and additional production to aug-

1. Joseph S. Nye, "Energy and Security," in David A. Deese and Joseph S. Nye, eds., *Energy and Security*, p. 3.

ment the U.S. Strategic Petroleum Reserve. Needless to say, the United States has not always been clear on which of these points was most important at any given moment. Most often, security of supply has taken precedence over price restraint when U.S. officials have talked to their Saudi counterparts. Relatively little emphasis has been placed on developing spare capacity.[2]

Some Americans have objected to the emphasis on keeping Saudi output high and maintaining price stability. This, they argue, ensures that the West will remain heavily dependent on Saudi oil and therefore vulnerable to a major disruption if Saudi Arabia goes the way of Iran. It would be better, they believe, to cut demand for Saudi oil, to let prices rise to the point where alternative sources of energy can be produced on a large scale and where non–Middle East oil producers will have an incentive to increase production. Even for Saudi Arabia, they argue, lower rates of oil production would reduce the strains of rapid development and thus would enhance stability.

These arguments have not gained a great deal of currency in U.S. official circles. Insofar as they represent a rational long-term calculus of Saudi economic interests, they involve many uncertainties that make it difficult for policymakers to embrace them. And the relationship between rates of Saudi oil production and internal stability is very hypothetical. Thus policy tends to be geared toward short-term needs for adequate, predictable supplies and price restraint.

Early in the Reagan administration a spate of articles appeared that took a radically different point of view, arguing that Saudi self-interest was enough to assure high rates of production and comparatively moderate prices. Noting that the Saudis have tended to spend most of their oil revenues no matter how large they have been, these analysts assume that the Saudis have a clear interest in maximizing current income. Thus production levels will remain high and slight price discounts will be offered to preserve the Saudi share of the market.[3]

2. During a visit to Saudi Arabia in 1977 Secretary of Energy James R. Schlesinger urged the Saudis not to expand capacity beyond 12 million to 14 million bpd. The reasons for this advice have remained unclear, although some U.S. officials have maintained that there was serious concern at the time that the Saudis might "overproduce" their fields and thereby reduce the ultimate amount of oil that could be recovered.

3. This is argued by Douglas J. Feith in "The Oil Weapon De-Mystified," pp. 19–39, and in the *Wall Street Journal*, March 30, 1981. Feith weakens the force of his argument by simplistically distinguishing between a "rational" oil producer, who will not use oil as a weapon, and an "irrational" one, who is not susceptible to per-

From a strategic perspective current Saudi production may be less important than Saudi willingness and ability to increase production during periods of crisis and uncertainty. In 1973–74 and in 1979 the actual loss of oil on the world market was modest, but the price effects were enormous and debilitating, in part because of uncertainty and panic among consumers. In 1980, during the Iraq-Iran war, the price effect of supply disruptions was less because of the large stocks of oil held in the consuming countries and Saudi willingness to increase production. These factors had a calming effect on the market and helped to prevent a sharp price hike.

The Saudis, however, have just about reached the limit of their ability to make up for supply disruptions unless they develop additional capacity. Thus a major U.S. interest in the future should be to encourage the Saudis to maintain spare capacity to be used in the event of major disruptions. Therefore, reducing world demand for Saudi oil well below levels of 10.5 million bpd is a desirable U.S. objective.

Security

The American and Western interest in access to Saudi oil entails a concern for the security of Saudi oil and of the kingdom itself. In light of the value of Saudi oil reserves it is remarkable that no serious threat has ever been aimed at occupying the oil fields, toppling the Saudi government, or trying to blackmail the Saudi government through sabotage of the oil facilities. Since the onset of oil production in Saudi Arabia, the flow of oil has never been disrupted by military action or terrorist attacks. For a resource conservatively valued in current dollars at over $5 trillion, this is remarkable.

Because of the enormous gap between the cost of production of Saudi oil—no more than several dollars a barrel—and its price, over $30, whoever controls Saudi production will acquire immense wealth. Thus it is not at all farfetched to assume that at some time in the 1980s Saudi oil will be a tempting target for outside powers as well as domestic conspirators.[4] Prudence dictates that the Saudis and their friends take steps

---

suasion and therefore should be ignored. The Saudis are viewed as rational and therefore to be taken for granted. After writing these articles, Feith became a member of the National Security Council staff, with responsibility for Middle East affairs.

4. See Yamani's remarks on the Soviets in appendix C.

to enhance the security of the oil fields, protect the regime from external threats, and create a balance of power in the Persian Gulf that will deter direct Soviet intervention.

In recent years Saudi Arabia has been rapidly modernizing its armed forces, largely with American assistance. But even when the modernization programs are well on their way toward completion in the mid-1980s, Saudi military strength will not be awesome. Manpower constraints are virtually insurmountable and advanced technology often aggravates the problem by increasing the need for skilled maintenance personnel, many of whom of necessity will be foreigners.

As the U.S.-Saudi security relationship becomes increasingly complex, points of friction are certain to arise. The Saudis, always anxious to avoid pressures from their neighbors and genuinely fearful of U.S.-Soviet confrontations in the gulf, will resist American requests for a larger military presence and will argue that arms to Saudi Arabia are all that is needed. U.S. officials are likely to conclude that responding positively to Saudi arms requests is essential if the American presence in the kingdom is to be maintained. And without that presence in the form of the U.S. Military Training Mission, the AWACS aircraft, the U.S. Army Corps of Engineers, and advisers to the national guard, the United States will have less influence, be less well informed about possible threats to Saudi Arabia, and less well prepared to bring military power into the region in the event of a serious threat from the Soviet Union or one of the regional powers.

For both countries, then, maintenance of the security relationship is of vital importance, but each party has different priorities. The Saudis want highly visible U.S. assistance in the form of sales of sophisticated weaponry. It is hoped that this alone will deter countries such as South Yemen from ever attacking Saudi territory. The Saudis want to be treated as belonging to the same league as Israel and Egypt, for whom the most advanced equipment is readily made available. This is partly a matter of pride and symbolism, and the fact that the Saudis pay for their arms adds to their sense that their requests should be honored. As a reminder to Washington that Saudi Arabia cannot be taken for granted, several large arms purchases from European sources have been made and Crown Prince Fahd has even raised the possibility of Saudi-Soviet arms deals.[5]

5. In comments to the press, Crown Prince Fahd said that Saudi Arabia was prepared to diversify sources of its weapons. Asked if this might involve purchases of

The Americans face a number of dilemmas in dealing with Saudi arms requests. Up to a point the Saudis have been taking U.S. advice in modernizing their armed forces. This makes it all the more difficult to say no to militarily justifiable arms requests. For Washington, the political constraint in responding to Saudi military demands is partly a function of domestic politics. The Saudis are not uniformly seen as a strong friend of the United States worthy of support. Memories of the oil embargo, oil price hikes, and hostility to Israel and Egypt have all undermined the image of Saudi Arabia as a moderate, pro-Western, anti-Soviet state. There is no strong or vocal pro-Saudi constituency in the United States, and an administration that seeks to sell arms to the Saudis will always have to overcome the skepticism of the friends of Israel in Congress.

The Saudis resent the fact that Israel appears to have such a strong say on arms to Riyadh. If any further proof were needed, they point to this as evidence that Persian Gulf security and the Arab-Israeli problem are indeed inextricably linked.

Another source of tension in the U.S.-Saudi relationship is the belief in some quarters that the lesson of Iran is that generous arms supplies can be destabilizing. Whether this is an accurate reading of the reasons for the shah's demise is debatable, but it leads to the conclusion that the United States should refuse to sell arms to the Saudis for their own good. The patronizing overtones of this posture are not lost on the Saudis. They know they are being told that they, unlike Israel and Egypt, cannot be entrusted with expensive and lethal military items. No self-respecting military establishment will admit this, and no political leadership that wants to keep the loyalty of its armed forces can appear to agree.

Finally, even when the United States does consent to sell arms to the Saudis, this does not guarantee easy relations in the future. In fact, the positive benefits of most arms sales are remarkably short-lived. In some instances the Saudis resent the advice and the restrictions that come with the arms. In their search for efficiency American advisers have on occasion pressed the Saudis to reorganize their armed forces on the U.S. model of a joint command of the various services. The Saudis have re-

---

arms from the Soviet Union, Fahd said, "Why not if there is a need for that? . . . If we find American and Western doors shut, why not? Purchasing arms from the Soviet Union means buying equipment, not principles." *Saudi Review* (Jidda), no. 4368 (February 23, 1981), p. 4.

sisted such advice, both because it would risk upsetting delicate political balances in the royal family and because it might enhance the coup-making capabilities of the military.

While the security dimension of the U.S.-Saudi relationship is likely to remain central throughout the 1980s, it will not be free of tensions and strain. The two countries may share broad objectives, but they have not worked out a common strategy, their priorities differ, and their political imperatives often clash. From time to time an issue like the sale of F-15 aircraft and associated equipment, or the AWACS, will be defined on both sides as a "litmus test," but the catch is that the test will be repeated over and over.[6] Success in passing one test is likely to raise expectations of comparable performance in the future. And high expectations can lead to frustrations and disappointment.

Nonetheless, the Saudis recognize the important role played by the United States in enhancing Saudi security. But many Saudis do not feel that this is a selfless American contribution for which the Saudis should be expected to pay a high price. After all, they argue, Saudi security is the guarantee that oil will be available to the West. If the Soviets were to threaten the oil, the United States would have to respond, not for the sake of Saudi Arabia, but in its own interests.[7] This leads some Saudis to wonder whether there is any American commitment to Saudi Arabia's security apart from the concern with oil. Is the United States, for example, committed to the regime, to the protection of Saudi territory, or just to the oil fields? The fate of the shah raised questions about both the value of U.S. arms and of U.S. commitments, and it will be some time before the Saudis feel reassured.[8]

6. After the successful conclusion of the F-15 sale to the Saudis in spring 1978, some observers thought that this would ensure Saudi cooperation on oil issues and on the peace process. When the Saudis refused to support the Camp David accords, many in Washington were especially angry since they had thought the F-15 issue had been a "test" that would automatically produce positive benefits across the full spectrum of U.S.-Saudi relations.

7. Saudi officials seem to believe that the Soviet Union can be deterred from direct military intervention in the gulf by means of the strategic balance of power. This assumes that a threat to the oil supplies of the West would be viewed as tantamount to a declaration of war and that the U.S. response would have to be global, not just regional.

8. For a somewhat alarmist but often insightful view of strains in the U.S.-Saudi relationship, see the article by a former American official, Anthony Cordesman, written under the pseudonym of Abdul Kasim Mansur, "The American Threat to Saudi Arabia," pp. 47-60.

Regional Stability

If oil and security have been the most tangible elements of the U.S.-Saudi relationship, the most elusive problems have been those involving efforts to enhance regional stability. Both countries profess to value stability and to oppose the extension of Soviet influence into the region. And yet policies in Washington and Riyadh often diverge. In the 1960s the United States backed the Republican forces in North Yemen, and Saudi Arabia aided the Royalists. After the 1967 Arab-Israeli war the United States sided with Israel, while the Saudis assisted the PLO. In 1977 Saudi Arabia argued for aid to Somalia, while Washington was reluctant to burn its bridges to Ethiopia. Even in the Iran-Iraq war of 1980–81 the United States slightly tilted toward Tehran, just as Saudi Arabia leaned toward Baghdad.

On occasion, of course, the United States and Saudi Arabia have coordinated their policies. Both worked for the expulsion of Soviet advisers from Egypt in the early 1970s. Both have tried to strengthen pro-Western governments in countries such as Turkey, Pakistan, and Morocco. And both rushed to aid North Yemen in spring 1979.

Nowhere has the gap between U.S. and Saudi regional policies been greater than on the Arab-Israeli conflict. Over and over the Saudis insist that the greatest threat to regional stability is the unresolved Palestinian question. Some will go so far as to imply that all problems in the area will disappear once the Palestinians have been domesticated by giving them a state of their own. Americans who tend to see regional instability as the result of the strains of modernization, normal interstate conflicts, or Soviet mischief-making often have little patience with the Saudi point of view and may dismiss it as little more than public rhetoric.

It is equally difficult for many Americans to understand why Saudi Arabia treated Egypt as an outcast just because Sadat made peace with Israel. Prone to see Arab states as "moderates" or "radicals," many Americans find the breach between two moderate friends of the United States inexplicable. Indeed, Saudi hostility to Sadat had a negative impact on U.S. public opinion toward the kingdom.

By the time Sadat was assassinated in October 1981, Saudi-Egyptian relations were still strained, but some high-level contacts had been resumed, especially with Vice President Husni Mubarak. The Saudis will doubtless seek to draw Egypt closer to a moderate Arab consensus now that Sadat is no longer alive, but it will be some time before the basic differences between the two countries can be overcome. For the United States, it is especially important to encourage the normalization of relations between Cairo and Riyadh.

On a host of other regional issues the United States and Saudi Arabia have not succeeded in developing a common approach. For example, North Yemen is a country of great importance to the Saudis, but Washington has found it to be extremely difficult to support fully Saudi policy toward Sanaa. As a result, the two countries have often worked at cross-purposes, providing an opportunity for the North Yemen government to play one off against the other.

Similarly, the United States has been slow in following the Saudi lead in cultivating the Iraqi regime of Saddam Hussein. Saudis believe that Baghdad can be lured away from its Soviet connections and that a strongly pragmatic streak lies behind Saddam's Baathist rhetoric. The United States, they believe, should encourage this trend. Thus far Washington has been reticent.

Recent history reveals little reason to expect strong congruence in U.S. and Saudi regional strategies for the Middle East. At a minimum the two countries should try to avoid working entirely at cross-purposes. Better yet, some division of labor may be attainable. But on issues involving the Arab-Israeli conflict and inter-Arab politics, the Saudis will almost certainly choose to pursue their own interests as they see them, not as Washington prefers. On occasion, as in the 1981 Lebanon crisis, a degree of congruence will permit some coordination, but just as often Washington and Riyadh will find it difficult to work closely together.

Beyond the immediate issues of the Arab world, the chances for U.S.-Saudi cooperation are somewhat better. Turkey, Pakistan, and Morocco are all good candidates for U.S. arms and technology and Saudi economic assistance. Somalia may now fit the same category, as well as Sudan. But expectations of developing a grandiose U.S.-Saudi strategy for the multiple ills of the Middle East region must be held in check. Neither Washington nor Riyadh has demonstrated the qualities of leadership, consistency, or foresight to ensure that such a strategy could be mutually beneficial. Instead, both have reacted to events, shifting policies to adjust to existing situations, improvising as much as planning, and counting on luck as much as consultation to prevent direct conflicts over how best to deal with regional problems.

If this uninspired pattern is to be broken, it will not be done by starting with the Arab-Israeli conflict, but rather by selecting an issue such as assistance to Pakistan, to the Afghan resistance, or to the North Yemen government as a testing ground for effective U.S.-Saudi cooperation. The payoffs are potentially high, the perceptions of the issues are not dramatically different, and the combination of Saudi money and U.S. arms may make a difference. These ingredients, unfortunately, are either absent or inadequate for dealing with most of the other regional problems of concern to both countries.

Economic Development

American assistance has been central to the transformation of Saudi Arabia from a poor, underdeveloped, isolated country into a rapidly modernizing, largely urban, and potentially very wealthy nation. Oil wealth was developed by American companies. Economic plans were designed in consultation with American experts. American technology flourishes throughout the kingdom. The national airline, the desalination projects, the hospitals, the national guard, and the vast petrochemical complexes at Jubayl and Yanbu all reflect American technology.

Unlike other dimensions of the U.S.-Saudi relationship, however, economic development has primarily involved the American private sector, not the government. For many years ARAMCO probably played a more important role in U.S.-Saudi relations than did the U.S. government. Despite the Saudi takeover of ARAMCO, it continues to be heavily staffed with Americans. Compared with most American corporate experiences in the developing world, ARAMCO has had a great success story in terms of both profits and relations with the local population and host government.

The U.S. private sector involvement in Saudi Arabia has led to the presence of some 40,000 American citizens, about 4,000 of whom (with 9,000 dependents) work with ARAMCO. Because of their conservative social code, the Saudis have placed severe restraints on the American community in Saudi Arabia. These restrictions, the harsh climate, and U.S. tax laws have discouraged some American businesses from trying to compete in the Saudi market. In recent years, U.S. companies have received a somewhat smaller percentage of contracts and there has been concern that the U.S. share of Saudi imports will drop. European and Japanese competition is keen. Korean, Filipino, and Pakistani workers are pouring into the kingdom to do unskilled and semiskilled work.

Nonetheless, U.S. business is still a strong factor in the kingdom's development.

While most Saudis show little resentment of the large U.S. presence in the country, it has drawn criticism from religious conservatives. One of the demands of the Mecca dissidents was the elimination of the Western presence in Saudi Arabia because of the negative effect it had on Islamic values. Since Mecca, restrictions on foreigners have been tightened. Religious services cannot be openly held and women's clubs cannot meet. As a result, the Western presence is less visible and probably less intrusive than it was in Iran.

Some Saudis are critical of U.S. and other Western companies for fostering the atmosphere in which Saudi officials are corrupted. They talk of large payments being offered to deputy ministers to secure contracts. It is widely assumed that most large business transactions are accompanied by some side payments or commissions. Those Saudis who bemoan the demise of traditional values place more of the blame on the companies who tempt officials to win their favors than on the Saudis who succumb to the lure of enriching themselves at no effort and little risk.

Few Saudis seem to have a nostalgic desire to turn the clock back, but many are alarmed by the pace of change, the rush for instant wealth, and the social upheavals that accompany instant development. Improved health care, better education, ample supplies of food and water, adequate housing, and electricity are desired and now are assumed as a birthright of all Saudis. The Saud family cannot reverse these expectations, and U.S. companies will remain essential to the development of these dimensions of the Saudi society and economy. But whatever credit is won by the regime by improving the prospects of the average Saudi citizen could be eroded by the frustration felt by Saudis as they see the country's wealth wasted on useless projects, as they hear lurid stories of corruption, and as the seamy side of Western culture makes itself felt in the kingdom. If these negative aspects of development outweigh the positive gains, Saudis could turn much of their resentment against the United States as the source of their unhappiness.

Finance

Since 1973 Saudi Arabia has acquired large surpluses of capital, thus increasing its stake in a stable international financial order and in the value of the dollar. By 1981 Saudi surpluses stood at more than $100 billion, most of it held in dollars and much of it invested in the United States. The rationale for investing in the United States is twofold: security of investments and capacity to absorb large sums. No other market seems as certain and nowhere else can large investments be made so easily.

The existence of such large sums provides the United States and Saudi Arabia with another common interest, but problems also exist. Americans want to ease the balance-of-payments problem by attracting surplus petrodollars back to the U.S. economy. To do so they must provide attractive investment opportunities. At the same time, many Americans have been reluctant to see foreigners buy into U.S. companies and banks and purchase real estate. Consequently most Saudi investments are in short-term certificates of deposit and Treasury bills, a situation that is probably less than optimal for both countries.

For the Saudis, holding large reserves in the United States creates a sense of vulnerability. Iranian assets, after all, were frozen by the United States during a political dispute. The same could happen, they fear, to Saudi assets. Thus the Saudis have shown a desire not to accumulate huge surpluses in recent years, preferring to spend most of what they earn. In addition more surplus capital is heading for European and especially Japanese markets to reduce Saudi exposure to U.S. pressures and to deflect domestic criticism that Saudi Arabia is making too many unreciprocated gestures of friendship to the United States.

The Saudis have also increased their contribution to the International Monetary Fund with loans of $11 billion for 1981–82, thus giving the Saudis the sixth largest voting share in the IMF after the United States, Britain, Germany, France, and Japan. Saudi foreign aid remains at high levels, approximately 5–6 percent of gross domestic product in 1980. These measures help to dampen hostility toward Saudi Arabia from the less developed countries.

Whatever their preferences, the Saudis cannot avoid a close connection with the U.S. economy and U.S. financial institutions. Much of their money placed in European banks will find its way to the American market because the investment opportunities are greater there. Nor can the Saudis afford to reduce by much their foreign holdings. At present rates of spending, Saudi reserves cover little more than one year of expenditures. If oil income were ever to be cut off entirely, the Saudis would not be able to continue for long by drawing on their reserves.

Thus despite all the talk of oil in the ground being a better investment than money in the bank, the latter remains essential, especially if the ability to market the former is ever called into question by events comparable to the Iran-Iraq war.

Cultural Barriers

U.S.-Saudi relations would be difficult to manage even if both parties shared the same values and cultural heritage. But despite endless professions of good will and friendship, American and Saudi officials have often had great difficulty in communicating with each other. As a result, serious misperceptions frequently occur, often resulting in charges of bad faith.

On one level, the problem is literally one of language. No Saudi leader of the older generation has chosen to conduct his meetings with American counterparts in English. King Faisal understood English but always spoke through an interpreter. Needless to say, it is a rare U.S. official who can deal with the Saudis in Arabic. Thus on most occasions direct contacts at the highest level have required the presence of an interpreter. In subtle ways this changes the nature of the dialogue and opens the way for misunderstandings.[9]

More important, however, than the problem of language is the style of communication. Americans tend to be direct, legalistic, and fairly pragmatic in their diplomatic exchanges. They expect yes or no answers; they value written documents; they expect punctuality and efficiency; and they require public manifestations of policies and agreements.

By contrast, the Saudis still adhere to a more indirect mode of discourse. Elaborate rituals of hospitality are still required to set the stage for serious talk. Decisions cannot be made under the pressure of time. Yes and no answers are avoided if at all possible, but infinite variations of "maybe" are available. Oral understandings are more important than written agreements. Secrecy is of the essence, and publicity is tantamount to a betrayal of trust.

9. The younger generation of Saudi officials, many schooled in the United States, is much better at bridging the cultural and linguistic gap than the senior princes are. At the same time, they are often more nationalistic and outspoken, so the effect of better communication is sometimes to create a greater sense of confrontation. Since they are often frustrated by the indirectness and politeness of their elders, the younger generation at times bends over backwards to speak bluntly in order to make sure Saudi concerns are taken seriously.

On several occasions U.S.-Saudi relations have been troubled by the difficulty of reading each other's intentions. After the Camp David agreements in September 1978, for example, the Carter administration tried to win Saudi support. In the face of persistent American appeals, Saudi officials said that they appreciated President Carter's efforts on behalf of peace, that they admired Sadat's courage, that they wished the Egyptian people well, and that all sincere efforts to bring peace to the Middle East would have Saudi support. They did not, however, say that they would support the Camp David approach and indeed had no intention of doing so. But the warm words of general encouragement convinced some in Washington that the Saudis would back Sadat. After all, some thought, they had no real alternative. Thus when the Saudis aligned themselves with the anti-Sadat forces at Baghdad in November 1978 the reaction in Washington was one of genuine anger. For several months thereafter the two countries were barely on speaking terms.

A second example involved a well-meaning cabinet member who was visiting Saudi Arabia to discuss economic relations. Like all emissaries, the secretary wanted to deliver a presidential message. Some vague but friendly sentences were agreed upon, but by the time the secretary arrived in Riyadh a new issue had arisen. The Saudis were reported—inaccurately—to be planning to reduce oil production by 1 million barrels a day. Without authorization from Washington, the secretary added some sharp words of warning to the presidential message concerning the effects of such a cutback in oil production. The Saudis listened politely, said little, implied they would be cooperative, and tried to hide their anger.

The following day two reports reached Washington almost simultaneously. One was from the secretary, reporting in euphoric terms the meeting with the Saudis and the great success in preventing a cut in oil production. The other was from another source. The Saudi official who had received the presidential message had immediately called an American official to protest the high-handed ways of the secretary. Never, he claimed, had he been talked to in such a patronizing way. If the secretary had not been a guest, he would have broken off the meeting. The report went on with exquisite details of how offended the Saudi prince had been. The participants in the meeting could hardly have had more widely divergent perceptions of what had taken place.

The problem of communicating across these cultural gaps is especially great for visiting emissaries, each of whom is intent on "solving" some problem in the course of a twenty-four hour visit. It is less of an issue for diplomats in Saudi Arabia who have become accustomed to the Saudi style, but Washington officials rarely succeed in catching the nuances of the Saudi position. The younger generation of Saudis, mostly educated in the United States, can help bridge the gap, but they are often not well informed on the policies of their elders. So while this is likely to remain a problem with no easy solution, an awareness of its potentially pernicious effects can go some distance in reducing its importance.

It is less likely that the Saudi allergy to publicity can be cured or accommodated. The United States is a remarkably open society. Government can rarely keep secrets. Congress and the press insist on their right to be informed. Since U.S.-Saudi relations engender controversy, the Saudis must expect careful scrutiny of important decisions. And with much of the world interested in the happenings of the gulf region, the Saudis cannot escape publicity.

In recent years the royal family has been acutely embarrassed and angered by some publicity. For example, in spring 1979 an unflattering article was written about Crown Prince Fahd in the *Washington Post*. The Saudis thought the story was deliberately planted by the administration to punish the Saudis for not supporting the Egypt-Israel peace treaty. Suspecting the U.S. Central Intelligence Agency of supplying some of the information in the story, the Saudis unceremoniously asked the embassy to remove the head of the CIA station in Jidda, an unusual step for a friendly country to take.

Later, the Saudis were again embarrassed by the screening of the film *Death of a Princess*, a dramatization of a true event involving the execution of the granddaughter of King Khalid's elder brother Muhammad. The Saudis were so angry at this unfavorable publicity that they tried, unsuccessfully, to block the showing of the film in Britain. Failing that, they sent the British ambassador home for several months. By the time the film aired in the United States the Saudis realized that they could not stop it and instead had merely succeeded in drawing attention to it. In retrospect the entire incident seemed overblown, but it left a residue of anger among Saudi officials.

Unfortunately for the Saudis, incidents of this sort are bound to recur. They cannot be expected to like the leaks to the press, congressional hearings, anti-Saudi propaganda, and politically motivated speeches against them. But in the real world of politics these are problems likely to confront anyone with power and money. In time perhaps the Saudis will develop a thicker skin. Perhaps they will learn to respond to criticism more effectively than has often been the case, or perhaps they will conclude that most of the sound and fury does not make much difference in any case.

Future Problems

The U.S.-Saudi relationship has fairly good prospects of continuing on a generally positive path through the 1980s, but differences of interest, compounded by cultural barriers, ensure that problems will periodically arise. Some of the divisive issues can easily be anticipated:

Arms supplies. No matter how generous the United States may be in responding to Saudi requests, the Saudis will always want something that goes beyond what Washington believes is prudent or politically feasible. While no easy solution exists for this problem, it helps to be able to tell the Saudis well in advance what they can and cannot expect. The worst combination is that of whetting their appetite with technical briefings on sophisticated new systems, then denying them access on political grounds. At some point in the overall security dialogue, the United States should also make a serious effort to demonstrate that relatively simple, easily maintained equipment, such as antitank weapons and antiaircraft missiles, may be as useful as sophisticated aircraft. The Iran-Iraq war, for example, seems to demonstrate some of the limits of airpower for third world countries. It is in the U.S. interest that the Saudis not waste their limited manpower on weapon systems that serve little real purpose and are poorly adapted to the realities of the region.

Bases. U.S. military planners invariably fantasize about the merits of bases in Saudi Arabia. On most military dimensions—logistics, nature of the threat, warning times—a U.S. base near Saudi oil fields makes sense. But politically the Saudis are likely to continue to refuse, arguing that it could be politically destabilizing and that it would serve as a magnet to draw more Soviet forces into the area. Instead of bases, the Saudis prefer an "over-the-horizon" presence, combined with some discreet understanding of how Saudi facilities might be made available in emergencies. For the United States to press for fully sovereign bases would be to jeopardize the type of security cooperation that is possible.

The Palestinians and Jerusalem. The Saudis still feel they need some indication that the United States will not indefinitely underwrite Israel's

occupation of the West Bank, Gaza, the Golan Heights, and East Jerusalem. At a minimum an independent U.S. position on the legality and
permanence of the Israeli occupation is expected. Preferably the Saudis
want some evidence of movement. It is not so much the precise details
of the U.S. position that count but the direction of policy. Prolonged
stalemate and visible U.S. disinterest will place the Saudis in an awkward
position as they have to justify their close relations with Washington.
Although the Palestinian issue is not necessarily the most important
problem in U.S.-Saudi relations, it can be ignored only at considerable
risk. Americans should not underestimate the depth of Saudi preoccupation with the Palestinians and the conflict with Israel.

Oil. The United States will continue to look to the Saudis to use their
oil production to moderate prices and to help meet emergency shortfalls
in supply. Very rapid price increases or overt use by Saudi Arabia of
the oil weapon could lead to deep strains in U.S.-Saudi relations. The
perception (largely inaccurate) that the Saudis oppose U.S. efforts to fill
the Strategic Petroleum Reserve could also create problems.

Petrodollars. How will the Saudis use their oil revenues? Will they
continue to spend large sums on contracts with American companies?
Will they aid friends of the United States? Will they invest in the U.S.
market? Any dramatic shift away from past practices could add strain
to the U.S.-Saudi relationship.

The Soviet Union. At some point in the future the Saudis will be
tempted to upgrade their dialogue with the USSR. Diplomatic relations
have never been broken in fact, but diplomatic representation in each
other's capital has not existed since the late 1930s. The exchange of
diplomats could well be a traumatic moment for the United States. The
early warning signs are already present. Polite words are being ex-
changed between Moscow and Riyadh. Occasional direct contacts take
place. Some trade ties exist. Sales of oil to East Europe may not be far off.
East European and Soviet military equipment has been allowed to pass
through Saudi territory to reach Iraq since early 1981. Soviet commercial aircraft are allowed occasional overflights of Saudi territory en route
to South Yemen. If the Saudis can see any benefit in establishing full
diplomatic relations with Moscow, they will do so, despite anxieties in
Washington. They may also take such action as a deliberate signal of
their displeasure over U.S. policies.

Crisis management. How will the United States and Saudi Arabia try
to coordinate policies in the event of a South Yemen threat against

North Yemen? Iranian threats against the Arab side of the gulf? Iraqi pressures on Kuwait? Some prior contingency planning is needed, along with consultations as the crises unfold. A quick reaction capability is essential for the United States, since in crises the Saudis will want immediate reassurance.

Guidelines for U.S. Policy

Few countries will rival Saudi Arabia in their importance to the United States in the 1980s. At stake is the economic well-being of much of the world, energy supplies, and the containment of Soviet expansion into the Persian Gulf region. For the United States to enhance the prospects of attaining its objectives, the effective management of the U.S.-Saudi relationship will be essential.

At the risk of oversimplification, some guidelines for U.S. policy can be suggested:

Be realistic about Saudi influence. Despite their wealth the Saudis are not very powerful. Aware of their own limitations and vulnerabilities, the Saudis behave cautiously in foreign policy. They are not leaders. At best, they are consensus builders.

On Arab-Israeli issues this means that the United States should not press the Saudis to adopt a public stand in support of American peace initiatives, at least not as long as those are limited to Camp David. The Saudis will not take the lead in negotiations with Israel. At most, they may operate discreetly in the right context to support Jordan and moderate Palestinians who are ready for peace with Israel.

On most inter-Arab issues the Saudis will similarly seek to use their limited influence through quiet diplomacy. American demands that they take a more active, highly visible role in the affairs of the Middle East in support of U.S. interests will produce little more than frustration and resentment. By all means, the United States should resist the temptation to see Saudi Arabia as the replacement for the shah's Iran as a regional power.

Keep the U.S. military presence modest. As much as American leaders might want full-fledged U.S. bases on Saudi soil to help protect the oil resources of the gulf, it would be an error to seek them. In present circumstances the Saudis will resist granting base rights to the United States, judging that to do so would expose them to unacceptable domestic and foreign pressures. Instead of bases in Saudi Arabia, the United States should seek to increase its capabilities to deter Soviet military threats to the gulf by other means. For example, the Saudis are prepared to cooperate in "overbuilding" some of their own military facilities and may agree to some "pre-positioning" of equipment. The two aircraft carriers that have been in the Indian Ocean since 1980 are both acceptable and reassuring to the Saudis. In addition the four AWACS aircraft now in Saudi Arabia are operated by Americans, the data are shared with the Saudis, and they provide a very useful intelligence and command-and-control capability. Combined with adequate airlift, these arrangements could provide the near equivalent, in military terms, of a base. They would have the great advantage, however, of being politically more acceptable to the Saudis and less destabilizing internally than sovereign American bases.

Be careful with arms sales. Somehow the United States has to break the pattern of whetting the Saudi appetite for state-of-the-art technology and then, because of U.S. domestic political considerations, dragging its heels in responding to Saudi requests. The debates over F-15s in 1978 and AWACS in 1981 are examples of what the United States should try to avoid.

The first order of business is to try to reach agreement on a military force posture that makes sense for the Saudis and that the United States in good conscience can defend before Congress and the American public as meeting legitimate security needs. When the Reagan administration first decided to sell five AWACS planes to Saudi Arabia, the rationale should have been cast in terms of meeting real threats to Saudi security—a very defensible proposition—and advancing U.S. national interests, not that President Carter had made a promise or that the sales would guarantee oil supplies or Saudi moderation toward the peace process.

If the United States cannot justify the sale of equipment in military terms, it should not make the sale, since other justifications are often ill-considered, misleading, and can leave a residue of bitterness. The United States cannot expect explicit, publicly acknowledged quid pro quos from the Saudis for arms that they are paying for. This does not work with the Israelis or Egyptians, who even get the arms on subsidized terms, and it will not work with the Saudis. The influence the United States buys by providing arms may be elusive, but insisting on apparent clarity will not enhance its real influence.

Don't forget the Palestinians. American credibility in the Middle East, especially with the Saudis, requires a strategy for resolving the remainder of the Arab-Israeli conflict. Camp David is not enough, and its symbolism has become a problem for much of the Arab world. While the positive gains of Camp David can and should be preserved, the United States will need to go beyond the "full autonomy" framework if movement toward peace is to be achieved.

The basic equations are not difficult to define and have long been part of U.S. policy: in return for credible assurances of peace and security from her Arab neighbors, Israel should agree in principle to the end of military rule over Palestinians in the West Bank and Gaza and phased withdrawal of troops from occupied territories. This, after all, is what UN Resolution 242 envisaged before Prime Minister Begin unilaterally redefined its meaning. Much would need to be negotiated, and problems would doubtless arise over the status of East Jerusalem and the precise form of Palestinian self-determination. But some indication from Washington that the status quo is not acceptable and that Arab-Israeli peace remains a high priority is central to developing an effective American strategy for the Middle East.

In addition to these substantive points, several procedural guidelines are also needed:

Don't panic over differences. The United States and Saudi Arabia are not destined to have identical views, especially on issues relating to inter-Arab politics and Israel. They will disagree in the future as they have in the past. Americans should not overreact. The essential interests —oil, security, containing Soviet power—should be carefully watched to ensure a complementarity of policies, but on other issues the United States sometimes will have to accept differences as inevitable.

Strike the right tone. The Saudis should not be coddled or shown excessive deference. They appreciate frankness and candor if offered in private. The United States should try to keep its dialogue with the Saudis on sensitive matters out of the press.

Don't rely on emissaries. The Saudis are slow to trust foreigners. Emissaries who sweep through Riyadh in the hope of solving problems will be disappointed. Instead, the U.S. government should maintain a first-rate ambassador in Saudi Arabia and rely heavily on him to conduct the dialogue, with a few other high-level officials maintaining regular contact with their Saudi counterparts. In addition, presidential letters should be sent only rarely, on matters of great importance. In the past too many presidential requests on too many issues have been made.

Reduce external pressures. The proper U.S. role is to shield Saudi Arabia from excessive pressures from outside, especially from the Soviet Union and its friends. American officials are less well positioned to advise the Saudis on how to reform their own society. If the United States has the irresistible urge to press for internal reforms, it should do so privately, not in public initiatives.

Don't play family favorites. It will not serve U.S. interests to become deeply involved in royal family politics. Some Americans favor Fahd, others Sultan, some Abdallah. The less said by American officials about such preferences the better. For the moment, no alternative to the royal family seems likely to be more friendly to the United States, nor is one member of the family so much better than others that Americans should become involved in their domestic politics.

Finally, it is worth remembering that no quick-fix, no single test will assure a harmonious U.S.-Saudi relationship. Each hurdle is a prelude to another, but a consistent pattern of mature U.S. handling of differences will provide a strong base for the relationship. Although the United States cannot take Saudi Arabia for granted, it should not be overwhelmed by the difficulty of winning Saudi cooperation on essential issues. Despite the many problems that exist and the inevitability of differences, the basic relationship is still surprisingly healthy. It will take a lot of mistakes on both sides to end what has become a very special and complex form of interdependency.

Conclusion

The future of Saudi Arabia depends in large measure on its relationship with the United States. Many internal developments, of course, will have a life of their own. But Saudi Arabia has in recent years been heavily influenced by events beyond its borders, and that reality will not change in the 1980s.

If the United States can develop an effective regional strategy for the Middle East that contains Soviet and radical pressures, helps resolve conflicts, provides security for friends, and eases the painful process of modernization, Saudi Arabia will be the beneficiary. If instead the

United States appears to be weak, uncertain, clumsy, or overbearing, it can greatly complicate the kingdom's problems. In that case the Al Saud would be tempted to take their distance from Washington and try as best they can to adapt to their immediate environment. This could be a very costly outcome for the world as a whole, and one that the United States has the capability to prevent. Few foreign policy matters deserve higher priority in Washington, for it is there that the future of U.S.-Saudi relations will largely be decided.

Appendix A

Economic Data

Table A-1. *Saudi Arabian Oil Revenues, 1970–80*
Billions

| | Revenue | |
| | Current dollars | 1980 dollars[a] |
Year		
1970	1.2	2.3
1971	1.9	3.5
1972	2.7	4.8
1973	4.3	7.2
1974	22.6	35.0
1975	25.7	36.3
1976	30.8	41.4
1977	36.5	46.3
1978	32.2	38.1
1979	60.0	65.4
1980	95.0	95.0

Source: *The Middle East and North Africa, 1980–81,* 27th ed. (London: Europa Publications, 1980), p. 654.

a. When the 1980 dollar figures are adjusted to reflect the import value to OPEC countries, the numbers are somewhat higher: 1973, $9 billion; 1974, $39.6 billion; 1975, $50.5 billion; 1977, $54.5 billion; 1978, $41.3 billion; 1979, $68.2 billion; 1980, $95.0 billion. See "International Economic Issues and Priorities," *World Financial Markets,* Morgan Guaranty Trust of New York (December 1980), table 4, p. 8; and "Implications of the New Oil Situation," ibid. (May 1979), table 1, p. 2.

Table A-2. *Saudi Arabian Imports and Exports, 1976–80*

Billions of dollars

Country	1976	1977	1978	1979	1980
			Imports to Saudi Arabia		
United States	2.80	3.60	4.40	4.90	5.80
Japan	1.90	2.40	3.30	3.80	n.a.
West Germany	1.20	1.70	2.01	2.40	n.a.
United Kingdom	0.71	1.00	1.50	1.90	n.a.
Italy	0.66	1.10	1.50	1.90	n.a.
France	0.34	0.62	0.88	1.10	n.a.
Other	3.19	4.28	6.32	7.60	n.a.
World total (f.o.b.)	10.80	14.70	20.00	23.60	34.70[a]
			Exports from Saudi Arabia		
United States	1.9	4.4	6.6	10.9	12.5
Japan	8.2	8.8	8.5	11.0	n.a.
West Germany	1.3	1.3	1.2	1.8	n.a.
United Kingdom	2.0	2.0	1.4	2.1	n.a.
Italy	2.6	3.4	2.8	5.2	n.a.
France	4.2	4.0	4.3	5.3	n.a.
Other	21.1	22.5	17.1	27.2	n.a.
World total (f.o.b.)	41.3	46.4	41.9	63.5	102.5[a]

Sources: Saudi Arabian Monetary Agency, Research and Statistics Department, *Annual Report 1400 (1980)* (Riyadh: Kingdom of Saudi Arabia, 1980), p. 63; *The Middle East and North Africa, 1980–81,* 27th ed. (London: Europa Publications, 1980), p. 658; Robin Allen, "U.S. Exporters Head for Pastures New," *Middle East Economic Digest,* March 13–19, 1981, p. 47; and Dennis Topping and Dennis Dwyer, *The Times* (London), December 9, 1980. Figures are rounded.

n.a. Not available.

a. Estimate.

Appendix B

The U.S.-Saudi Military Relationship

Table B-1. *U.S. Military Sales and Deliveries to Saudi Arabia, 1971–80*

Millions of dollars

| Fiscal year | Sales | | | Commercial exports licensed under Arms Export Control Act |
	Total agreements	Corps of Engineers projects	Actual deliveries	
1971	15.2	...	64.0	20.8
1972	305.4	...	159.6	3.6
1973	1,152.0	1,064.3	211.0	5.7
1974	2,048.2	1,389.4	331.7	18.0
1975	5,776.0	3,937.7	329.6	20.2
1976[a]	7,742.1	3,745.0	926.9	92.7
1977	1,888.2	550.6	1,502.1	44.0
1978	4,121.5	701.6	2,368.9	166.3
1979	6,468.7	1,522.1	2,471.5	44.4
1980	4,536.8	2,393.4	2,724.7	29.0

Source: U.S. Department of Defense, Security Assistance Agency, *Foreign Military Sales and Military Assistance Facts* (DOD, December 1980), pp. 1–2, 5, 7–8, 27–28. Figures are rounded.

a. Includes transitional quarter, July–September 1976.

Appendix C

Petroleum: A Look into the Future

AHMAD ZAKI YAMANI

I WOULD LIKE US to go back a little bit to the past to remember two important facts that will help us see the way.

The first is that there is a relationship between oil prices and oil consumption rates. Whenever prices go down, consumption goes up, and vice versa. In the sixties and early seventies, when the oil prices were low and were controlled by the oil companies, which manipulated the prices under the direction of their respective Western governments, the consuming countries tended to overuse this vital material. Consumption was greatly increasing at a yearly rate of about 7 percent to 8 percent during the period of 1961–73. In 1973 the price of oil started to increase and approach realistic levels; thus the rate of oil consumption started to decrease in 1974, and by 1978 the increase was only 1.4 percent per annum. Again, when prices increased in 1979–80 as a result of another corrective move, the rates of oil consumption went down, and we expect a further decrease in oil consumption in 1981 compared with 1980.

The second fact is that whenever oil prices increase, larger amounts of capital are invested in search of alternative sources of energy and in the search for oil in different areas. After the 1973 price increase, huge capital investments were made available. Also, coal consumption increased. In the seventies, consumption of coal, as a source of energy, reached 18 percent of total energy requirements compared to 7 percent prior to that. Likewise, there was an increase in nuclear energy, as well as in the rates of oil well drilling. . . .

In light of these two facts, let us predict together how things will be in the future. Predicting the near future may not be difficult. In spite of the Iraqi-Iranian war, and thanks to the increase in production by Saudi Arabia, Kuwait, and the United Arab Emirates, oil supplies are almost sufficient to meet the world's demand except during wintertime when consumers have to depend on stored oil, which is meant for use under such circumstances. After the wintertime, there will be a balance between supply and demand. There may be a relative surplus from which consumers can store oil to replace what they have used during the winter.

THIS edited version of a lecture given by Minister Yamani at the University of Petroleum and Minerals in Dammam, Saudi Arabia, on January 31, 1981, is based on an unofficial translation and portions of the original Arabic transcript.

In 1982, if the Iraqi-Iranian war were to continue, we expect a surplus in the summer of that year. This is the easy part of our prediction of what will happen in the near future. But if we try to look further ahead, we come up against contradictions. Yet we have to know about the future as much as we can so as to build our policy in light of whatever facts and figures are available to us.

We do not know now how the situation will be in the consuming countries. If we go back to the year 1973, for example, when the price of oil sharply increased, we find a great interest in investments for alternative sources of energy as well as investments for controlling consumption. However, this zeal started to fade away because the producing countries did not continue to raise prices in terms of actual currency value. For the increases in the price of oil were not large enough even to cover the prevailing inflation rates during the period 1973–79. A price of over $12 per barrel in 1979 actually represented no more than $7.80 in terms of the 1974 dollar value. This meant in fact that oil prices started to decrease instead of increasing, which definitely led the people in the petroleum industry to discontinue further investments in means for developing their industry and reducing oil consumption. Once again the American gas-guzzling luxury cars returned to dominate the street and highway scenes. Here we might be blamed, and Saudi Arabia, which led the campaign of not raising the prices, might be accused of bringing this state of affairs upon us.

As for the future, if the oil-producing countries could finally approve the formula submitted by the Strategy Planning Committee calling for a gradual but real-value increase in oil prices that would exceed the rate of inflation by a certain percentage, then those who shelved their plans for reducing oil consumption would have to reactivate those plans. If this takes place, the incentive might again spend itself out, as in 1974, and we may see another period of increase in oil consumption followed by a price reduction resulting in yet another sharp increase in prices that will weigh very heavily on world economy.

This, however, is an incomplete picture. We will discover this as we approach the year 1982 and enter it, for then we will most likely encounter a big glut in the oil market at a time when we are not ready for it and have not definitely decided to increase oil prices by rates that exceed those of inflation. Then the chances of a price collapse will be great for those consuming countries that seek a reduction in prices, even if such a collapse would be costly to them too.

The OPEC countries, which produced over 31 million barrels per day in 1979, decreased their production to 27 million bpd in 1980. This production will further decrease this year in the absence of two big producers, namely, Iraq and Iran. But when the war ends, the first thing these two countries will do is produce the maximum amount possible to make up for their losses and rebuild what has been destroyed by the war. We expect that the production of these two countries will be no less than 6 million or 7 million bpd in 1982. Now, if all the OPEC countries produce a total not exceeding 2 million bpd,

the kingdom will have no choice but to decrease its production. This is undoubtedly welcome to us. Nevertheless, even when we lower our production,
there will arise technical difficulties and an opportunity for repricing.

This is one side of the picture. The other side is the Soviet bloc and the extent of its oil needs. All the available studies point to the fact that the Soviet
bloc will be definitely importing oil sometime in the eighties, most probably
in 1987. If this will be the case, we would lose a little more than 1 million bpd
of oil supplies that were flowing from Russia to the West and to the Eastern
bloc. In addition, the Soviet bloc countries will be seeking some supplies from
the OPEC countries. We cannot here discuss in detail the political consequences of such a development, but they undoubtedly will be very significant
since Russia, which now obtains 50 percent of its foreign currency from selling oil, will have to find hard currency to buy for itself or for others in dollars
rather than in rubles. The countries under Russian influence, which currently
obtain cheap oil from Russia, will be deprived of such oil, and Russia itself
will lose thereby an important hold on them. The Eastern bloc will have to
turn to the West, of which OPEC is a part, which conducts its dealings with
dollars. This situation will force them to increase their trade relations with the
West in order to get dollars. This increase in trade relations will strengthen
the common commercial interests, which in turn will foster common political
interests. At this point the danger of East-West confrontation will multiply.
The main arena of such a struggle will be the oil sources.

Again, I cannot with any precision predict what will happen if OPEC continues to raise the real sale value of its oil and to what extent the Western
countries will be able to reduce their oil consumption and increase their consumption of alternative sources of energy. However, in spite of all the ob-
stacles that stand in the way of such a situation, we will reach the stage when
the Western countries will succeed in achieving this goal and thus will elimi-
nate energy problems—unless political storms emerge and affect the oil supplies. Such storms are expected. In the near past, in 1978, when there was a surplus in the oil market, the world was expecting OPEC to collapse. But then the
Iranian revolution occurred, and the resultant oil shortage strengthened
OPEC. Turmoil happened again, and in 1980, when oil supplies increased and
people spoke about a glut, the Iran-Iraq war broke out and people were scared.

The elements of future political storms in the area are there. Such storms
will occur unless efforts are unified to defuse them and put an end to the
struggle over this sensitive part of the world. Thus in spite of the poor visibility, we can predict that we will reach agreement over the pricing of oil, that
the Western countries will continue their efforts toward reducing energy
consumption, and that OPEC will continue to be the main exporter of oil,
increasing or reducing its production as necessary until the world discovers an
alternative source of energy.

As far as Saudi Arabia is concerned, our interests are clear. First, we do not
intend to exhaust this wealth quickly and deprive our future generations of
it. On the other hand, we do not want to shorten the life span of oil as a source
of energy before we complete the elements of our industrial and economic

development, and before we build our country to be able to depend on sources of income other than oil. In this respect the kingdom's interests might differ from those of its OPEC colleagues. In OPEC there are countries that will stop exporting oil toward the end of the eighties; for such countries the life span of oil should not extend beyond that time. But if the life span of oil as a source of energy ends at the close of the present decade, this will spell disaster for Saudi Arabia. The line that separates the two situations is a matter of judgment. Our behavior should be guided by what we perceive of the future. What we ought to do now is stop this depletion as soon as possible and go step by step in order to prolong the life span of oil for a period sufficient to put our economic and developmental house in order. As the coming century arrives, we will have diversified our sources of income, and we will still have enough oil, which we and the coming generations will utilize as a source of energy and as feedstock for the various industries we intend to establish.

[*Questions and Minister Yamani's answers followed the remarks above.*]

Q: The Saudi citizen who looks at his country's current oil policy finds that the country is producing more than its economy needs and is selling at prices lower than current prices, even lower than the prices received by other gulf states. Such sacrifice is rewarded by hostile attacks and threats by the press, media, and even certain high government officials in Western countries. Don't you think the time has come for us to stop sacrificing ourselves for the sake of the oil consumers?

A: Let us set emotions aside and look at the facts. Saudi Arabia's interest may appear to be served by lower production rates and higher prices irrespective of the outcome. Regardless of the political reasons that lie behind the calls for higher or lower prices, for fighting such increases, or for higher or lower production rates, let me remind you of my earlier statement regarding the link between price and consumption rates. As the price rises, consumption falls and capital is invested in searching for alternative sources of energy. Had you been with us on OPEC's Strategy Planning Committee, where we spent more than two and a half years assisted by some of the best-qualified individuals and scientific institutions in the world, you would have been surprised to find out that raising prices excessively and without restrictions or limits will not be in the interest of certain OPEC members, including Saudi Arabia and Iraq. You may have noticed that Iraq, which until 1977 or 1978 had pioneered the call for raising and amending prices, has begun to reconsider, inasmuch as the study, made with the benefit of computer data, indicates that we have reached a crucial point and that going beyond it would jeopardize the interests of Iraq, Saudi Arabia, and the UAE.

If we force Western countries to invest heavily in finding alternative sources of energy, they will. This would take no more than seven to ten years and would result in reducing dependence on oil as a source of energy to a point that would jeopardize Saudi Arabia's interests. Saudi Arabia would then be unable to find markets to sell enough oil to meet its financial requirements. This picture should be well understood.

I realize that the question was motivated by the passionate concern that we are being cheated: we are selling at prices lower than those received by others, and we are producing at rates far above our needs. Believe me, I understand and appreciate your concern. Your concern is perfectly valid, although its grounds are not. Let us look at the facts objectively and with clear minds. Let us not rashly toe the line behind other countries with definite interests in receiving the highest possible price per barrel of oil in the shortest possible time during which they have marketable oil. To clarify my point, let me take the case of Algeria. Algeria at present sells 1 million bpd. In 1985 it will be selling only one-half million, and in 1990 its sales will drop to zero. If I were Algerian, I would certainly wish the price per barrel of oil to reach $100 this very day even at the risk of driving the world to an economic depression, because no matter how bad the world is economically, it will still buy that million barrels of oil from me. And if by so doing I encourage and drive the world to invest in finding alternative sources of energy, such investments will not bear fruit in less than ten years, at which time the matter would be of no concern to me.

Let us look at past records that I have already mentioned. Before 1972 the increase in the rate of oil consumption was over 7.8 percent annually. As a result of the increase in prices, this annual increase fell to 1.4 percent. And in 1980 we had a decrease of 4.7 percent in consumption, compared with 1979.

What does this mean? Let me once more return to OPEC and review some details. This year OPEC member countries will produce 25 million bpd. This is OPEC's share of the world market. Leaving Saudi Arabia aside—Iran and Iraq as well—we have Kuwait, which produces approximately 2 million bpd including its production from the Neutral Zone, and the UAE and Qatar, which produce just over 2 million. This brings the total to 4 million. Venezuela produces 2 million bpd, which brings the total to 6 million. Add Nigeria's 2 million bpd and you have a total of 8 million bpd. One and one-half million from Libya and 1 million from Algeria brings the total to 10.5 million. If we add the 1.5 million produced by Indonesia and the combined production of Ecuador and Gabon, plus Saudi Arabia's production from the Neutral Zone, we have 13 million bpd. Iran currently exports—as of three weeks ago—1 million bpd, which brings the total to 14 million bpd. Iraq also exports small amounts to Turkey, France, and Italy. Let us say that the total is 14 million bpd. Saudi Arabia's 10 million bpd brings the total to 24 million. The additional 1 million required is obtained from stockpiles.

When Iran and Iraq resume their normal production of 7 million bpd, and when OPEC's share of the market is reduced to less than 24 million bpd, Saudi Arabia will have to reduce its production to an average of no more than 5 million bpd. Technical experts among you realize that the gas that will be used in fueling our industry and running our desalination and power plants is an associated gas that can only be produced with oil. This is a technical handicap.

We have reached a point in our growth and development where we are engaged in a race against time to build various industries that use up billions of dollars. What would be our situation if OPEC's share of the world market

continued to decline—as is concluded by some studies done by neutral parties
—to 22 million bpd? Do we ask Iraq and Iran, which have come out of a
ruinous war and are entitled to build up their war-ravaged economies, to
lower their production? Shall we ask Algeria, Nigeria, or Indonesia—countries that need every dollar they can lay their hands on for their own development—to reduce their production? The burden will fall on Saudi Arabia,
which may have to reduce its production to 4 million or even 3 million bpd.
This picture is based on scientific studies and is supported by facts and figures
available to OPEC and to agencies of our Ministry of Petroleum. Therefore,
while we all share this passionate concern over the high rate of production and
the price issue, we must not forget the results of exaggeration. We must therefore be reasonable and decisive. Saudi Arabia's interests lie in extending the
life span of oil to the longest period possible to enable us to build a diversified
economy supported by industry, agriculture, and other endeavors. Unless we
do that there will come a time when this developing country will receive a
violent shock.

I hope that I have clearly explained the situation. We have observed that the
price of oil is gradually rising at a higher rate than we had expected or than the
so-called hawks in OPEC had ever dreamed of.

Q: Do you expect a change in Saudi Arabia's oil policy by the end of the
1980s when the USSR and its satellite countries require oil?

A: At present Saudi Arabia does not sell oil to Eastern bloc countries. The
problem of the USSR and its satellite countries does not lie only in finding a
continuous and stable source of oil but also in their hard-currency shortages.
It remains to be seen whether the Soviet bloc will be satisfied by ensuring its
oil requirements through controlling certain oil supply routes or whether it
will try to acquire the oil sources and pay for its oil in rubles instead of dollars.
The possibility that the USSR will occupy the oil sources is a matter observers
and researchers have speculated on for a long time. As to Saudi Arabia, the
USSR will not only have a hard time reaching it, but it will also have to face
a world war doing so. If the matter was confined to commercial dealings, I
do not foresee any great difficulty in reaching certain understandings that
would govern any future relations, irrespective of whether such relations concern only one country or the entire Eastern bloc. Moreover, the Eastern bloc
countries can obtain their needs from other OPEC member states besides
Saudi Arabia, such as Iran, Iraq, Libya, and Algeria, from which they buy at
present. Such need is therefore not urgent, because they can secure a source of
supply elsewhere.

Q: ... Why don't European countries attempt to dispel the misconception
prevailing in the Western world that OPEC is responsible for the world's
economic difficulties? Why do certain countries buy more oil than they actually need and stockpile it? And why do we sell them that oil? Why don't
we keep it in our fields and sell it to them when it is needed?

A: ... OPEC has sustained many attacks in the past and is likely to sustain
more in the future. Even Saudi Arabia, which has sacrificed and sold its oil at
the lowest price possible and produced at rates higher than it needs, is por-

trayed by the U.S. press as a bloodsucker taking from the West what it has no right to take. Recently, however, there has been a noticeable change in this attitude toward Saudi Arabia as well as OPEC. Previously OPEC was portrayed as a beast with an Arab headdress. But officials in both the United States and Europe have begun to realize that OPEC was performing a service not only to its member states but also to the world.

Just before we went to Bali recently, there was fear and apprehension among Western officials that the Iraqi-Iranian war would lead to a confrontation within OPEC and bring about its collapse, thus releasing the oil demon from its OPEC bonds. For the first time, the Western authorities felt the importance of OPEC and candidly expressed it to me. The very same newspapers that had attacked OPEC in the past have started to sing OPEC's praises and to commend its importance to the world economy and its constructive role in serving that economy.

Q: What about stockpiling?

A: In 1978, stockpiles had reached the lowest level known in the history of the oil industry. The companies and consumer countries were trying to pressure OPEC to refrain from raising its prices more than necessary. But the Iranian revolution took them all by surprise and they all went through a period of shortages. The Iranian revolution and the short supply created a new market condition. Many of the so-called independent companies, which in the past relied on the large international oil companies for their oil supplies, suddenly found themselves deprived of oil and were forced to buy their supplies directly from the spot market at very high prices since they had to compete with the large companies. As the pressure eased, these independent companies began to stockpile to ease their reliance on the large companies. As the independent companies' fears of further turbulence increased, their stockpiles rose until they reached a level unprecedented in the history of the oil industry. This phenomenon was expected to produce a price collapse, inasmuch as the stockpilers are merchants who just want to sell for profit. But stockpiling costs more than $6 per barrel a year. Add to this the financing, the lease of storage facilities, and the high interest rates and you have more than 50 cents per month per barrel in storage costs. When this merchant realizes that the price per barrel of oil is not going to rise more than $6 per year, he is going to stop stockpiling and to use what he already has instead of buying on world markets. Many factors enter into what happened in the past, the most important of which are psychological and political. Commercial factors have led to a change in the type of relationship between the big companies and the independents.

As to the future, if we can establish an era of stability governed by OPEC's pricing guidelines, then I do not expect excessive stockpiling except for political reasons, such as the strategic reasons used by the United States to build its stockpiles. Stockpiling for political reasons is governed by principles of politics and is outside the scope of commerce. Current stockpile levels caused by commercial and psychological factors are not likely to be maintained under stable conditions beyond 1982.

Appendix D

Genealogy of the Al Saud

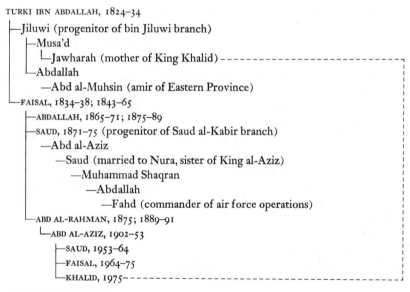

TURKI IBN ABDALLAH, 1824–34
- Jiluwi (progenitor of bin Jiluwi branch)
  - Musa'd
    - Jawharah (mother of King Khalid) ------------------------
  - Abdallah
    - Abd al-Muhsin (amir of Eastern Province)
- FAISAL, 1834–38; 1843–65
  - ABDALLAH, 1865–71; 1875–89
  - SAUD, 1871–75 (progenitor of Saud al-Kabir branch)
    - Abd al-Aziz
      - Saud (married to Nura, sister of King al-Aziz)
        - Muhammad Shaqran
          - Abdallah
            - Fahd (commander of air force operations)
  - ABD AL-RAHMAN, 1875; 1889–91
    - ABD AL-AZIZ, 1902–53
      - SAUD, 1953–64
      - FAISAL, 1964–75
      - KHALID, 1975- ------------------------------------

Dates denote periods of rule.

Sources: Adapted from H. StJ. B. Philby, *Arabian Jubilee* (London: Robert Hale, 1952), pp. 250–71; R. Bayly Winder, *Saudi Arabia in the Nineteenth Century* (New York: St. Martin's Press, 1965), p. 279; and David E. Long, *Saudi Arabia*, Washington Papers 39 (Beverly Hills: Sage Publications for the Center for Strategic and International Studies, Georgetown University, 1976), p. 259.

Appendix E

Key Members of the Family of King Abd al-Aziz

ABD AL-AZIZ IBN ABD AL-RAHMAN (b. 1880; r. 1902–53; d. 1953)

	MOTHER'S NAME
—SAUD (b. 1902; r. 1953–64; d. 1969)	*Wadhba bint Muhammad*
—FAISAL (b. 1906; r. 1964–75; d. 1975)	*Tarfah bint al-Shaykh*
—Abdallah (b. 1921; former minister of interior)	*Sultana bint Ahmad al-Sudayri*
—Khalid (b. 1941; governor of Asir)	*Haya bint Turki bin Jiluwi*
—Muhammad (b. 1937)	*Iffat bint Ahmad al-Thunayan*
—Saud (b. 1941; foreign minister)	" " " "
—Abd al-Rahman (b. 1942; army officer)	" " " "
—Bandar (b. 1943; air force)	" " " "
—Turki (b. 1945; intelligence)	" " " "
—Muhammad (b. 1910)	*Jawharah bint Musa'd bin Jiluwi*
—KHALID (b. 1912; r. 1975–)	" " " " "
—Nasir (b. 1920; former governor of Riyadh)	*Bazza*
—Sa'd (b. 1920)	*Jawharah bint Sa'd al-Sudayri*
—Musa'id (b. 1923; his son killed Faisal)	" " " "
—Abd al-Muhsin (b. 1925; governor of Medina; "free prince")	" " " "
—Fahd (b. 1921; crown prince)	*Hussah bint al-Sudayri*
—Sultan (b. 1924; minister of defense)	" " "
—Abd al-Rahman (b. 1926)	" " "
—Nayif (b. 1933; minister of interior)	" " "
—Turki (b. 1934)	" " "
—Salman (b. 1936; governor of Riyadh)	" " "
—Ahmad (b. 1940; deputy minister of interior)	" " "
—Abdallah (b. 1923; national guard)	*Al Fahda bint Asi al-Shuraym*
—Fawwaz (b. 1934; former governor of Mecca; "free prince")	*Bazza*
—Mish'al (b. 1926; former governor of Mecca; minister of defense, 1951–56)	*Shahida*
—Mit'ab (b. 1928; minister of public works and housing)	"

	MOTHER'S NAME
—Talal (b. 1931; "free prince")	*Munayir*
—Nawwaf (b. 1934; head of royal palace under Saud)	"
—Badr (b. 1933; deputy commander of the national guard)	*Haya bint Sa'd al-Sudayri*
—Abd al-Ilah (b. 1935; governor of Qasim)	" " " "
—Abd al-Majid (b. 1940; governor of Tabuk)	" " " "
—Majid (b. 1934; governor of Mecca; former minister of municipal affairs)	*Muhdi*
—Sattam (b. 1943; deputy governor of Riyadh)	"
—Muqrin (b. 1943; governor of Hail)	*Barakah al-Yamaniyah*

Sources: Adapted from Brian Lees, *A Handbook of the Al Sa'ud Ruling Family of Saudi Arabia* (London: Royal Genealogies, 1980); H. StJ. B. Philby, *Arabian Jubilee* (London: Robert Hale, 1952), pp. 250–71; David E. Long, *Saudi Arabia*, Washington Papers 39 (Beverly Hills: Sage Publications for the Center for Strategic and International Studies, Georgetown University, 1976), pp. 66–68; and "The Royal House of Saud," *Financial Times* (London), March 20, 1978.

Appendix F

Saudi Arabia's Military Capabilities

THE DATA in this appendix were obtained from numerous sources, including conversations with U.S. Department of Defense officials. The following publications were particularly helpful: International Institute for Strategic Studies, *The Military Balance, 1980–1981* (London: IISS, 1980), p. 47; and Abdul Kasim Mansur (pseud.), "The American Threat to Saudi Arabia," *Armed Forces Journal International*, September 1980, pp. 52–53.

TOTAL DEFENSE SPENDING, 1980–81: $21 billion

ARMY (30,000+ personnel)

Equipment
380 tanks (520 on order)
200 armored personnel carriers (200 on order)
250 scout cars (144 on order)
  10 batteries Improved-Hawk surface-to-air missiles (6 on order)

Organization
  2 armored brigades
  2 mechanized brigades
  2 infantry brigades
  3 battalions of royal guards
  3 artillery battalions
  2 paratroop battalions
33 antiaircraft artillery batteries
10 surface-to-air missile batteries

AIR FORCE (14,000 personnel, 130 experienced pilots)

Equipment
105 F-5 aircraft
  27 Lightning interceptors
  62 F-15 Eagles on order
  59 C-130 transports (20 other transports on order)
      Sidewinder, Maverick missiles
      AIM 9-L air-to-air missiles on order
    5 AWACS on order

Organization
   3 fighter-bomber squadrons
   1 interceptor squadron (1 to be organized)
   2 helicopter squadrons

NAVY (2,000 personnel)
   10 surface attack (3 more on order)—with harpoon missiles
   3 surface attack—torpedo
   4 minesweepers
   53 patrol craft (large and medium)
   4 landing craft

NATIONAL GUARD (17,000 personnel)
   20 battalions (4 modernized; 4 more to be modernized 1982–85)

MAJOR MODERNIZATION PROGRAMS
   "Peace Sun": 62 F-15 Eagle interceptors (1981–83)
   AWACS: 5 E3-A aircraft, 1985
   Armored brigades: French AMX-30 tank
   Naval expansion: possible French program of $3.5 billion

Appendix G

Chronology of Saudi Oil Production and Policies

Table G-1. *Saudi Oil Production, Prices, and Policies*

Year and quarter	Production level[a] (millions of barrels per day)	Selling price, Arabian light crude (dollars per barrel)	OPEC price decisions
1973	7.6	2.00–3.60	October 16, 1973: Six OPEC members met in Kuwait; increased posted prices from $3.01 to $5.12 per barrel during Arab-Israeli war.
1974	8.5	8.32–10.46	December 23–24, 1973: OPEC met in Tehran; increased posted price to $11.65 during Arab embargo and production cuts.
1975	7.1	10.46–11.51	October 1975: OPEC met in Vienna; increased price by 10 percent, compromising between 5 percent sought by Saudis and 15 percent by Iran.
1976	8.6	11.51	December 1976: OPEC met in Doha; Saudis and UAE agreed to 5 percent price increase; others increased by 10 percent.
1977:I	9.3	12.09	
1977:II	9.4	12.09	July 1977: OPEC met in Stockholm to reunify prices. Saudis increased by
1977:III	9.0	12.70	5 percent; others dropped demands for additional July increases.
1977:IV	9.0	12.70	
1978:I	8.0	12.70	
1978:II	7.6	12.70	
1978:III	7.7	12.70	December 1978: OPEC at Abu Dhabi agreed on gradual price increases on quarterly basis through 1979, 10 percent increase for year as a whole.
1978:IV	10.0	12.70	
1979:I	9.8	13.34	March–June 1979: Aftermath of Iranian revolution and temporary reduction in Saudi production to 8.5 million bpd created tight market. In March OPEC accelerated schedule of price increases, bringing barrel to $14.55 for second quarter. OPEC at Geneva in June decided on price increases from $14.55 to $18.
1979:II	8.8	14.55–18.00	

Period	Production	Price	Events
1979:III	9.8	18.00	
1979:IV	9.8	18.00–24.00	December 1979: OPEC in Caracas failed to reach unified price structure. Saudis increased price to $24, retroactive to November 1, 1979.
1980:I	9.8	26.00	January 1980: Saudis unilaterally raised price to $26, retroactive to January 1, 1980, to align their price with effective OPEC "marker."
1980:II	9.8	28.00	May–June 1980: OPEC ministers met at Taif in May; Saudi price increased from $26 to $28, retroactive to April 1. In Algiers in June OPEC prices went from $32 to $37; Saudi price stayed at $28.
1980:III	9.8	28.00–30.00	
1980:IV	10.3	30.00–32.00	September–December 1980: OPEC ministers met in Vienna in September; Saudis increased price to $30, retroactive to August 1. Iraq-Iran war began in late September. OPEC met in Bali in December; Saudis increased to $32, retroactive to November 1, but declared intention to keep production high to bring other OPEC prices down to Saudi level.
1981:I	10.3	32.00	
1981:II	10.3	32.00	June 1981: OPEC ministers met in Geneva; decided on price freeze. Surplus production was major problem, with spot prices falling sharply. Saudis continued high level of production to narrow price spread within OPEC.
1981:III	10.0	32.00	August 1981: OPEC ministers met in Geneva to try to reach unified price. Saudi Arabia refused to go above $34 per barrel; others held out for $35 or more. Meeting ended without agreement. Yamani said Saudi price would remain $32 through 1982; production level would be reduced to a 9 million bpd ceiling in September 1981, with monthly adjustments to follow.

Sources: *Middle East Oil*, **Exxon** Background Series, 2d ed. (New York: Exxon Public Affairs Department, 1980); selected issues of *Petroleum Intelligence Weekly* (New York), *Middle East Economic Digest* (London), and *Middle East Economic Survey* (Nicosia); and U.S. Department of Energy, Energy Information Administration, *Monthly Energy Review*, DOE/EIA-0035 (81/03) (DOE, March 1981), p. 78. Figures are rounded.
a. Includes Saudi share of **Neutral Zone** oil, about 275,000 barrels per day.

Bibliography

Abir, Mordechai. *Oil, Power and Politics: Conflict in Arabia, the Red Sea and the Gulf*. London: Frank Cass, 1974.

Abu al-Khail, Mohammed. "The Oil Price in Perspective," *International Affairs* (London), vol. 55 (October 1979).

Aburdene, Odeh. "OPEC Investments in the West," *OAPEC News Bulletin*, vol. 3 (January 1977).

Adelman, M. A. "Is the Oil Shortage Real? Oil Companies as OPEC Tax-Collectors," *Foreign Policy*, no. 9 (Winter 1972–73).

———. *The World Petroleum Market*. Baltimore: Johns Hopkins University Press for Resources for the Future, 1972.

Akins, James E. "The Oil Crisis: This Time the Wolf Is Here," *Foreign Affairs*, vol. 51 (April 1973).

Ali, Sheikh Rustum. *Saudi Arabia and Oil Diplomacy*. New York: Praeger, 1976.

Almana, Muhammed. *Arabia Unified: A Portrait of Ibn Saud*. London: Hutchinson Benham, 1980.

Anderson, Irvine H. *ARAMCO, the United States and Saudi Arabia: A Study of the Dynamics of Foreign Oil Policy, 1933–1950*. Princeton: Princeton University Press, 1981.

Badeau, John S. *The American Approach to the Arab World*. New York: Harper and Row for the Council on Foreign Relations, 1968.

Al-Banyan, Abdullah Saleh. *Saudi Students in the United States: A Study of Cross Cultural Education and Attitude Change*. London: Ithaca Press, 1980.

Beling, Willard A., ed. *King Faisal and the Modernization of Saudi Arabia*. Boulder, Colo.: Westview Press, 1980; London: Croom Helm, 1980.

Braibanti, Ralph, and Fouad Abdul-Salam Al Farsy. "Saudi Arabia: A Developmental Perspective," *Journal of South Asian and Middle Eastern Studies*, vol. 1 (Fall 1977).

Al-Chalabi, Fadhil J. "The Concept of Conservation in OPEC Member Countries," *OPEC Review*, vol. 3 (Fall 1979).

———. *OPEC and the International Oil Industry: A Changing Structure*. Oxford: Oxford University Press, 1980.

Chubin, Shahram. "Soviet Policy towards Iran and the Gulf," *Adelphi Papers*, no. 157. London: International Institute for Strategic Studies, 1979.

Collins, John M., and Clyde R. Mark. "Petroleum Imports from the Persian Gulf: Use of U.S. Armed Force to Ensure Supplies." Washington, D.C.: Congressional Research Service, Library of Congress, 1979.

Collins, Michael. "Riyadh: The Saud Balance," *Washington Quarterly*, vol. 4 (Winter 1981).

Cottrell, Alvin J., ed. *The Persian Gulf: A General Survey.* Baltimore: Johns Hopkins University Press, 1980.

Cummings, John Thomas, Hossein G. Askari, and Michael Skinner. "Military Expenditures and Manpower Requirements in the Arabian Peninsula," *Arab Studies Quarterly*, vol. 2 (Winter 1980).

Davis, E. "The Political Economy of the Arab Oil-Producing Nations: Convergence with Western Interests," *Studies of Comparative International Development*, vol. 14 (Summer 1979).

Dawisha, Adeed I. "Internal Values and External Threats: The Making of Saudi Policy," *Orbis*, vol. 23 (Spring 1979).

————. "Saudi Arabia's Search for Security," *Adelphi Papers*, no. 158. London: International Institute for Strategic Studies, 1979–80.

Deese, David A., and Joseph S. Nye, eds. *Energy and Security.* Cambridge, Mass.: Ballinger, 1981.

DeGaury, Gerald. *Faisal: King of Saudi Arabia.* New York: Praeger, 1966.

Duguid, Stephen. "A Biographical Approach to the Study of Social Change in the Middle East: Abdullah Tariki as a New Man," *International Journal of Middle East Studies*, vol. 1 (July 1970).

Eilts, Hermann F., "Security Considerations in the Persian Gulf," *International Security*, vol. 5 (Fall 1980).

Eisenhower, Dwight D., *Waging Peace, 1956–1961.* Garden City, N.Y.: Doubleday, 1965.

Al-Farsy, Fouad. *Saudi Arabia: A Case Study in Development.* London: Stacey International, 1978.

Feith, Douglas J. "The Oil Weapon De-Mystified," *Policy Review*, no. 15 (Winter 1981).

Feotistov, A. "Saudi Arabia and the Arab World," *International Affairs* (Moscow), no. 7 (July 1977).

Halliday, Fred. *Arabia without Sultans: A Political Survey of Instability in the Arab World.* New York: Vintage Books, 1975.

Helms, Christine Moss. *The Cohesion of Saudi Arabia: Evolution of Political Identity.* London: Croom Helm, 1981.

Holden, David. *Farewell to Arabia.* London: Faber and Faber, 1966.

Hopwood, Derek, ed. *The Arabian Peninsula: Society and Politics.* Totowa, N.J.: Rowman and Littlefield, 1972.

Howarth, David. *The Desert King: Ibn Saud and His Arabia.* New York: McGraw-Hill, 1964.

Ignotus, Miles (pseud.). "Seizing Arab Oil," *Harpers*, March 1975.

Al-Janabi, Adnan A. "The Supply of OPEC Oil in the 1980s," *OPEC Review*, vol. 4 (Summer 1980).

Johany, Ali D. *The Myth of the OPEC Cartel: The Role of Saudi Arabia*. Dhahran: University of Petroleum and Minerals, 1980; New York: Wiley, 1980.

————. "OPEC and the Price of Oil: Cartelization or Alteration of Property Rights?" *Journal of Energy and Development*, vol. 5 (Autumn 1979).

Kanovsky, Eliyahu. "Deficits in Saudi Arabia: Their Meaning and Possible Implications," in Colin Legum and Haim Shaked, eds. *Middle East Contemporary Survey*. Vol. 2: *1977–78*. New York: Holmes and Meier, 1979.

————. "An Economic Analysis of Middle East Oil: A Look Backward and a Look Ahead," in Colin Legum and Haim Shaked, eds., *Middle East Contemporary Survey*. Vol. 4: *1979–80*. New York: Holmes and Meier, 1981.

Keddie, Nikki R. "Iran: Change in Islam, Islam and Change," *International Journal of Middle East Studies*, vol. 11 (July 1980).

Kelly, J. B. *Arabia, the Gulf and the West*. New York: Basic Books, 1980.

Khoury, Enver M. *The Arabian Peninsula, Red Sea, and Gulf: Strategic Considerations*. Hyattsville, Md.: Institute of Middle Eastern and North African Affairs, 1979.

Kingdom of Saudi Arabia. Ministry of Planning. *Third Development Plan: 1400–1405 A.H.—1980–1985 A.D.* Riyadh: Ministry of Planning, 1980.

Knauerhase, Ramon. *The Saudi Arabian Economy*. New York: Praeger, 1975.

Lackner, Helen. *A House Built on Sand: The Political Economy of Saudi Arabia*. London: Ithaca Press, 1978.

Lees, Brian. *A Handbook of the Al Sa'ud Ruling Family of Saudi Arabia*. London: Royal Genealogies, 1980.

Long, David E. *The Persian Gulf: An Introduction to Its Peoples, Politics, and Economics*. 2d ed. Boulder, Colo.: Westview Press, 1978.

————. *Saudi Arabia*. Washington Papers 39. Beverly Hills: Sage Publications for the Center for Strategic and International Studies, 1976.

————. "Saudi Oil Policy," *Wilson Quarterly*, vol. 3 (Winter 1979).

Long, David Edwin. *The Hajj Today: A Survey of the Contemporary Makkah Pilgrimage*. Washington, D.C.: Middle East Institute, 1979; Albany: State University of New York Press, 1979.

Mabro, Roger. "Oil Revenues and the Cost of Social and Economic Development" (in Arabic), *Al-Mustaqbil al-Arabi*, no. 7 (May 1979).

MacDonald, Charles G. *Iran, Saudi Arabia, and the Law of the Sea: Political Interaction and Legal Development in the Persian Gulf*. Westport, Conn.: Greenwood Press, 1980.

McHale, T. R. "A Prospect of Saudi Arabia," *International Affairs* (London), vol. 56 (Autumn 1980).

Mansur, Abdul Kasim (pseud.). "The American Threat to Saudi Arabia," *Armed Forces Journal International*, September 1980.

Miller, Aaron David. *Search for Security: Saudi Arabian Oil and American Foreign Policy, 1939–1949*. Chapel Hill: University of North Carolina Press, 1980.

Moran, Theodore H. "Modeling OPEC Behavior: Economic and Political Alternatives," *International Organizations*, vol. 35 (Spring 1981).

Mosley, Leonard. *Power Play: Oil in the Middle East*. New York: Random House, 1973.

Nakhleh, Emile A. *Arab-American Relations in the Persian Gulf*. Washington, D.C.: American Enterprise Institute for Public Policy Research, 1975.

———. *The United States and Saudi Arabia: A Policy Analysis*. Washington, D.C.: American Enterprise Institute for Public Policy Research, 1975.

Nyrop, Richard F., and others. *Area Handbook for Saudi Arabia*. 3d ed. Washington, D.C.: Government Printing Office, 1977.

Ortiz, Raul, "The World Energy Outlook in the 1980s and the Role of OPEC," *OPEC Review*, vol. 3 (Fall 1979).

Page, Stephen. *The USSR and Arabia: The Development of Soviet Policies and Attitudes towards the Countries of the Arabian Peninsula, 1955–1970*. London: Central Asian Research Centre in association with the Canadian Institute of International Affairs, 1971.

Park, T., and M. Ward. "Petroleum-Related Foreign Policy: Analytics and Empirical Analyses of Iranian and Saudi Behavior 1948–1974," *Journal of Conflict Resolution*, vol. 23 (September 1979).

Peck, Malcolm C. "Saudi Arabia in United States Foreign Policy to 1958: A Study in the Sources and Determinants of American Policy." Ph.D. dissertation, Harvard University, 1970.

Peterson, J. E. "Tribes and Politics in Eastern Arabia," *Middle East Journal*, vol. 31 (Summer 1977).

"Petromin: General Petroleum and Mineral Organization, Saudi Arabia," *OPEC Bulletin Supplement*, vol. 11 (February 25, 1980).

Philby, H. StJ. B. *Arabian Jubilee*. London: Robert Hale, 1952.

———. *Saudi Arabia*. London: Benn, 1955.

Presley, J. R. "Saudi Arabia: A Decade of Economic Progress," *Three Banks Review*, no. 127 (September 1980).

Quandt, William B., Fuad Jabber, and Ann Mosley Lesch. *The Politics of Palestinian Nationalism*. Berkeley: University of California Press, 1973.

Rihani, Ameen. *Ibn Sa'oud of Arabia: His Land and His People*. London: Constable, 1928.

Rouhani, Fuad. *A History of O.P.E.C.* New York: Praeger, 1971.

"The Royal House of Saud," *Financial Times* (London), March 20, 1978.

Rugh, William. "The Emergence of a New Middle Class in Saudi Arabia," *Middle East Journal*, vol. 27 (Winter 1973).

Salameh, Ghassane. "Political Power and the Saudi State," *MERIP Reports*, no. 91 (October 1950).

Saudi Arabia 1980: A MEED Special Report (London), June 1980.

Sheehan, Edward R. F. *The Arabs, Israelis, and Kissinger*. New York: Reader's Digest Press, 1976.

Solaim, Soliman A. "Constitutional and Judicial Organization in Saudi Arabia." Ph.D. dissertation, Johns Hopkins University, 1970.

Sullivan, Robert R. "Saudi Arabia in International Politics," *Review of Politics*, vol. 32 (October 1970).

Tahtinen, Dale R. *National Security Challenges to Saudi Arabia*. Washington, D.C.: American Enterprise Institute for Public Policy Research, 1978.

Troeller, Gary. *The Birth of Saudi Arabia: Britain and the Rise of the House of Sa'ud*. London: Frank Cass, 1976.

Tucker, Robert W. "Further Reflections on Oil and Force," *Commentary*, March 1975.

———. "Oil: The Issue of American Intervention," *Commentary*, January 1975.

Turner, Louis, and James Bedore. "Saudi Arabia: The Power of the Purse-Strings," *International Affairs* (London), vol. 54 (July 1978).

U.S. Central Intelligence Agency. National Foreign Assessment Center. *The World Oil Market in the Years Ahead*. ER79-10327U. Washington, D.C.: Central Intelligence Agency, 1979.

U.S. General Accounting Office. *Critical Factors Affecting Saudi Arabia's Oil Decisions*. Report by the Comptroller General of the United States. ID-78-32. Washington, D.C.: General Accounting Office, May 12, 1978.

U.S. Congress. House. Committee on Foreign Affairs. *U.S. Security Interests in the Persian Gulf*. Report of a Staff Study Mission to the Persian Gulf, Middle East, and Horn of Africa, October 21–November 13, 1980. 97 Cong. 1 sess. Washington, D.C.: Government Printing Office, 1981.

———. ———. ———. Subcommittee on Europe and the Middle East. *Proposed Arms Sales for Countries in the Middle East*. 96 Cong. 1 sess. Washington, D.C.: Government Printing Office, 1979.

———. ———. ———. ———. *Saudi Arabia and the United States: The New Context in an Evolving "Special Relationship."* Committee Print. Report prepared by the Foreign Affairs and National Defense Division, Congressional Research Service, Library of Congress. 97 Cong. 1 sess. Washington, D.C.: Government Printing Office, 1981.

———. ———. ———. ———. *U.S. Interests in, and Policies toward, the Persian Gulf, 1980*. Hearings. 96 Cong. 2 sess. Washington, D.C.: Government Printing Office, 1980.

U.S. Congress. Senate. Committee on Foreign Relations. Subcommittee on International Economic Policy. *The Future of Saudi Arabian Oil Production*. Staff Report. 96 Cong. 1 sess. Washington, D.C.: Government Printing Office, 1979.

———. ———. ———. Subcommittee on Near Eastern and South Asian Affairs. *U.S. Security Interests and Policies in Southwest Asia*. Hearings. 96 Cong. 2 sess. Washington, D.C.: Government Printing Office, 1980.

Valkova, A. "Saudi Arabia: Internal Position and Foreign Policy" (in Russian), *Narodi Azii i Afriki*, no. 6 (1975).

Vasil'yev, A. "Saudi Arabia between Archaism and Contemporaneity" (in Russian), *Aziya i Afrika Segodnya*, nos. 8–9 (August 1980).

Vidal, F. S. *The Oasis of Al-Hasa*. Dhahran: Arabian American Oil Company, 1955.

Wahba, Hafiz. *Arabian Days*. London: Arthur Baker, 1965.

Wein, Jake. *Saudi-Egyptian Relations: The Political and Military Dimensions of Saudi Financial Flows to Egypt*. Santa Monica: Rand Corporation, 1980.

Weisberg, Richard Chadbourn. *The Politics of Crude Oil Pricing in the Middle East*. Berkeley: Institute of International Studies, University of California, 1977.

Wells, Donald A. *Saudi Arabian Development Strategy*. Washington, D.C.: American Enterprise Institute for Public Policy Research, 1976.

Wenner, Manfred W. "Saudi Arabia: Survival of Traditional Elites," in Frank Tachau, ed. *Political Elites and Political Development in the Middle East*. New York: Wiley, 1975.

Winder, R. Bayly. *Saudi Arabia in the Nineteenth Century*. New York: St. Martins Press, 1965.

Yamani, Ahmad Zaki. "Energy Outlook: The Year 2000," *Journal of Energy and Development*, vol. 5 (Autumn 1979).

Yorke, Valerie. *The Gulf in the 1980s*. London: Royal Institute of International Affairs, 1980.

Index

Aba al-Khayl, Muhammad, 87, 124
Abd al-Aziz ibn Abd al-Rahman Al
    Saud, 4, 13, 47–49, 65, 77, 79, 88, 93
Abdallah ibn Abd al-Aziz, 81–83, 91, 99
Abu an-Nasir, Abd al-Karim, 71n
Aden, 18, 22
Adham, Kamal, 78, 84
Afghanistan, 42–43, 68–70
Aid: Egyptian, 15; Saudi, 19–20, 22, 24,
    26–29, 41–43, 51, 67, 115–16; U.S., 11,
    17–18, 49, 147–48
Airborne warning and control system
    (AWACS), 18, 53, 57, 85, 121, 156
Al al-Shaykh, 88
Algeria, 18
Allen, Robin, 72n
Amin, Idi, 10
Angola, 67
Arab Gulf Cooperation Council, 26
Arabian American Oil Company (AR-
    AMCO), 48, 100, 125, 147
Arab-Israeli conflict: Camp David sum-
    mit, 21, 28, 59–60, 68–69, 114, 151;
    Egyptian peace initiative, 16–17, 59–60,
    68, 113–14, 151; June 1967 war, 61–62;
    October 1973 war, 20, 50–51, 67, 112,
    128–29; Saudi policy, 9–10, 20, 29–33,
    35, 38, 48, 58–62, 84, 112–17, 128, 145–
    46; U.S. role, 47, 49–51, 59, 68–69, 112–
    15, 129, 145–46, 151, 153–55, 157
Arab League, 15, 115, 131
Arab radicalism, 18–22, 27, 60
Arafat, Yasir, 32–33
Armed forces: arms purchases, 18, 52, 57,
    61, 72, 84–85, 117–21, 142–44, 156; de-
    velopment, 51–53, 61, 102, 142; Paki-
    stani, 41; political role, 7, 99–105; U.S.
    military presence, 11, 49, 52, 55–58, 142,
    153, 155–56
Arms sales, 18, 52, 72, 142–44, 156. See also
    AWACS, F-15 aircraft, F-5E aircraft

Assad, Hafiz al-, 19, 20, 81, 112
Assad, Rifaat al-, 81

Badeau, John S., 49n
Baghdad summit, 114–15
Bahrain, 24–26
Bandar ibn Sultan, 84, 85, 119
Banyan, Abdullah Saleh Al-, 99n
Bashir, Faisal al-, 87
Begin, Menachem, 60, 68, 113
Beling, Willard A., 78n
Belyayev, Igor, 69, 70n
Ben Bella, Ahmad, 18
bin Baz, Shaykh, 94
Blechman, Barry M., 66n
Bourret, Jean-Claude, 73n
Braibanti, Ralph, 77n
Brown, Harold, 61n, 120, 121

Camp David summit, 21, 28, 59–60, 68–69,
    114, 151
Carter, Jimmy, 26, 57, 59, 68, 113, 118–21
Central Intelligence Agency (CIA), 152
Church, Frank, 120
Collins, Michael, 79n
Cordesman, Anthony, 144n
Corruption, 91, 148

Dawisha, Adeed, 21n
Death of a Princess, 152
Deese, David A., 139n
Dhahran airfield, 11, 49
Doha decision, 129–30
Domestic issues, 97–98; corruption, 91,
    148; economic development, 147–48;
    foreign influences, 6–7, 99–101; leader-
    ship continuity, 98–99; Mecca incident,
    83, 88, 93–96, 148; military role, 101–04;
    political system, 92–93, 100, 109; Shiite
    disturbances, 96–97; stability, 6–8, 104–
    06

187